ESSENCE OF MANAGERIAL ECONOMICS AND MANAGEMENT SCIENCE

ESSENCE OF MANAGERIAL ECONOMICS AND MANAGEMENT SCIENCE

(A Twenty First Century Approach)

(For Students of Commerce and Management)

By

B. N. NARAYAN

Prof. of Economics, (Retd) A. P. S. College
Director of Studies, NCMS, Bangalore
Visiting Professor, Management Studies, Bangalore University
Ex-Secretary, FKCCI, Bangalore.

ANMOL PUBLICATIONS PVT LTD
NEW DELHI-110 002 (INDIA)

ANMOL PUBLICATIONS PVT LTD
4374/4B, Ansari Road, Daryaganj
New Delhi-110 002

Essence of Managerial Economics and Management Science

First Edition 1997

ISBN 81-7488-490-4

PRINTED IN INDIA

Published by J. L. Kumar for Anmol Publications Pvt Ltd, New Delhi and Printed at Mehra Offset Press, Delhi.

With Love and Affection

To My Children and Grand Children

Shubha and Anand

and

Deepak, Nitya and Akina

CONTENTS

PART-B: MANAGEMENT SCIENCE

B. Elasticity of supply - Laws of supply - Assumptions

C. Input and output analysis - Main features - Assumptions - Working operation - Methodology - utility of the analysis.

D. Cost - Benefit analysis - Meaning and importance - classification of the analysis - conclusion.

E. Multiple products - new products - policy on adding New products - policy on dropping of old products

F. Multiplier and Accelerator Mechanism - Utility of the concept.

G. Capital Budgeting - Its importance to managerial economics.

H. Matrix Organisation (Project organisation)

I. An analysis of selling cost.

J. Management Education and Training in India.

K. Selected Readings

PREFACE

This book is written in two parts A and B with a view to satisfy the requirements of students of Business Management and Commerce both at the post-graduate level and Post-Graduate Diploma in Business Management (PGDBA) and to those interested in Management studies.

We are on the threshold of the 21st century, when the subject of "Economics of Management" demands a very careful and an in-depth study to achieve the target of "Economies of Management." Modern Business trends and industrial management have assumed gigantic proportions necessitating a penetrating and comprehensive knowledge and study in several fields of Management.

The concept of demand analysis, price elasticities, input-output ratio; investment - return ratios; the problems of modern industrial organisation; the economies of scale; the price determination under different market structure; product differentiation, price discrimination; demand forecasting, profit determination and analysis; assessment of national income measurement; capital budgeting and the economic fluctuations haunting the developed and the developing countries and production management are some of the major problems to be tackled by a managerial economist, if one has to survive in the challenging modern business world. Hence, a detailed study of this subject in its different manifestations is absolutely necessary.

Most of the developing countries have resorted to economic liberalisation programs with a view to keep pace with the developed countries. As such, they require a well knowledgeable and efficient managers, who could meet the challenges of the 21st century. Thus a detailed study of this subject can be of great advantage to a student, who would like to carve his future in this field of management education.

With the advent of 21st Century, Scientific Management of Industrial Sector and Business Houses would become indispensable both for acceleration of total output and reduction of cost of production. We are very shortly entering an era of economic dynamism, when international forces and national environment would be a challenge.

Productivity being a major concern of Managers, the operation of management system through operation research, automation and computerisation would be a dire necessity. Hence, an in-depth study of this subject of management in its various dimensional facts is necessary for every modern student, immaterial whether he is a scientist, engineer, business manager, captain of the industry of even a doctor. Efficiency, effectiveness and austerity should be the guiding principles. Let us remember that every producer has to develop "Cost consciousness" production may be in Public sector, Joint sector or Cooperative sector.

Against this background using my academic theoretical knowledge and practical experience, I have written this book. Hope the students will be satisfied.

In the preparation of this book, I have consulted many different authors and other publications for information on the subtle issues and graphs. I am highly thankful to them.

I will be failing in my duty, if I am not indebted to my wife Mrs. Champaka Narayan for her encouragement and continued support in drafting this book.

Bindiganavalae Narasimha Narayan

PART - A

CHAPTER - 1

MANAGERIAL ECONOMICS

INTRODUCTION:

Managerial Economics had its beginning in the early part of 1950's. The term managerial Economics has progressively displaced the term business economics. Managerial Economics refers to the firm's decision making process. It could be also interpreted as " Economics of Management" or "Economies of Management". The way used towards solving business problems of management constitutes the subject matter of managerial economics. Business involves risks and uncertainty. Risk arises from uncertainty about future.

Market demand and consumer behaviour have much uncertainty influencing revenues, production schedule and the employment of resources and costs. These in turn create price uncertainties. Financing involves uncertainties about raising adequate capital and credit. Environmental factors also create problems in business management. The business executives have to take decisions carefully and formulate plans for the future. The managerial economics with concepts and principles relating to profit, demand, cost, pricing, etc., aided by commerce, statistics or mathematics can help to solve the problems of business management.

Managers' problems are decision problems. These problems may be major or minor, simple or complex. Once the decision is taken, the manager's job is to ensure that it is put into effect quickly and economically. The prime functions of a business executive is decision-making and forward planning. Decisions making implies the process of selecting once action out of two or more alternatives; while forward planning means "establishing plans for the future". All decision problems are, how to get the best out of expensive and scarce resources . The business firm wants to make sure that the resources are used to bring a satisfactory return. The scarcer they are, the more expensive they will be. The firms have to take decision under conditions of uncertainty. The business managers do not have complete information about future sales, costs, profits, capital flow, demand and other important economic variables.

Economics deals with men and their methods. Man exhibits certain fundamental characteristic features. He seeks various competitive ends, objectives or wants. The means of satisfying these ends are limited and subject to alternative uses. He has to exercise choice in the selection of resources depending up on their relative importance. "Scarcity is the most important factor in economic science. He has to make a choice as regards "ends" and "Scarce resources". Prof. Loinel Robbins says "Economics is the science which studies human behaviour as a relationship between ends and scarce means which have alternative uses". Prof. Wickstead observes "Economics is the study of those principles of which the resources of the community should be so regulated and administered so as to secure the common ends without waste". So also Prof. Stigler points out that "Economics is the study of principles governing the allocation of scarce means among competing ends when the objective of allocation is to maximise the attainment of ends".

Managerial Economics is also called as Industrial Economics or Business Economics. Some of the tools applied by managerial Economics are also used by industrial economics in the management of business firm.

2. MEANING-DEFINITION

Managerial Economics is "Applied Economics" used in decision making. It bridges the gap between economic theory and managerial practice. It emphasies the use of economic analysis in clarifying problems, in organising and evaluating information and comparing alternative courses of action. It provides application in managing non-profit organisations and public sector undertakings. To some managerial economics is applied economics, the application of economic theory and methodology to business administration practice. It uses the tools and techniques of economic analysis to solve business problems. It provides the link between traditional economics and the managerial decision making. Business administration declares the targets and decision problem to the manager,who utilises traditional economics decision science to carry the given targets. He applies theory and methodology of traditional economics and technique of decision science like linear programming and stastical techniques. Thus,managerial economics is the application of economic theory and methodology to solve business problems. The problems of business management are mainly two,namely,-

1. Decision making with reference to current problems;and

2. Forward planning to take care of future course of business.

The business goals could be of five types,namely,- production goal,inventory goal sales goals,market share goal and profit goals.

Economics is defined as the study of allocation of scarce resources among unlimited ends,managerial economics is the study of allocation of the resources available to a firm or management. It is concerned with choice. It is goal- oriented and prescriptive and aims at maximising the achievement of objectives. Economic theory deals with a number of concepts relating to profits,demand,cost,pricing,business cycles,national income etc., and aided by accounting,statistics,operations research for solving problems of business management. The manner through which economic analysis is used to solve business problems constitutes the subject matter of managerial economics. Business administration declares the targets and decision problems to the manager,who uses traditional economics to carry the given targets. Managerial economics can be defined as normative micro- economics,which deals with smallest units,like individual consumers,single producer or a factor of production. Micro -economics has both a normative approach and a positive approach. A positive approach deals with the description and theory; it deals with what it is; while the normative approach deals with what to do and how to do. Since a manager is concerned with the latter, the managerial economics is a normative micro-economics. A manager has to study the society, the economy, the behaviour of the consumers and the political climate, otherwise he cannot be a successful manager. He has to make an integrated approach to solve the business problems.

Managerial economics is defined as economic theory and operation research and it deals with the methodology that could be applied to scarce resources. Operations research deals with the various techniques with which one can estimate and forecast the variables like demand, supply, price, cost of production etc., . Managerial Economics is a fundamental academic subject to understand and analyse the problems of business decision making. Operation research is a functional activity, whose aim is to help the manager to do his day to day job.

Mac Nair and Merian define managerial economics as "consisting of the use of economic modes of thought to analyse business situations". Spencer and seigleman state that "the integration of economic theory with business practice for the purpose of facilitating decision making and forward planning by management. Managers take decisions and they determine the nature and extent of economic activity. Decision implies a deliberate choice of alternative courses of action. Business decisions are directed towards certain objectives. Managerial economics provides a link between traditional economics and managerial decision making. It is pragmatic concerned with the promise to improve decision making in the future.

3. SCOPE AND NATURE

Prof.Hayes points out that managerial economics does not extend to macro-economic theory; while others argue that it extends to aspects of macro-economic theory like public economics, National income analysis, trade cycles, etc., which affects business decisions. The scope is widening with the time and with the increasing business complexities. It covers -

1. Demand analysis and forecasting;
2. production and cost analysis;
3. Principle powers in different market conditions;
4. National income analysis;
5. Profit management;
6. Capital Management, and
7. Business cycles. (Economic Fluctuations) etc.,

The subject matter of managerial economics consists of applying economic principles and concepts towards adjusting the various uncertainties faced by a business firm.

1. Demand analysis and forecasting.

The business involves accurate estimation of demand both in the present and future. Demand analysis and forecasting form an integral part of managerial economics. Then market demand schedule needs the study of individual demand of consumers. Consumer behaviour is an important part of demand analysis, which identifies various factors affecting demand, like price, incomes, substitutes, tastes, likes and dislikes, habits etc. On this basis demand forecasting is made for specified period. A business firm is an economic organism, which transforms productive resources into goods to be sold in the market. A forecast of future sales and demand is very necessary for the preparation of production schedules. The forecast is also important for the firm for maintaining or strengthening market position and improving profits. Accuracy in demand forecasting is necessary for the firm to produce the required quantities and to arrange the various infrastructure in advance. The demand forecasting could be short term and long term. The forecast may be at macro-level taking in to consideration the entire economy. It could be at industry level or firm level. The forecast could be general or specified, and it should take into account the nature of competition; risk factors involved in production and sales, etc. There seems to be uncertainty regarding the methods of forecasting, since no one can precisely predict the future with certainty. Thus, there is need for combining both the scientific technique and the human judgement, while resorting to forecast. Many important factors like -survey of buyers intention,collective opinion and trend projection relating to market position etc., have to be considered. The secular trends, the seasonal trends, the cylical trends etc. have to be accounted for clearly since these trends are interrelated and very irregular in their movements. Economic indicators relating to the behaviour of products to certain other allied transaction also have to be considered. Thus, demand forecasting is a major issue for the firm and the methods used to forecast should be updated from time to time to suit the changing market conditions and consumer's behaviour.

2. Production and Cost Analysis:

The study of production and cost of firm is an essential part of managerial economics. Profit depend upon the total output and cost of production. To achieve maximum profits the firms have to arrive at maximum output at minimum cost. Analysis of production and cost behaviour enables the business to take right decision to fulfill the objectives of maximum profits. The manager has to determine the optimum output where the cost of production is minimum. The cost estimates are useful for management decisions. Discovering economic cost and able to measure them are necessary steps for more effective profit planning. Production analysis is in physical terms, while the cost analysis is in monetary terms. Cost concepts and classifications, cost - output relationships, economies and diseconomies of scale and production functions are some of the points constituting cost and production analysis.

3. Pricing decisions, policies and practices:

Pricing is a very important element in the economic system and it is the basis of revenue of a firm and it is price that is fixed that determines the profits and in turn the success of a business enterprise. Price determination; pricing methods; pricing policies, profit line pricing and price forecasting are important factors that constitute pricing decisions. Price of the product, other thongs remaining constant, determines the level of profits. The firm's decisions about price depend upon the market structure. Once the market structure is provided, the firm is free to follow any method or price fixation that will be equal to the cost or more.

4. National Income Analysis:

The economic environment prevailing in a country decides the profits earned by a business firm. The economic conditions determine the demand for a product and the working operations of factors. A detailed analysis and study of the trends of national income and its components are very essential for Managerial economics. Besides national income analysis, the nature and causes of trade cycles are also important factors to be studied.

Managerial economics derives tools and techniques from decision sciences to analyse business problems. To achieve pre-determined established goals, the managerial economics draws from the area of optimisation techniques and statistical tools are made use of for estimating relationship among important economic variables in decision making problems. Financing, production and sales are very important factors and their inter -relationships are to be studied and operation research provides the company with the necessary models.

Statistics provides probability theory to understand the quantitative relationships among different variables connected in decision making process. The profit and loss account is an indicator of the performance of a business firm.

It also throws light on the future course of action to be taken to streamline the administrative machinery to keep the firm going in case accounting details indicate a downward slope in the operational field.

5. Profit Management:

Profit is consequence and causation factors are very many like maximum output; cost minimisation; involvement of science and technology; good industrial relations etc. Profit making is the Universal objective of any firm. Production and profit always go together. There is always an element of uncertainty about profit due to variation in cost and revenues caused by internal and external factors. Thus, a study and nature of profits and theories of profits form the subject matter of managerial economics.

6. Capital Management:

One of the major inputs in the productive process is capital and a very scarce factor of production. The future and prospects of business depends upon capital. It is the responsibility of the business firm to mobilise enough to the optimum point. A proper capital management includes efficient planning and control of capital expenditure. The most complex problem of a business enterprise is to find out sufficient capital investments. Cost of capital, rate of return and selection of projects are important formation.

4. IMPORTANCE AND USEFULNESS OF MANAGERIAL ECONOMICS

Business firms play a vital role in the society. Managerial economics can point out the role of business firms to improve the society's benefits. It helps the society in making the best use of scarce economic resources. Managers are helped to solve their problems of profit making and business promotions. Profit is the difference between total revenue and total cost. A manager can increase his profits either by decreasing cost or by increasing the revenue or both. 'The law of diminishing returns' and 'Returns to scale' help the managers to determine the level of output at which the unit cost is the minimum. Depending upon the models of price determination under various market conditions, the manager can sell the product at the highest profit level. Economic theory helps in determining the equilibrium point at which the firm can get maximum profits. Managerial economics also covers other disciplines like Mathematics, Statistics,Psychology,Sociology and politics, which helps the manager to manage the firm efficiently and effectively. Mathematics help to understand production techniques. Statistics helps to study the trends of cost, demand and prices. Politics helps to understand the political environment which can influence economic conditions in which the organisation has to operate. The business has to operate within the laws and regulations imposed by government.

The Management economist can help the management relating to decision making and forward planning by supplying skills and techniques. Big 'Industrial Houses' make use of the services of managerial economists to determine the methodology and models that are necessary to improve the operational efficiency of their firms. A managerial economist can contribute effectively to the external and internal factors that affect the working operations of a business firm. The volume of trade, national income, output and price affect every organisation. The outlook of national economy, the demand prospects; the prices of raw materials and finished products, the government economic policies etc., have all an impact on the business firm. The managements seek the advise of managerial economists in meeting the situation. Even with regard to internal factors like sales and profit budgets, the wage and price structures, market research, capital projects, production programmes etc., the managerial economists can render yoeman service. He must have a strong personal conviction that profits are essential and he has an obligation and responsibility in that direction. He should make the best forecast and aim at minimising the risks involved in uncertainties. He should be, so to say a watch-dog of the organisation, and extend the management in successful decision-making and forward planning, then only he becomes an asset to organisation.

5. GOALS OF A BUSINESS FIRM

Dr. Alfred Marshall emphasised 'short-term profit maximisation' as the sole goal of a business firm. This concept held good at a time when business men were share-holders and as well as top managers; and they ignored other interest group like employees, consumers etc.,

Dr. Barthwell observes that "profit maximisation is the most conventional and widely used business motive in the theory of industrial economics."

These concepts have not been accepted by modern economists. The group of public sector industries in the underdeveloped countries have rejected this concept that is not motivated by profit maximisation.

The managerial revolution in the industrially advanced countries has brought about seperation of ownership and management control. It is now realised that profit maximisation is harmful to the stability and survival and growth of the firm.

Prof. William Baumal says that a firm is interested in "Sales Maximisation" and it is involved in "Scale of operations rather than profits". Minimum profit and growth is the slogan today.

Prof.Marris points out that "a modern business firm is more inclined towards not profit maximization but by multiple objectives of which sales maximisation is an important objective".

Prof Galrbraith stated that the growth objective is central to many modern business firm managed by "Technostructure". The growth of the firm is opposed to profit maximisation: The accepted business objective today is secured minimum profit, survival, growth and technological development.

Though opinions differ on this issue, still the element of profit is always there. So long the profits are at the satisfactory level, the management devote a major part of its effort and resources to the expansion of its sales. Besides profit maximisation and sales, there are other objectives namely maintaining and increasing market shares, maintaining stability, maintenance of public image, fulfillment of social obligations and responsibilities, maintaining desirable financial position, achieving and stablising good labour reactions, etc., that are primarily in the minds of management.

Prof. Higgins pointed out that "profit maximisation is a survival condition in perfect competition, and under imperfect competition, it is weaker.

***Summarization (points at a glance)**

1. *Managerial Economics is the integration of economic theory with business practice for the purpose of facilitating decision making and forward planning by the management. It is a process of selecting one action from two or more alternative courses. It consists of the use of economic models to analyse business situations.*

2. *It applies theoretical concepts into the practical field of business behavior under different field of business behavior under different existing conditions. It makes an attempt to estimate economic relationships; predict important economic quantities; makes use of these economic quantities in the process of decision making and forward planning and analysing the various significant external forces influencing demand, production, process, profits, etc.*

3. *It is micro-economics in character related to firms and its various attendant problems. It studies in detail the theory of firms and the principles underlying the distribution theory based on profit. It considers and makes an indepth study of the macro-environment in which the business firm has to function with the ultimate objective of not only profit-making but also to serve for the firm in particular and society in general.*

4. *The economic theory supplies general principles, while the managerial economics applies them to practical problems and make them more objective. The Managerial economics*

deals with firm and not individual. While economics deals with rent, interest and wages, the managerial economics deals with profit only.

5. *The scope of managerial economics comprises of demand analysis, cost analysis, pricing of products and prices, profit earning and management and capital budgeting. It also deals with cyclical fluctuations, which have an impact on firms and industries having number of firms. It deals with the concept of the selling cost and the input-output ratio.*

6. *Decision making and forward planning are the main problems of the managerial economist. He has to forecast the future, plan the productive process in such a way as to derive profits from the investment. Decision making relates to two factors namely,- internal factors and external factors. The internal factors relate to price determination, rat e of operation of the unit, investment portfolio, quantity of products to be produced, expansion or contraction of business unit etc. the external factors relate to prices at international markets, national income and output. volume of trade and international and national economic environment. The internal factors lie with in the business, while the external factors have to be forecast and analysed with reference to general business conditions prevailing.*

7. *the management has to shoulder greater responsibilities to make the best profit from the invested capital, the managerial economist should have a sound knowledge of business and keep himself well equipped with upto-date knowledge and trends. He should take all possible precautions to avoid hasty decisions. He should analyse all the possible alternatives logically and scientifically to avoid taking wrong decisions. He should aim at economies of management.*

CHAPTER - **2**

DEMAND ANALYSIS

Any desire cannot be a demand. Only those desires that are backed up with sufficient purchasing capacity are termed as Demand in Economics. Demand is one of the factors determining price. Demand is related to consumption and the process through which a consumer obtains good and services is called as demand. Demand and price are interrelated, inter-connected and mutually influential. Prof.Benham observes that "the demand for anything at a given price is the amount of it which will be brought per unit of time at that price". If demand has to exist, three things are necessary namely,- (1) the price of a commodity; (2) the amount of the commodity (3) and the willingness to buy at a given price. There is always an inverse relationship between the price of a commodity and the quantity demanded and this relationship is known as the Law of Demand. Ordinarily when prices fall demand increases and vice-versa. Prof. Samuelson says "Law of Demand states that people will buy more at lower prices and buy less at higher prices, other things remaining the same". Prof. Bilas and Prof. Ferguson also hold the same view.

Prof. Stigler and Prof. Boulding explain the law as follows based on certain assumption:

1. Consumer's tastes and preferences should not change;
2. Consumer's income to remain constant; Prof. Marshall refers to money incomes and prof.Milton Fried Man refers to the real income;
3. The prices of the commodities related to the commodity in demand to remain constant.

The response of amount demanded to changes in price of a commodity is known as the demand schedule. The demand schedule may be an individual demand schedule or a market demand schedule, but in price theory the managerial economists is interested in the market demand schedule. "The market demand schedule is defined as"the quantities offered at a given moment of time". The summation of individual demand schedules is called as the market demand schedule. When the demand schedule is graphically represented, it becomes a 'demand curve'. The individual demand curve has a negative slope and the market demand curve also slopes downwards.

The law of demand has theoretical as well as practical advantages.

1. A monopolist with the help of law of demand fixes his price for the product, and he is able to decide the most profitable amount of output for himself.

2. The Finance Minister takes the help of this law to know the effects of his tax reforms and policies. Only those commodities which have relatively inelastic demand should be taxed.

3. The demand schedule has great importance in planning for individual commodities and industries.

Broadly speaking price determines demand. There are several other factors like desire, purchasing power(Income), Prices of related goods, etc., affect demand on one side and the supply side on the other. "The action and inter-action of the forces of demand and supply determine prices" This price has a close relationship to demand and sales and this could be termed as 'law of demand' also. The contraction and the expansion of demand is always related to price line, provided other things remain constant. The size of population; the income levels of the community; the composition of population;

the prices of substitute; the prices of complimentary goods and services; the habits, customs,tastes,fashions,traditions, likes and dislikes of consumers should not change; weather and climatic environment; advertisement and salesmanship; etc., are other factors having an impact on demand.

Exceptions to the law of Demand:

There are certain exceptions to the law of demand and economists have identified that in the case of items like precious metals, antiques, old paintings etc., even though prices go up, demand continuous to increase. Especially the wealthy communities resort to such purchases as they carry prestige value. This is also known as "Vebten effect" since it was Prof. Vebten of U.S.A. who enunciated this point.

In the case of speculative transactions this law does not operate. When consumers anticipate a further increase in price at a future date, they buy commodities even at higher price with the fear complex that the commodity may not be available. So also when consumers anticipate fall in prices, they cut down their purchase at present and postpone their current demand.

The operation of 'griffin's paradox' is another exception to the law of demand. Ireland was a poor country during the 19th century and people mainly subsisted on potato and meat. Poor people consumed potatoes more than meat, since the price of former was lower to that of meat. Prof. Griffin observed that people purchased more potatoes when the price went-up because meat was already costly to them. Thus they reduced their expenditure on meat and diverted the money to the purchase of more potatoes. Where inferior items are consumed with superior items together, and if the price of inferior items increases, consumers have a tendency to buy more of inferior items only.

In a stock exchange this type of activity is very common. When prices of shares and stocks increase, people buy more of them anticipating a further increase in price at a future date and to make profits; but if prices fall they sell the shares and stocks anticipating a further fall in price at a future date to avoid loss; thus when prices increase, demand increases and when prices fall, demand decreases. This type of peculiar situations are common leading to exceptions in the Law of Demand. (the activities of bulls and bears in stock exchanges and share markets).

A. Demand Elasticity:

Demand moves upwards and downwards in response to price changes.But the law of demand fails to explain how much the quantity demanded varies in response to price changes. It only explains the direction of the change and not the rate at which the change takes place. "Elasticity of Demand can be defined as the degree of responsiveness of quantity Demanded to a change in price".Demand may be elastic or inelastic. In the case of salt any change in price,upwards and downwards, will not bring about any change in demand and demand remains constant;and this is a case of inelastic demand. It is a commodity absolutely essential,without substitutes. In the case of goods like woolen etc., Luxury commodities with substitutes,a change in consumers income are some of the factors that bring about a degree of change in the amount demanded. From the above it is clear that demand can be _ (1)Price elasticity;(2)Income elasticity; and (3) Cross elasticity (that is to say the responsiveness of commodity 'A' to changes in the price of a related commodity 'B' of late,some economists have considered that the outlay on advertisement also may bring about changes in demand. A great publicity campaign can alter the course of demand. This is very true in Japan and other Western countries, Where a sizeable portion of investments by management is earmarked for salesmanship and advertisement to bring about a tremendous influence on sales promotion. This is another factor that could be considered for bringing about a change in demand besides prices,incomes and prices of related goods.

1. Price Elasticity of Demand:

Prof. Marshal says "The elasticity (or responsiveness) of demand in a market is great or small according as the amount demanded increases much or little for a given fall in price and diminishes much or little for a given raise in price".

Prof.K. Bouldings observes " Elasticity of Demand measures the responsiveness of demand to change in price".

Prof. Cairncross points out "the elasticity of demand for a commodity is the rate at which quantity bought changes as the price changes".

$$\text{Elasticity of Demand} = \frac{\text{proportionate change in demand}}{\text{proportionate change in price}}$$

The degree of responsiveness of demand to price changes differs from commodity to commodity and from individual to individual. Economists elaborate five kinds of price elasticity of demand.

A. PERFECTLY ELASTIC DEMAND:

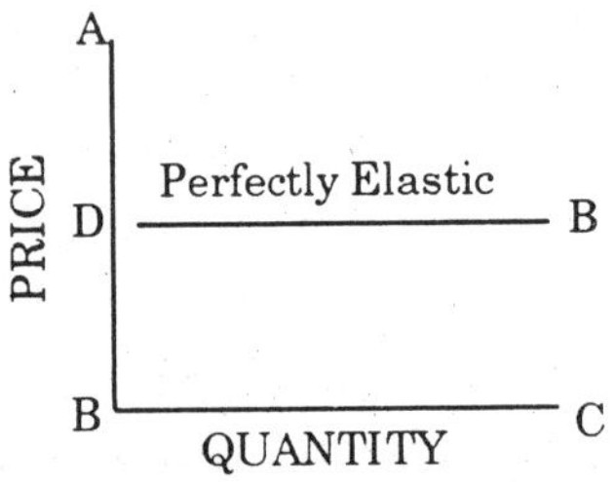

This is a situation where no reduction in price is needed to cause an increase in demand. Cases of perfectly elastic demand are exceedingly rare and hence not of much practical importance.

B. PERFECTLY IN-ELASTIC DEMAND:

In this situation a change in price causes no change in quantity demanded. When the quantity demanded of a

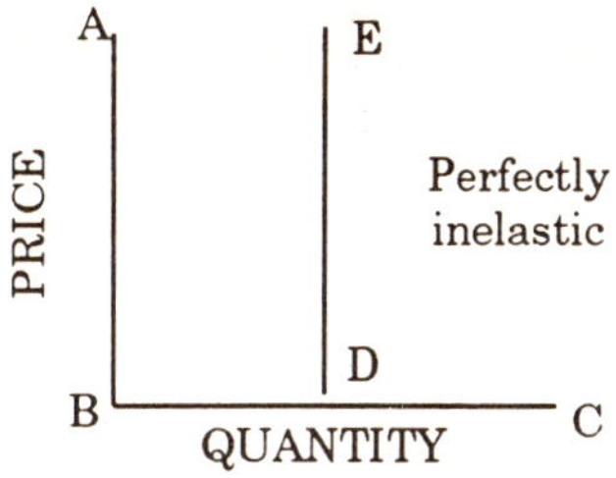

commodity remains the same,irrespective of any rise or fall in price of a commodity, then the demand is perfectly inelastic. This is also a rare case.

C. UNITY ELASTICITY DEMAND:

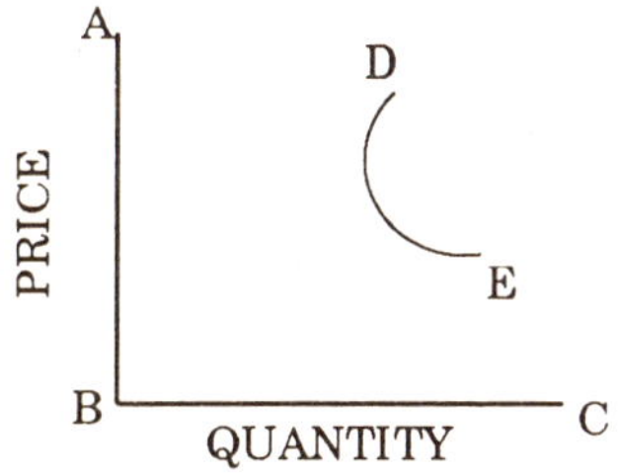

This is a situation when a given proportionate change in price causes equal proportionate change in the quantity demanded. If the price of commodity A goes up by 20%,if it results in the contraction of demand by exactly 20%, Demand curve slopes from left to right.

D. RELATIVELY MORE ELASTIC DEMAND:

This is a situation when reduction in a price leads to more than proportionate change in demand. A proportionate fall in price accompanied by a relatively large proportionate increase in the quality demanded and vice-versa.

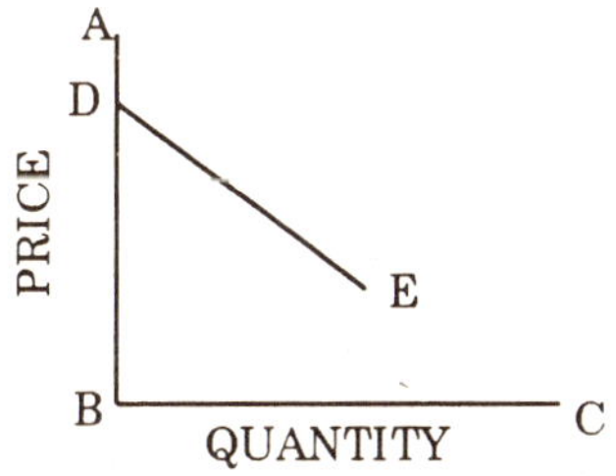

Demand is more sensitive to price changes and change in price bring a about a large distortion in demand. The demand curve would be more inclined to appear like horizontal curve.

E. RELATIVELY INELASTIC DEMAND:

This is a situation when a reduction in price leads to less than proportionate change in demand. Demand is inelastic when a given proportionate fall in the price of a commodity causes a relatively small proportionate increase in the quantity

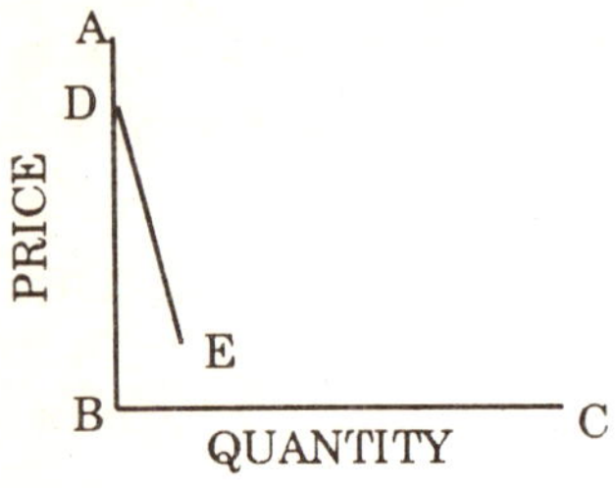

demanded and vice-versa. In such a situation, the demand curve would be inclined to look vertical and look more parallel to AB axis.

If the prices go-up by 50%, the demand reduces by less than 50%.

The elasticity of demand depends upon the following factors:

1. Nature of the commodity;
2. Extent of use the commodity is put into;
3. Range of substitutes;
4. Income levels;
5. What proportion of income is ear-marked for the community;
6. Frequency of a product entering the market;
7. Durability of the commodity decides the quantity to be purchased;
8. Urgency of demand;etc.,

To understand demand analysis clearly,it is necessary to know the distinguishing features of revenue,which have an affect on demand.

Average revenue refers to the total receipts from sales divided by the number of units sold.

Total Revenue means the total sale proceeds.

Marginal Revenue is the additional revenue which could be earned by selling an additional unit (marginal unit) of a firm's product.

Incremental Revenue measures the difference between the new total revenue and the existing total revenue.

PRICE ELASTICITY OF DEMAND-BUSINESS DECISIONS:

The concept of price elasticity has practical application in managerial business decision making. The manager,who is the captain of the Industry,should know whether a lowering of price will lead to increase in demand for the product and if so to what extent his profits would increase .If the increase in sales is more than proportionate to the declines in price,the total revenue will increase resulting in greater profits. A knowledge of the concept of elasticity of demand for a business man to decide whether he should cut his price or not in a particular case. In general,for items where the demand is elastic, it will profit him to charge relatively low prices;and on those commodities where the demand is inelastic,the manager would be better at a higher price.

A good knowledge of elasticity of demand of a commodity as well as the brand produced by the company and the way the total outlay (expenditure) responds to price changes is essential for the management to effectively analyse a wide range of business problems especially with reference to pricing and marketing problems.

IMPORTANCE OF PRICE ELASTICITY OF DEMAND:

Dr. Lord Keynes considered that price elasticity of demand to be the most important contribution of Dr.Alfred Marshall to economic theory.

It is necessary for every producer to determine about the quantity to be produced and the price he has to fix up for selling the product. Elasticity of demand helps him to take a decision.

A monopolist adopts a price discrimination policy only when the elasticity of demand from different consumers or sub-markets are different. These consumers in whose case the demand is inelastic,a higher price could be charged than those with more elastic demand.

In the case of joint supply, wool and mutton, the price determination is little difficult due to joint costs of production. Under such cases, this concept is of great importance. If the demand for wool is inelastic as compared to the demand for mutton, a higher price for wool could be charged.

The paradox of poverty always exists in the incomes of farmers though there is higher PRODUCTION. The inelasticity nature of demand explains this paradox. Since the demand for agriculture products is inelastic, prices are lower when their supply is high. Thus, this concept is of great importance to agriculture as an industry.

2. Income Elasticity of Demand:

Buyers, income is a basic demand determinant and along with price, they account for bringing variation in the sales of many commodities when the demand changes in response to the change in income, but not to the changes in the price, it is called Income elasticity of demand. According to Prof. Watson - "Income elasticity of demand means the ratio of the percentage change in the quantity demanded to the percentage change in income". The income elasticity measures the responsiveness of demand to changes in income. To what extent a consumer is sensitive to demand for a commodity when his income changes, is revealed by this concept. A knowledge of this concept helps in predicting and planning the changes in demand due to changes in income of the people. There are three types of income elasticity.

A. ZERO INCOME ELASTICITY

Where a change in income has no effect on the quantities demanded. Salt could be very good example. In this case the income demand curve is a straight line parallel to the vertical axis.

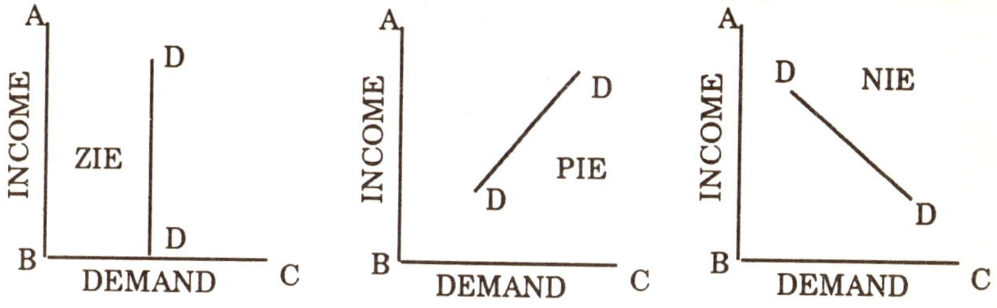

X Y Z

B. POSITIVE INCOME ELASTICITY

Where an increase in income may lead to an increase in quantities demanded and vice-versa. Such elasticity is said to exists for superior goods. This concept helps the planners and manufacturers to anticipate an increase in demand due to increase in income. The positive elasticity could be -

a) ***Unit elasticity,-*** when the increase in income brings about a proportionate change in the quantities demanded;

b) ***More than Unit Elasticity,*** - when an increase in income brings about more than proportionate increase in the quantity demanded, and lastly,

c) ***Less than Unit Elasticity,*** - when an increase in income brings about less than proportionate change in quantities demanded.

The income demand curve will be positively stopping from left upwards to the right as shown in figure (Y).

C. NEGATIVE INCOME ELASTICITY

Where increase in income may lead to a reduction in the quantity demanded; Generally foreign goods are said to have this effect. When the income increases, the buyer may shift his demand to a superior commodity. (From beedi to cigarettes).

The income demand curve for inferior goods slope from left down to the right indicating that demand reduces, when income increases. Fig indicates the position.

The knowledge of this concept is useful in forecasting the effect of changes in economic activity on demand. The businessmen may be interested in knowing whether his product will lead or lag economic growth. This concept is an important tool applied in business research. If the planners are aware of the income elasticity of demand of at least the goods and services of general use, they could take necessary steps to balance demand and supplies through controls and thereby contain inflation.

3. CROSS ELASTICITY OF DEMAND:

The cross elasticity of demand refers to a change in the demand for a product due to the changes in the price of a related product (which could be a substitute or complimentary). If the cross elasticity is positive, the related commodity is a "substitute" and if the cross elasticity is "negative" the related commodity is 'complimentary'. Thus, the price of one commodity is the independent variable, where as the quantity of another commodity is a dependent variable. Prof. Ferguson observes - "the cross elasticity of demand is the proportional change in the quantity of 'x' demanded resulting from a given relative change in the price of the related good 'Y'.

This concept is important in handling intercommodity relations and as such it forms the basis for the general equilibrium analysis.

The classification of markets and services is mainly based on this concept of one seller in relation to the other. Under perfect competition, the cross elasticity between products of different sellers is infinite, since the products are perfect substitutes. The lesser the cross elasticity of demand, the greater the monopoly power. This is a basic concept for drawing a clear cut line between fair competition and monopoly; and hence it is important for anti-monopoly legislation, that is recorded to in U.S.A. To a manufacturer for making price decisions, this is an important concept.

4. ADVERTISING ELASTICITY OF DEMAND

Modern Economists are of the view that besides prices, incomes and prices of related goods; the outlay earmarked for salesmanship and advertisement do play an important role in bringing about changes in demand. Advertising is an important tool for promoting sales of a product. There is a relationship existing between advertisement and volume of sales. In western countries like Europe, U.K., U.S.A., and also in japan a substantial out lay is provided for the advertisement sector to accelerate sales. Sales is possible even without advertisement, but up to a certain point an increase in advertisement can bring about more than proportionate increase in sales and beyond a particular point it may not click, and even may become negative.

Prof. Joel Dean has identified that several methods determine advertisement outlay and followed by businessmen in practice. Percentage of sales approach, return on investments, competitive parity approach etc., are some of the methods for advertisements outlay.

B. DEMAND FORECASTING

Accurate demand forecasting is necessary for a firm to enable it to produce the required quantities at the right time well in advance for the various factors of production. The area of production planning and control aim at two important objectives namely the production at the appropriate time. This calls for forecasting the future demand of a given production. This also involves arrangement well in advance the various infrastructure like men, material, money, machinery etc., which help to produce to meet the probable demand. In industrially advanced countries, where demand conditions are always uncertain than the supply conditions, demand forecasting is very significant and popular; where as in developing countries, supply is a major limiting factor.

There are several factors involved in demand forecasting and it could be classified under two categories.

1) Short-term demand forecasting, and

2) Long-term demand forecasting,

1. *short term demand forecasting*

This is limited to short period not exceeding a year. This forecasting relates to policies regarding sales, purchases, pricing and finance and with reference to existing production capacity of the firm. The firm may face violent fluctuations, especially in a dynamic society. It, therefore becomes necessary to plan accurately and formulate a suitable sales policy assuming that the prevailing conditions would continue. Proper price forecasting may help the firm to reduce the cost of operation.

To determine the price policy, demand forecasting is very helpful to the businessman. A balanced price determination with reference to determination of demand fluctuations, would help the firm to maintain its profit levels.

In a capital intensive industry, where the gestation period is long and the capital assets have a long fixed life, the demand forecasting has to be spread over from 10 to 20 years. It is rather difficult in a short period to alter production to meet the fluctuating demand.

Some companies use forecasting for setting sales targets and for establishing controls and incentives. If sales targets are too high, it discourages those who have to meet them; and if it is very low, it is easily met and all incentives prove meaningless. In the absence of demand forecasting, the financial planning gets upset and both production schedules and inventory accommodation are affected. In the preparation of budgets for the firm, short-term forecasting is very important.

2. *Long term Demand Forecasting*

When the company is using the existing production capacity, short-term planning is sufficient; but if the firm is involved in long-term planning, where the gestation period is too long, long-term planning is necessary to determine demand. Demand is the fundamental basis for any organisation. Planning of a new product unit or the expansion of an existing unit has to take into consideration the long-term demand potential of the product. A multi-product firm should ascertain not only the total demand situation but also the demand for different items. In obtaining this information, the firm has to study the consumer preferences and the trends, the economy, the technological developments, the trend projections to assess the demand potential. When once this is done, the firm has to engage itself in long-term financial planning. The man-power planning is another very important central factor in production for the existing as well as for the new firms have to be based on long term forecasts of the company's growth and expansion. Larger the period of forecasting, the probability of error is high; and this is because the factors that are taken into consideration at the time of forecasting cannot be always be constant and are subject to change. That too in a fast changing economy the probability of error is higher. Items like the trend of prices, costs of production and the nature of competition cannot be predicted accurately in long-term demand forecasting. Besides national factors, even international factors, which are beyond the control of the company like wars, natural calamities, depressions and prosperity, inventions and technology development etc., upset the calculations. Thus, it becomes obligatory for each firm to decide the span of time to be covered in demand forecasting. If the volume of demand has remained constant for a fairly long period, long-term forecasting is preferable, otherwise, if the demand is inconsistent and erratic, the forecasting period should be for shorter period.

1. Demand forecasting may be undertaken at three different levels, namely -

   a) Macro-Level forecasting.

   b) Industry level forecasting, and

   c) Firm level forecasting.

   depending upon the business conditions existing in the entire economy; from the different trades point of view and from the managerial point of view respectively.

2. The forecast could be general or specific. The firm always prefers a general forecast, but requires to be classified under commodity and sales.

3. The peculiarity of the product and the extent of market decide the type of forecast.

4. The products should be classified as consumer's goods or producer's goods, the pattern of demand varies for each of these categories.

C. DETERMINANTS OF DEMAND

It would be rather difficult to prepare a list of demand factors that are important for every commodity; and one can identify the possible common demand determinants for specific or particular product.

1. *Non-durable consumer goods:*

There are three basic factors influencing the demand for non-durable consumer goods. They are

a) purchasing power;
b) price; and
c) demography.

a) Purchasing power (income)

The purchasing power of the consumer, which is determined by income, is one of the major determinants of demand. In India due to non-availability of statistical information, it is difficult to determine the actual disposable income for estimating demand.

b) Price

The economists emphasise on the importance of price of a particular product and its substitutes in determining the demand. The concept of 'Elasticity of Demand' explains the measure of price-demand relationship of a product.

c) Demography

The population characteristics also determine the demand for a product. Demography does not always refer exclusively to human population. Demographic or population groups can be defined in terms of educational background, sex, age, income, social status, etc., Each segment can be used as an independent factor affecting the demand for the product.

2. Durable consumer goods:

In the case of durable consumer goods three purchase characteristics can be identified, and they are :

a) Time use characteristics,
b) Use facilities characteristics,
c) Demographic characteristics.

Consumer durables are never used up in a single act like match sticks. They could be used for a long time by repairing or replacing with new ones after scraping them. The decision to replace is influenced by other considerations such as social prestige, status, income, etc.

Use facilities relate to special facilities provided for the use of the product in question. For example good roads for cars and electricity supply for refrigerators. Thus the existence of facilities determine the demand potential.

Size of family, age distribution, population groups based on income, price etc., and demographic considerations determining the demand for consumer durables. It must be remembered that in the case of durable goods, demand has a saturation point. Merely because with income increase, a person will not by two radios at a time. Thus, the total demand consists of new owner demand and replacement demand.

3. Capital Goods:

The capital goods are used for further production. Since the demand is derived, it will depend on the profitability of industries. Capital goods are "produced means of further production". The demand for capital goods are determined by the profitability position of the industries using the capital goods; the ratio of production to capacity in user industries; the level of wage rates, the policy of the government; business prospects etc., In the case of certain capital goods, demand will depend upon particular markets they serve and the purpose for which they are bought. Two factors determine in forecasting the demand for capital goods, namely-

1) the growth prospects of the user industries;

2) the norm of consumption of the capital goods per unit of each end use, or installed capacity.

Thus, we find that there are many factors determining demand and among them the following are a few important variables;

a) Price of the commodity;

b) general price level prevailing in the market;

c) size and growth of population;

d) the composition of population;

e) stocks of durable goods;

f) the buyers disposable income;

g) the process of substitutes;

h) the scientific and technological changes and their impact on taxation, etc., etc.

D. METHODS OF FORECASTING

Industries or firms use same methods for forecasting demand for established goods. The starting point is general business forecasts relating to the economy for the period under consideration. Macro-economic forecasting is highly developed technique in western countries. In India the planning division periodically prepares forecast of national income and its components to be used by firms and industries for their own use.

There are several methods of forecasting, namely,-

1) Trend projections:

When an industry or firm has been in existence for some time, it will have the capacity to accumulate some data relating to sale or production of a certain commodity at different time periods. When such data is chronologically arranged, it gives out some trend projection, which is called "Time Series". In this approach, a company analyses its past sales to determine the nature of existing trend; and this trend is extrapolated into the future, which becomes the basis for a forecast. This could be well understood by means of an example; suppose a car manufacturer decides to fore-cast the next year sales of his product by this method, he has to collect data on his sales for the previous 5 to 6 years to get an idea.

Year	Sales (in thousand of unit)
1987	60
1988	65
1989	55
1990	70
1991	75

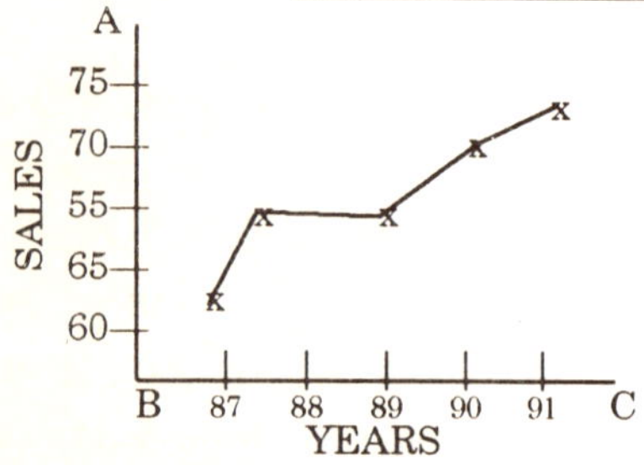

If the sales are projected, a graph representing the time series is obtained.

An examination of this graph indicates that the sales are following an up-ward trend, Thus, the firm can determine the future demand and act accordingly.

2) Opinion Surveys:

It is a subjective method of prediction based on weighted or un-weighted averaging of attitudes and expectations. Surveys may be attempted for purposes of planning at the level of the firms, industry or the economy. Forecasting is essentially the art of anticipating what buyers are likely to do under a given set of conditions. A list of potential prospective buyers are prepared and an individual approach is made to ascertain about the quantity he would buy in a stipulated time under the given conditions. The various factors that would influence his choice also will be considered. In the event of getting this information correctly, the firm would seem to have an ideal basis for forecasting its demand. A firm may plan a survey of its potential buyers through a sample or a census basis depending upon cost considerations.

It is dangerous to depend totally on buyers estimates. This method is passive and does not expose and measure the variables under managements control. This method is not useful in the case of household consumers for various reasons.

3) Expert opinion:

Another method of forecasting is obtaining the opinion from persons such as distributors or outside experts, dealers,etc., Prof. Philip Kotler says that the estimates obtained from dealers are subject to the same strengths and weakness as salesmen estimates. In U.S.A. various public and private agencies issue periodic forecasts of short term or long term business conditions. These opinions may be the outcome of surveys condensed with the help of statistical and mathematical analysis of past data.

4) Delphi Technique Method:

This method counters the limitations of traditional quantitative methods. This technique is the result of systematic analysis of opinion and value judgements. Delphi offers a systematic and scientific procedure for evaluation. It is a sophisticated statistical method. Delphi is capable of incorporating behaviour elements like personality, intuition and retrospection. It was developed in 1940 by Mr. Helmer and Gordon and applied in technological and environmental forecasting, and also in the defence field. In the business management field, its importance could be seen in manpower planning, business forecasting and demand estimation, Delphi can be used in civil defence policy, computer applications, education, urban planning, evaluation of research projects, foreign affairs and information processing. Thus, Delphi technique method is of great value in arriving at the concensus.

5) Barometric Technique:

Simple Trend Projections are incapable of forecasting turning points. The barometric technique is based on the idea that certain events of the present can be used to predict the directions of change in future, This could be obtained by the use of economic and statistical indicators, which are select time series related to the variables to be predicted. Personal income; non-agricultural placements; gross national income; prices of industrial materials; wholesale commodity prices; industrial production; Bank deposits etc., are some of the most commonly used indicators.

6) Econometric Model Building:

It is a branch of applied science based on the idea that changes in economic activity can be explained by a set of relationships between the relevent economic variables. A major objective of this concept is to identify functional relationship between variables and to measure them by statistical techniques. Functional relationship envisages that a change in the value of one variable is associated with change in the value of another. If the quantity demanded of a product is dependent on its price, demand is dependent variable and price is independent variable. If demand depends on income and price, then dependent variable is a function of two independent variables, whether the number of variables the function can be expressed as an equation. Economic model builders use statistical tool like "correlation and regression analysis" to predict probability course of events.

Certain companies in advanced countries use other methods of forecasting also, namely, -

1) controlled experiments method;

2) Input-output model method;

3) chain Ratio method; and

4) Computer assisted forecasting method.

No single method is fool proof; and it is better not to rely entirely upon a single method. It is better to solve the problem from a number of different angles.

In business decision making in recent times forecasting has come to play an important role. In a well organised production control system, determination of the type of forecast requires a fundamental step. Firms are interested both in short-term and long-term demand. For estimating long-term demand, the firm may use any combination of the following forecasting method, namely opinion surveys, expert opinion, chain ratio method, trend projections, barometric techniques, econometric models, input-output model, computer assisted forecasting, etc. The success of forecast under the above methods depends upon the type of product, the availability and reliability of data. Demand forecasting for new products depends upon ingenuity and skills of the organiser. According to prof. Joel Dean the ideal forecasting method is one that yields returns over cost in accuracy, consisting with existing knowledge.

Summarization (points at a glance)

1. *Demand means a desire backed-up by sufficient purchasing capacity. Demand varies inversely with price and demand is always at a price. Demand analysis studies the various factors that influence the demand of a commodity or service.*

2. *The demand analysis has certain objects. It has to analyse the factors which affect demand. The following factors affect demand, price, price of complimentaries and substitutes; future trend of prices, change in tastes and fashions, climatic factors, change in population, change in real income, level of income, change in savings, conditions of trade, distribution of income and wealth; product improvement, educational standards, geographical position of buyers, etc.*

   Demand analysis has to measure the elasticity of demand. It has to prepare forecast of demand sales through trend analysis, correlation and regression analysis, customers opinion survey, substitute approach, buyers point of view, experts opinion and market analysis, it has to properly allocate resources and manipulate demand.

3. *Law of demand, explains the relationship of price and demand of a commodity. Other things remaining constant, a higher price results in lower demand and vice versa. Demand is a dependent variable while price is an independent variable. The law of demand is influenced by price effect, income effect and substitution effect. The demand curve slope downwards due to the operation of law of diminishing marginal utility, income effect, substitution effect and change in the number of consumers.*

4. *Inferior goods, conspicuous consumption, future changes in prices, emergencies, change in fashion, and consumer's ignorance are exception to the law of demand.*

5. *Elasticity of demand is the Degree of responsiveness of commodities demanded to a change in demand determinants. The demand elasticity is of four types, namely - price elasticity, income elasticity, cross elasticity and advertising elasticity. Nature of commodity,*

availability of substitutes, durability of the commodity share in total expenditure, inexpensive goods, different uses of the commodity, consumer's behaviour, level of income and range of prices are the factors influencing. Price elasticity helps in determining pricing policy, it is useful to monopolist, to the government, to the theory of international trade, to determine factor pricing and also explains the paradox of poverty in the midst of plenty.

6. *The income elasticity of demand measures the degree of responsiveness of quantities demanded to a given change in income. The income elasticity may be zero, when a change in income has no effect on the quantity demanded, it may be positive, when increase in income leads to an increase in the quantity demanded, and it may be negative, when an increase in income leads to a reduction in the quantity demanded. The income sales demand relationship is based on consumption function, product consumption function, differences in regional incomes and income expectation.*

7. *the cross elasticity of demand is the effect of a change in prices of related goods on the demand for a particular commodity and these related goods may be competitive or complementary.*

8. *The advertising elasticity of demand measures the responsiveness of demand to change in advertising and other promotional expenses.*

9. *Demand could be classified as follows:-*

   a) Derived demand and autonomous demand, if the demand for a product is linked with the purchase of some main product, it is said to be derived demand. The demand for cement to construct a house is derived demand. If the demand is not linked, it is autonomous demand.

b) *The demand by all the consumers in the market is total demand. Market segment demand means, the demand for the product by the consumers of a particular segment based on geographical location, status,age,sex,etc. Likewise,there are short term and long-term demand,industry and company demand, etc.*

As regards demand forecasting,there are three levels of forecasting, namely the macro-level forecasting based on national income, national expenditure and index of industrial production; industry level forecasting prepared by several trade associations on the basis of industry; land and firm level forecasting, that is at the micro-level related to the requirements of a firm.

With the classification of goods as capital goods, consumer durables and consumer nondurables goods, there is need for forecasting for each type.

10) *A short term forecasting aims at a suitable production policy, reduction in the costs of purchases, determination of appropriate price policy, establishment of controls, preparation of financial requirements and regular availability of labour force.*

11) *Different methods are followed for sales forecasting and they are:-*

   a) *Survey of buyers intentions;*

   b) *Collective opinion*

   c) *trend projections;*

   d) *economic indicators*

   e) *experts opinions; and*

   f) *controlled experiments,etc.,*

12) *Accuracy, reliability, simplicity, comprehensive, economy,durability,availability,etc. are some of the factors forming criteria for good forecasting.*

13) *The success of forecasting depends upon,*

    a) *Identification of objective;*

    b) *Selection of appropriate method;*

    c) *Identification of variables;*

    d) *Collection of relevant, reliable and exhaustive data;*

    e) *Preparation and proper interpretation of results;*

    f) *Forecasts in physical units, product groups,*

    g) *Correct and accurate financial requirements and fund allocation.*

CHAPTER - 3

PRODUCTION FUNCTION

The relationship between inputs and the consequent output is generally termed as production function. The term 'Inputs' is the composition of the term 'Factors of production' and resources interchangeably used. The relationship ignores the prices of inputs and outputs. The production function formalities the relationship between the maximum quantity of output (dependent variable) obtained by a process to obtain the yield. The production function could be expressed in the form of an equation.

$$Y = f(a1, a2, a3, a4) \quad \text{etc.,}$$

Here the term, 'Y' stands for the yield or the output and 'f stands for function of the inputs a1,a2,a3,a4 or variables that are absolutely necessary to obtain the yield or output 'Y' and a1 to a4 would be the various infrastructure like men, material, money, management, machinery, marketing, science, technology, technical know-how etc., employed in the production process by the Industry or firms. The production function relates the various amount of inputs with the maximum possible output which can be obtained out of the inputs. Every producer is interested in maximising the output from a given combination of inputs. Production is therefor, a statement of technical facts which the producer uses to obtain the least-cost combination of inputs to produce an output. The state of technology determines the form of production is function. A short period production function is different from a long period production. With the advancement of science and technology,new production functions come into being and this results in a greater flow of outputs from the same inputs, or smaller quantity of inputs for the same output. Production function differs from firm to firm and from industry to industry. The technologist gives the data the economist and this data is very essential to the production function. The economic theorist presents two kinds of input - output relations in the production function.

1. The relation where quantities of some inputs are fixed while quantities of other inputs vary;

2 Where all the inputs are variable and the relationship is between changes in the amount of all inputs and the resulting outputs.

Cobb - Dougl as production Function (PF)
Measurement of P.F

Economists have examined many production functions to measure relation between changes in physical inputs and physical outputs. The measurement dates back to a century when initial studies were made in the field of agriculture. A famous statistical production function is associated with the names of Prof. Cobb and Mr. Douglas. This Cobb and Douglas function is applied to the American manufacturing industries from 1899 to 1922 to labour and capital inputs.

The cobb-Douglas function can be stated as follows:

P = b l (k) c(k) in which

P = Actual input

L = Labour

C = Capital

b = Number of units of labour

k = Exponent of labour and capital.

The exponents of 'K' are the elasticities of production, that is they measure the percentage changes in labour and capital respectively. A 1% change in labour input, capital remaining constant, results with 0.75% change in output. Similarly 1% change in capital, labour remaining constant, results with 0.25% change in output. Prof. Douglas made a time series study for the manufacturing industry of U.S.A., Canada, Australia, etc., The Labour exponents, he observed, was about two thirds and the capital exponent was about one-third . Cobb-Douglas function indicates that labour's share of national product tends to be constant under competitive market conditions.

Though the concept looks highly abstract and unrealistic they are useful and logical. Production function can be used as aids in decision - making , namely,-(1) how to obtain the maximum output from a given set of inputs, and secondly, (2) how to obtain a given output from the minimum aggregate of inputs.

The cobb-Douglas function is critisised on the ground that labour and capital alone are taken into consideration, while treating raw - materials as an automatic subtraction from the total value of output. Secondly, all labour units are treated as homogeneous, which is not the case. Thirdly, the concept has not considered the increasing returns to scale. Forthly, the concept is based on industry to industry variations, leaving aside plant to plant and firm to firm variations with in the industry. However ,in the history of econometrics, their concept in the statical investigation into the laws of production are the most useful and celebrated.

Economies of scale

With the concept of the importance of division of labour in the productive process, economists are still discussing the forces responsible for determining the economies of scale and the optimum size of business units. The major problem even today is the problem of determining the optimum size of the industry or firm; because at the optimum point an industry or firm yield the highest output with maximum profits.

In a crude way, economies of scale are said to be "reduction in average cost attributed to increase in scale".

But economies of scale are the potential reductions in average unit cost, which are associated with higher levels of productive capacity, measured in terms of the number of units of the standard product produced per unit of time. Since quantitative estimates are very important in modern times either to meet the growing domestic demand or for export purpose to international markets, the concept of measuring economies of scale has been given great attention.

Business require a knowledge of the economies of scale, since it is one of the forces and a factor which determine the optimum method of organising production. To find out the sources of growth, an estimate of the forces of economies of scale is necessary. The developing countries to organise an industry and to decide the nature of industries should consider the economies of scale . Some research is necessary in the field of economies of scale that can throw some light on the economic policies of the government which affect the scale of production. This concept of economies of scale is an important tool for the managerial economist. There are various factors contributing for the optimisation of output for example, the demand conditions in the market; the level of technology, internal as well as external, the process of production; availability of infrastructure; the size of the firm; their cost of inputs etc. One of the factors is economics of scale, which refers to the advantage that accrue to a firm as a result of increases in the scale of production. From the data available of a firm, it is possible to estimate the short run cost curves for each firm and the long run average cost curve for new factories in the industry, which shows the lowest possible cost of production at any scale of output.

The economies of scale are inter-related. There are many costs which are partly independent of scale over certain ranges of output. The initial development and design costs and partly or wholly indivisible in relation to the output of product. So also research and development costs associated with new products and the cost of indivisible factor of production are independent of the level of output; and these indivisible costs could be spread over a larger scale through-out the process of production. For many types of capital equipment both initial and operating costs increase less rapidly than capacity. The larger the output of a product, factory or firm, the greater will be the opportunities for specification of both labour and capital equipments. The operation of the law of large numbers may result in economies of massed resources. A firm operating in a number of industries and producing a wide range of products may benefit from the cross fertilisation of ideas and experience between its various divisions. Increased scale may help to use more efficient techniques or methods of organising production. A faster rate of production reduces unit costs of stocks and work in progress resulting in economies. The learning experience can reduce unit costs since it is a force contributing for economies of large output. A vertical expansion of the firm may help the manufacturer to control a market and thereby reduce the uncertainty enabling him to invest more in capital intensive methods of production creating economies of scale.

The economies of scale are of two types:

a) Internal Economies:

These economies are entirely dependent upon the growth of the firm, and they are different for different firms. These internal economies are of five kinds namely, -Technical, managerial, commercial, financial, and technological, which are uncertainty bearing. Scientific and technological improvements and their application to the productive process could reduce per unit cost. Specialisation in a bigger unit can not only increase productivity but also reduce cost per unit.

Administrative,directive,supervisory and controlling abilities of a professionally trained manager can help the firm to produce the product at a lesser cost more efficiently.

Marketing is a very important factor, because it is in the market the firm has to buy the raw materials, stock,science,technology other infrastructure necessary for production. The purchase department is entrused with this task. "Buy in the cheapest market and sell in the dearest market" is the Watch-word in a business enterprise. So also, the Sales Department should sell the finished products at a competitive rate in a competitive market at a competitive price. Thus commercial economies refer to economies in the purchase and sales departments and these economies have impact on the cost of production.

Finance is the back-bone for industrial organisation and development. It is the responsibility of management to mobilise sufficient and adequate financial capital for the firm or industry. The management should accrue capital with minimum liability to the industry and should see that this mobilised finance is efficiently and effectively utilized to keep down the cost of production. Interest payment on borrowed capital is a charge and an element of cost of production. Financial economies arise when a big firm enjoys better credit facilities and borrow funds on more favorable terms. The cost of borrowing should not be too high. The firm or the industry should be neither over capitalied nor under-capitalised. The management should see that there is balanced supply of capital to the firm or the industry. Unnecessary payment of interest on capital is a drain on the profits of the institution.

With the rapid revolutions in the field of science and technology,and in a dynamic economy risks are always there. Risk and uncertainty are the two factors always threatening the firm. A big firm can afford to distribute or spread its risks. Through the process of diversification of products risks could be even eliminated; and this diversification relate to products, markets,prices of manufacture,sources of supply,etc. The problem of risk and and survival always threaten the firm or industry in view of the fact that the products manufactured by the firm has to face competitive goods, competitive price at competitive markets.

With the rapid revolutions in the field of science and technology, and in a dynamic economy risks are always there. Risk and uncertainty are the two factors always threatening the firm. A big firm can afford to distribute or spread its risks. Though the process of diversification of products risks could bring even eliminated; and this diversification relate to products, markets, prices of manufacture,sources of supply,etc. The problem of risk and survival always threaten the firm or industry in view of the fact that the products manufactured by the firm has to face competitive goods, competitive prices at competitive markets.

Thus,internal economies have a tremendous and relative impact on prices and costs. Prof. Stonier and Hague point out "These are those economies in production- those reductions in the production costs-which can be carried within the firm itself when output increases". These economies are particular to the individual firms and do not reach the whole industry. To conclude two factors, indivisibilities and specialisation, give rise to internal economies.

b) External Economies:

They are not related to individual firm's own cost reduction. They arise as a result of the expansion of an industry as a whole. They are common to all the firms in the industry. Whenever an industry expands transport facilities, road and railways amenities; commercial services like banking, ware-housing, accounting, become available at lower prices. Ancillary units and subsidary industries spring up in neighborhood and all these advantages are jointly shared by each of the firm. The subsidiary industries may even make use of the products of the larger industries profitably. Economies of information,research,market news and market research could be jointly made use of,and as such the cost per unit might go down. According to Stonier and Hague "External economies are those economies in production and increase in the out put of the whole industry rather than on increase in the output of the individual firm. Internal economies occur when a increase in the size of an industry leads to lower costs for the individual firms composing the industry."

These economies lead to cost savings; they are not monopolised by any single firm. They are shared by all the firms in the industry.

Industrial location or the scientific location of the industry and specialisation are the contributing factors for external economies.

Some contend that internal economies are a micro-approach and external economies are a Macro-approach. But when international situations are considered, even this macro-approach could become, a micro-approach. Prof. Roobertson analyses a situation when a firm enjoys both internal as well as external economies simultaneously. They are closely related and inter- dependent on each other.

c) Diseconomies of Scale:

There are certain forces which cause increases in unit cost as scale increases leading to diseconomies of scale. For all firms and industries there is an optimum point beyond which the scale of production cannot be indefnitely expanded. Beyond the point of optimum capacity a firm is subject to diseconomies of scale. The supply of a factor of production is fixed and if the demand for that factor increases, the supply cost of that factor rises. Even the efficiency in the use of a factor of production declines as that factor is subject to excessive use. There are several forces which are sources of diseconomies of scale. Beyond the point of optimum capacity economies yield place to diseconomies.

Basically there are three methods used for measuring the economies of scale. Of these the Engineering approach is most commonly used. Method of production are disintegrated into individual processes and operations. Whenever possible the technical basis for economies of scale are investigated. In most cases it is necessary to base estimates of cost of production and finally estimate the relationship between unit costs and the various dimensions of scale. The main advantage of the engineering approach is that it holds other conditions constant, while making estimates of the economies of scale.

d) The Law of variable proportions.

The laws of returns state clearly the functional relationship between inputs and outputs. The concept of return to scale becomes relevent only in the long period when all the inputs could be varied. This is because that during short period the factor input cannot be changed.

The law of variable proportions explains to us the behaviour of output when the changes are made in factor proportions. The level of output of a firm depend on the combination of different factors. To bring about a charge in the level of production, it becomes necessary to vary the quantities of various factors engaged in production. The law which examines the relationship between one variable factor and output, Keeping the quantities of other factors fixed, is called the Law of variable proportions.

Prof. Benham says "As the proportion of one factor in a combination of factors is increased, after a point, first the marginal and then the average product of that factor will diminish".

Prof. Stigler observes "As equal increment of one input is added, the inputs of these productivity services being held constant beyond a certain point the resulting increments of product will decrease, that is the marginal product will diminish".

Prof. Samuelson explains "An increase in some inputs, will, in a given state of technology, cause output to increase; but after a point the extra inputs will become less and less effective".

This law of variable proportions, which is very important for the production function, is based on certain assumptions:-

a) The state of technology in production remains constant;

b) Only one factor of input in production is made variable and other factors kept constant;

c) All units of the variable factors are homogeneous; and

d) The entire operation is for short-run, in the long run all inputs can be variable.

Three stages of laws:

Fixed factor	Variable factor	Total production in units.	Average production units.	Marginal production in units.
1	2	3	4	5
(Machines)	(labour)			
1	1	10	10	10
1	2	22	11.0	12
1	3	36	12.0	14
1	4	52	13.0	16
1	5	66	13.2	14
1	6	76	12.6	10
1	7	80	11.4	4
1	8	82	10.2	2
1	9	82	9.2	0
1	10	78	7.8	-4

Stage - I:

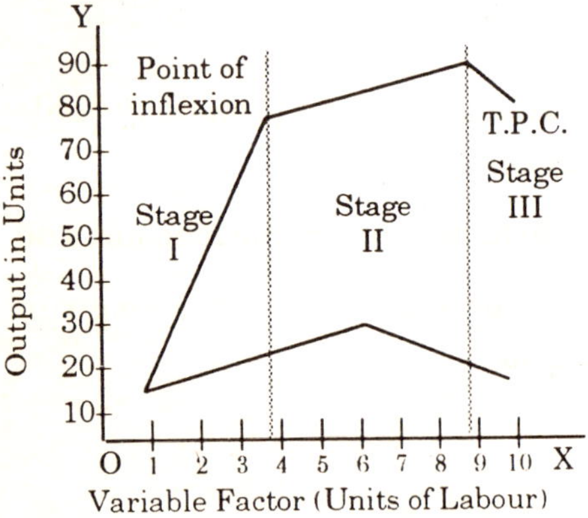

In this stage the total product increases at an increasing rate. The total product curve TPC increases sharply upto the point of inflexion (F), that is 4th combination, where the marginal product (MP) is at the maximum. Afterwards, that is beyond the point of inflexion (F), the TPC increases at a diminishing rate as the MP falls but is positive. The point of F where the total product stops increasing at a diminishing rate is called the point of inflexion. At this point the MP is at maximum. So stage - I refers to the increasing stage, where the TP, MP and AP are increasing. It is increasing Returns stage.

Stage - II

In the second stage, the TP continues to increase, but at a diminishing rate until it reaches the point S, where it completely stops to increase any further. At this the second stage ends. In this stage, the marginal product MP and the Average product (AP) are declining but are positive. At the end of the second stage at point S, the TP is at the maximum and the MP is zero. It is cutting the X axis. this is the stage of Diminishing Returns.

Stage - III

In this stage, the TPC declines and therefore the TPC slopes downwards. The MP becomes negative cutting the x axis. This stage is called the Negative Returns stage.

Thus, the TP, MP and AP pass through three stages. The law of variable proportion is nothing but the combination of the Law of increasing and Diminishing Returns.

A rational producer will not come to the 3rd Stage, where the MP becomes negative. The producer will also not choose to produce in the second stage, as he will not be making the best use of the fixed factor. Stage I and Stage III are stages of economic absurdity representing non-economic region in production function. In stage II, the TPC leads to maximum. Prices of factors determine the point of production in Stage II, which represents the range of rational production.

Returns to Scale :

This studies the behaviour of output to the change in input of all factors. In the law of variable proportions, we keep one or more factors constant and the other factors variable in increasing the input and to increase the output. But in the case of 'Returns of Scale', the entire input (all factors) is increased so that the proportion between factors will remain constant after increase. When all the inputs are increased on the existing ratio between the factors, it is said that the scale of input has been increased and then we study the output to the increase in scale. Here also, we meet with increasing constant and diminishing returns.

This concept explains changes in output when all factors of input are increased in the same proportion. That is to say, the concept deals with the behaviour of output in response to changes in the scale of production. It should be noted that factor proportions do not change when the scale of production changes in the scale, this constitute the subject matter of "Return to Scale".

In a dynamic society, the modern industries have to face a number of problems; and these problems are highly complicated demanding reasonable solutions. The following are the major problems.

1. The problem of Industrial location;
2. The problem of ownership and control;
3. The problem of optimum firm;
4. The problem of Rationalisation;
5. The problem of Industrial Relations;
6. The problem of marketing;
7. The problem of Industrial Financing
8. The problem of Risk and Survival;
9. The problem of Imperfect competition;
10. The problem of Governmental constraints and Restraints;
11. The problem of Transport and Communications;
12. The problem of Corporate taxes,etc.

These are some of the major problems that modern industries, especially the corporate sectors are facing today.

Production and profits always go together. In a capitalistic economy, the consumer is the king. Maintenance or increase of profits are the result of either increasing the selling price or the reduction of cost of production. In a consumer supremacy, profit cannot be increased by increasing the selling price. Consumer's demand is never constant but ever changing. Therefore, the modern producer has to adjust himself to the changing circumstances to maintain himself. Thus, production function is a major factor demanding constant attention. The laws of variable proportions operate continuously in the productive process and the entrepreneur has to shoulder the responsibility to bring down the cost of production by utilising the various infrastructure and exploit them to the optimum point, that is, capacity utilization through a rational, reasonable, systematic and scientific way.

CHAPTER - 4

COST ANALYSIS

A. In a productive process the production of goods and service involves costs of production. The utilisation of various infrastructure in the productive process like men, material, money (capital) machinery, marketing, energy etc., are to be compensated through payment. The Scarcity of factors of production and their alternative use make the payment more essential. The means or potentialities available to produce goods and service ar very much limited, where as the demand for products, both consumers goods and durable use goods, is increasing day by day with the growth of population and with the development of science and technology. The resources are not only scarce but they are subject to alternative uses.

The traditional methods of estimating costs are not of much use to the entrepreneur. Business decisions involve not only the present cost but also future costs and demand the choice of alternative plans to determine future expenses and revenues.

The determinants of costs differ from firm to firm and from problem to problem. A few determinants like rate of output, the size of plant, prices of inputs, technology, efficiency of management and labour are of special importance. In the price theory, different concepts of costs are used. To determine the cost of equilibrium firm, it is necessary to know clearly the working operations of these costs:

a) Real cost;
b) Opportunity cost
c) Implicit cost;
d) Explicit cost; and
e) money cost.

Cost behaviour is the result of many forces and the functional relationship of cost to each major force helps to provide the informational foundation for various cost forecasts and estimates of the alternative cost or rival programmes, which characterise cost analysis in managerial economics.

1. Money Cost:

The money outlays constitute a major item of a firm in the production process and its output. These include wages and salaries paid to labour; the expenditure on machinery and equipment and their maintenance; the payment made towards materials; power, fuel, and transportation, rent payments; advertisement, insurance and taxes etc. While calculating the costs of the firm, management remuneration, a reasonable rate of return on bloc capital like land and buildings, provision for depreciation and bad debts should also be considered. The economists consider the real costs from the social-view point. Dr.Marshall observed that "the exertions of the different kinds of labour that are directly or indirectly involved in making it; together with abstinences or rather the waitings required for saving the capital used in making it; all these efforts and sacrifices together will be called the real cost of production of the commodity".

According to Prof.Hanson, "The money cost of producing a certain output of commodity is the sum of all the payments to the factors of production engaged in the production of that commodity". Thus, money costs enter the records of the accountants of a company.

2. Opportunity Cost:

The concept of opportunity cost is more important and useful to management in making a decision among alternatives. According to Leftwitch " Opportunity cost of a particular product is the value of the foregone alternative products that resources used in its production could have produced". From the point of view of an individual, the sacrifice of an opportunity of using it for some purpose other than the one to which it is being put, constitutes the opportunity cost. The resources used in production have many alternative uses. Opportunity cost has to be stated in relative terms. They take the form of profits from alternative ventures that are foregone by using limited facilities for a particular purpose. In the Final Accounts they are not recorded, since they represent only sacrificed alternatives. Opportunity cost concept is used only when the supply of input factors is limited. According to Prof. Ferguson. "The alternative or opportunity cost of producing one unit of commodity X is the amount of commodity Y that must be sacrificed in order to use resources to produce X rather than Y".

In price theory the money cost of production is considered and other are considered only in Welfare economics.

3. Imputed costs:

there are certain costs that do not take the form of cash outlays, nor do they enter in the accounting system. such costs are called as imputed costs or implicit costs. Imputed costs may be defined as the earning of owner's resources employed in their best alternative uses. For example, suppose an entrepreneur does not utilise his services in his own business, and works as a manager in some other firm on a salary basis. If he joins his own business, he foregoes his salary as manager. This Loss of salary which is opportunity cost of his services utilised in his own firm becomes an implicit cost of his own business. While calculating the loss or gains of the business, imputed costs are not taken into account but considered while making a business decision.

4. Cost curves in the short and the Long run

Larger the product produced, Lower will be the cost incurred and Vice-versa;and this is the main advantage of a large scale production. The costs of production of a commodity are payment made to the inputs (factors) of production. Since the nature of production is different in short-run period from that in the long run period, it is necessary to build up cost analysis in both the periods.

In the short-run, some factors of production are fixed, while others are variable; in the long run, all inputs are variable. In the short-run period only the proportion of inputs can be changed while in the long run period, Scale of production can be varied. The short run cost are costs which vary with out put when fixed plant and capital equipment remain the same. Long-run costs are those which vary with output, if all input factors vary. When there is perfect flexibility in the size of plant, labour force, executive talent etc.long run cost behaviour is involved.

Short-run costs become relevent when a firm has to decide whether or not to produce more in the immediate future;when setting up of a new plant is ruled out, the firm has to manage with the given plant. The distinction is based upon the degree of adoptation of all input factors to rate and type of output. The duration of the shortrun longrun differs from industry to industry according to the nature of equipment and inputs required, the techniques employed, and the stage of development of the area.

a) Short-run cost analysis

(Cost-output relationship)

The short run costs could be divided in to two types,namely,-

1) Fixed Costs

2) Variable costs

1) Fixed Costs:

According to Prof.Benham "The fixed costs of a firm are those costs that do not vary with the size of the output". These are the cost of fixed plant and equipment of the firm. The fixed costs are unavoidable contractual costs. The fixed costs are the cost which a firm has to bear even when it is temporarily shutdown and produces nothing. For example;interest on investments in plant and equipment;property tax;Insurance premium; depreciation and maintenance;and the salaries to workers whose services can not be dispensed with even when the firm is temporarily shutdown. Prof.Marshall refers to fixed cost as supplement or over head costs. They also include the opportunity costs of the owners of the firm,as well as normal profits. They remain constant irrespective of changes in volume up to a certain level of output. Since they are constant in total,they vary per unit without rate. There is an inverse relationship between the volume and fixed costs.

2) Variable Costs:

These costs change with changes in the volume of output. These are variable,contractual costs. Prof.Benham observes that "The variable costs of a firm are those costs that do vary with the size of its output". Dr.Marshall called these costs as "Prime Costs",for example;Wages;payments to raw materials, fuel and power;excise;interest on short term loans etc.,are variable costs. Variable costs vary in total in direct proportion to changes in volume,and these costs are subject to reduction. Many costs fall between these extremes varying less than proportionately, or changing by jumps.

The distinction between these two costs is important in forecasting the effect of short-run changes in volume upon costs and profits. The break-even charge illustrates this application in predicting profits. During short period,the total cost of a firm are split in to fixed costs and variable costs,since it is important in the determination of price theory.

A producer while selling his output tries to cover both fixed cost and variable cost. During short period due to some reason price may fall, hence he will not be in a position to cover his costs leading to loss. Thus, he is forced to decide whether to continue production or not. If the firm is closed consequent to the above reason,the firm may not incur variable cost,but the fixed cost can not be avoided. The maximum loss it can suffer is equal to fixed costs. Thus,the firm will decide to shutdown if the price is less than the average variable cost, because the total loss will be greater than its fixed costs. On the opposite way, if the price is greater than the average,variable costs,the firm will be covering a part of its fixed costs also. Then it is advantageous to the firm to continue the production. This distinction is important only for the short period;because in the long period, all costs are variable and must be covered. Thus,the equilibrium conditions of the firm differ in the short period and long period.

Average Fixed Cost (AFC) & Average Variable Cost (AVC)

In price theory, it is necessary to know the average fixed costs and the average variable costs, so that they could be compared directly with the price of the product at which it could be sold in the market. It is also necessary to know the behaviour of AFC as output changes

$$\text{Average Fixed Cost (AFC)} = \frac{\text{Total Fixed Cost (TFC)}}{\text{output (O)}}$$

The fixed costs of a firm are constant, when output is changed, hence the impact of fixed cost per unit of output will continue to fall as output is increased. Thus, with increasing output the average fixed cost will continue to fall.

$$\text{Average Variable Cost (AVC)} = \frac{\text{Total Variable Cost (TVC)}}{\text{output (O)}}$$

The behaviour of average product of the variable factors determines the behaviour of average variable cost. It is clear in the theory of production, in the short period, that the average product of the variable factors rises in the beginning, remains constant for some time and starts falling latter resulting in the average cost increasing beyond a point.

It is necessary to know the average of both the fixed and variable costs combined, in order to find out the profit or loss to a firm at a particular level of output with the given price of the product.

The short run average cost is equal to AFC+AVC i.e., EAC=AFC+AVC; and hence the behaviour of SAc with changes in output depends directly on the behaviour of AFC and AVC. AFC goes on decreasing as output increases. AVC falls at first, reaches a minimum and then starts increasing. SAC and AVC are closely inter related.

AVC=SAC-AFC or AFC=SAC-AVC.

Both SAC and AVC are U-shaped.

Marginal Cost:

The Marginal Cost (MC) happens to be the third most important concept in the short run cost analysis. The addition made to the total cost by the production of one more unit of output is called Marginal Cost. Prof. Dooley observes that "the marginal cost is the change in total cost associated with a change in output."

$$\text{Marginal Cost (MC)} = \frac{\text{Change in Total Cost (TC)}}{\text{Change in Output (O)}}$$

Marginal cost is governed by variable costs which change whenever there is a change in output.

$$MC = \frac{V}{O} = \frac{\text{(Variable cost)}}{\text{Output}}$$

The behaviour of Marginal cost must be derived from the behaviour of AVC alone, because the MC is directly dependent upon the behaviour of AVC. The MC falls at first, reaches a minimum level then starts rising.

Relation between Marginal Cost and Average Cost:

The relationship between AC and MC in the price theory is of very great importance. The entire marginal analysis of pricing the product is dependent on that. Both AC and MC are calculated from the same source.

$$\text{Average Cost} = \frac{\text{Total Cost}}{\text{Total Output}}$$

$$\text{Marginal Cost} = \frac{\text{Change in total cost}}{\text{Change in Unit of Output}}$$

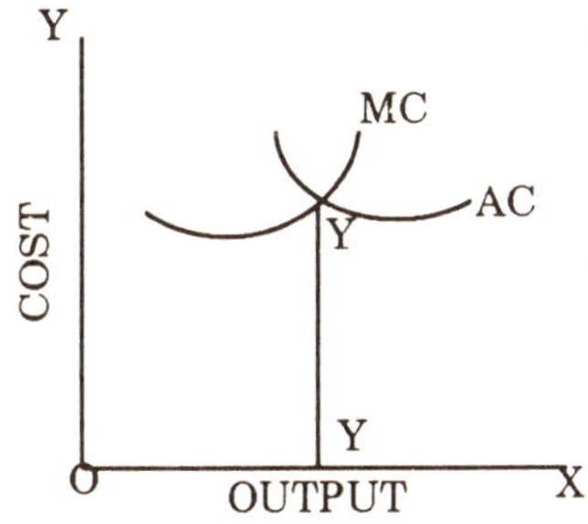

When average cost is falling, the Marginal cost is always lower than the average cost. When AC falls, MC falls faster. When MC reaches a minimum, it starts rising again even when the AC is falling. It should be noted that the Mc lies above AC and rises faster than AC. The MC curve must cut the AC curve at AC's minimum point. When AC is constant MC is equal to AC. The minimum point of the AC curve is that from which the perpendicular to the x axis is the shortest. The output OM is produced at the lowest average cost.

b) Long Run cost analysis :

In the long run no factor is fixed. Every thing including the plant size is variable. The firm can change to suit its needs, where as in the short run, a firm has no choice, but to adjust its production to the demand for its product by changing the proportion of variable factors relative to the fixed factors. The long run is a period long enough to make all costs variable including such costs as are fixed in the short run. The firm has sufficient time to fully adjust itself, hence all costs become variable. In the long run the firm will like to change its scale of production to suit its needs. It is always profitable to change the scale of the plant, rather than changing the proportions of inputs, so that the output is adjusted to demand in the long period. Prof. Leftwitch says "the long run average curves show the least possible cost per unit of producing various outputs, when the firm has time to build any desired scale of plant". Prof. J.S. Bain observes that "the long run average cost curve shows for each possible output, the lowest cost of producing the output in the longrun".

'U-shaped' short-run and long-run average cost curves are due to the operation of the Law of Variable proportion and the varying returns to scale. In the short-run, the plant of the firm is fixed, while other inputs are variable, and the production is subject to the law of variable proportions. As output is increased to reach the capacity, overhead costs per unit continue to fall. After the capacity output is reached, average cost will begin to rise, because the variable inputs become too much for the plant, whose size is fixed Thus, the 'U' shape of the SAC curve is due to the non- proportional returns at a given scale of the plant.

The reason for the 'U' shape of the LAC curve is a debated propositions. Most production functions exhibit constant returns to scale. This 'U'shape implies lower and lower average cost in the beginning until the optimum scale of the enterprise is reached and successively higher average cost thereafter. The LAC curve is faster compared to SAC curve. The 'U' shape of the LAC curve is less pronounced, because in the long run economies are possible, which cannot be had in the short run. A firm is interested in producing a given output at the maximum cost. The LAC curve helps a firm to decide the size of the plant that could produce the given output. Thus, in managerial decision-making, the usefulness of the LAC curve helps to assist the management to determine the best size of the plant. At the planning stage, the management is faced with the problem of selecting the best size of the plant that could give the largest output at the minimum cost.

B. Equilibrium of the firm and industry

Equilibrium is a 'position of balance' or 'a position of rest' or 'the stage of no change'. A firm refers to a Unit of control producing similar commodities competing with each other in the market.

A firm is said to be in equilibrium, when it has reached its most profitable position. In that position of equilibrium there will be no tendency on the part of the firm either to increase or decrease the output, as that level of output gives the firm maximum profit.

A consumer is said to be in equilibrium, when he spends his limited income on different commodities in such a way that he gets maximum satisfaction. Just as the consumer attempts to maximise his output at the minimum possible cost, so also a firm, while selling its finished products, attempts to maximise its profits.

The concept of equilibrium firm is based on two assumptions. Firstly, the firm is assumed to have only one aim, that is, to get maximum possible profit and it is not satisfied with normal or fair profits.

Secondly, it is assumed that the firm has full knowledge of the profit - making position. The firm through a series of experiments has been able to find out that level of output, which can secure the maximum possible profit.

In practice, these two assumptions may not hold good and practicable. The business firms may not be in a position to alter their output continuosly to find out that level of output to secure the maximum possible profit.

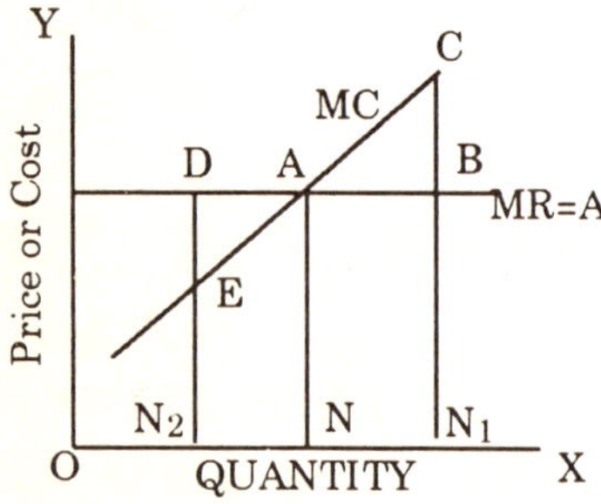

The firm is said to be in equilibrium, when the Marginal Revenue is equal to the Marginal Cost (MR=MC). Marginal Revenue is the addition to the total revenue obtained by selling one more unit of the output. Marginal cost means addition to the total cost, when one more unit is produced. When MR is greater than MC, there is scope for more gains. When MC is greater than MR, it is a losing position. So, the maximum gain will accure when MR=MC.

Equilibrium of a competitive firm

A competitive firm has a horizontal price line (Since the price is determined by the industry and the firm accepts it) and obviously, the average and marginal revenues coincide. The point 'A' shows the equality of MC and MR. ON is the maximum quantity which the firm can produce and this is the profit maximising quantity. Output beyond this point, ON, will mean loss to the firm, as the MR for this output is N'.B., but the MC is higher at N'.C. If the firm produces ON', it will incur a loss indicated by the triangle ABC, and no firm is prepared for this. On the other hand, if the firm produces ON2 quantity, the MR is higher than MC., and this is to the advantage of the firm. But, the firm can increase its total profit by producing additional unit of output N2N and there by gain additional profits shown in the triangle DAE. So no firm will stop producing at ON2. The best output is ON indicated by the equality of MR and MC.

The second condition necessary for an equilibrium firm is that MC curve should cut the MR curve from below. If MC curve cuts the MR curve from above, the point of intersection is not an equilibrium point, because after cutting MR curve, the Mc curve becomes lower to MR curve. This means with the incease in output, the difference between MR and MC persists, so as to give further profits. So, there is scope for increasing output maximising profits.

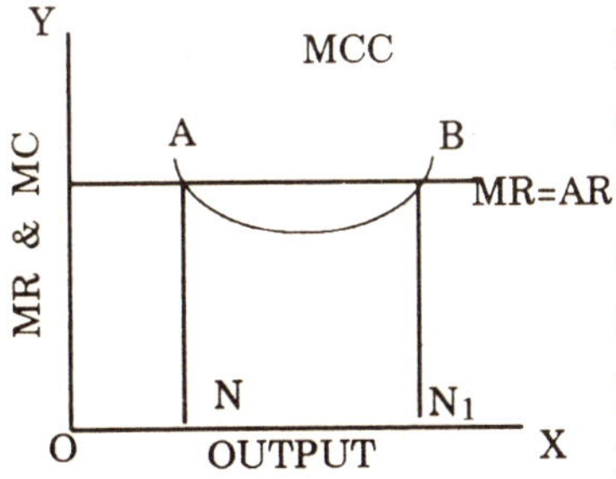

Some times the condition of MR=MC may not be sufficient enough and hence the second condition namely that MCC should cut MRC from below is to be insisted upon. An equilibrium for a perfect competitive firm is possible only if MCC cuts the MRC from below. For a competitive firm, the MRC is horizontal. (showing constant cost condition) coinciding with the MRC, then there is fixed output, which will either maximise profits or minimise the losses. Thus, there cannot be a horizontal MCC. Then, the two other possibilities are, the MCC can be sloping upwards, or downwards upto a point and upwards later.

In the above diagram, the MCC cuts MRC at points A and B. At point A, it cuts from above and at point B from below. Point A cannot be a determinate equilibrium point, since beyond this point MC is lower than MR and therefore it is advantageous to the firm to produce more and secure profits shown between A and B. At both these points MR=MC and the point of equilibrium lies only at B and not at A. The equilibrium output is 'ON', because after A, the MCC falls below MRC only at B, the MCC rises above MR and beyond that cost will be higher than revenue for marginal output. Hence, the equilibrium point is B and the equilibrium output is ON1.

The formula MR=MC holds good to any kind of producer, whether he is a monopolist, a firm in the monopolistic competition or a firm in the perfect competition.

Summarization (points ata glance)

COST ANALYSIS

1. *Business units use different types of costs to arrive at decision making;*

   a) *private cost - cost of production to individual producer and social cost-related to resources consumed in production.*

   b) *Actual cost-actual expenses incurred in production and opportunity cost - which refers to the revenue that could have been earned had the resources been employed elsewhere.*

   c) *Past cost -actual cost incurred in the past and recorded in account books and future cost-expected costs to be incurred in the future.*

   d) *Explicit cost- which include actual expenses made and implicit cost- those costs that are shouldered by the employer himself.*

   e) *Incremental costs- they are additional costs due to change in the nature of business and sunk costs -which do not change with the change in business.*

   f) *Fixed costs -which remain unaffected by the change in output or sales, and variable costs that varies proportionately with the increase or decrease in sales or output.*

Like wise, there are average cost, marginal cost, total cost, historical cost, replacement cost, controllable and noncontrollable costs, direct cost, indirect costs, etc.

2. *The following factors have an impact on cost behaviour;*

   a) *Locational factor, that is the scientific location of the business of the unit, which is determined by-*

      a) *Abailability of raw-materials;*
      b) *Nearness to the market.*
      c) *Energy supply,*
      d) *Efficient and economic labour,*
      e) *Network of transport system,*
      f) *Historical factors,*
      g) *Easy and cheap credit facilities,*
      h) *Nearness to the port,*
      i) *Climatic conditions,*
      J) *Personal preferences,etc.*

   b) *Scope of the business project, that is the various activities that the business unit is undertaking considering the techniques to be employed, the responsiveness of the market, after-sales service, the field of specialisation, NTC;and*

   c) *Size,-that is the size of the business unit, since an optimum size of the unit can reduce the cost of production.*

3. *The cost determination is influenced by the relationship among the variable costs, namely, the marginal cost, average cost and total costs. When the marginal cost falls, the total cost increases at a declining rate and vice-versa. When marginal cost curve is U-shaped, the marginal cost*

would be equal to average cost at a point, when average variable costs, the average variable costs would fall. If marginal cost first falls and then rises, it will be equal to the average cost at a point where

average variable cost is minimum.

4. a) *The cost output relationship in short run is based on:*

   i) *Average fixed costs, that is the total fixed costs divided by number of units produced;*

   II) *Average variable cost, that is the total variable cost divided by the number of units produced;and*

   III) *Average total cost, that is the total cost(fixed and variable)divided by the number of units produced.*

   b) *The long run period should be long enough to make all costs variable including those costs that are fixed in the short run. The long-run cost curve covers all SAC curves; U-shaped; it cannot cut a short-run average cost curve,etc.*

CHAPTER - 5

MARKET STRUCTURE

Business decisions are invariably competitive in nature. Competition has many different meanings. For competition to be present, there should be in the market two or more sellers or buyers of a definite commodity, each participant acting independently of every other one.

A. PRICING UNDER PERFECT COMPETITION

The concept of perfect competition is of great theoretical importance in the price theory. In a perfectly competitive market, the buyers and sellers have no rivalry since they are in large number and individually they have no influence over the price of the commodity. According to Prof. Leftwitch "perfect competition is a market in which there are many firms selling industrial products with no firm large enough relative in the entire market to be able to influence market price:. Prof. Ferguson has defined that "perfect competition describes a market in which there is complete absence of direct competition among economic group". Mr.Bilas says "the perfect competition is characterised by the presence of many firms. They all sell identically the same product. The seller is a price taker". Mrs. Joan Robinson has defined perfect competition in terms of the elasticity of demand. She says "perfect competition prevails when the demand for the output of each producer is perfectly elastic".

Conditions necessary for perfect competition:

1. Large number of small, un-organised firms:

The market must have such a larger number of sellers that no one seller is able to dominate in the market. The sellers will be the firm producing the product for sale in the market. Their individual output should be just a fraction of the total output in the market, so that none of them is capable of influencing the market price by its individual action. The firms should not have any kind of association or organisation with regard to price or sales.

2. Large Number of small, unorganised buyers:

On the buyers side, there should be large number of buyers, but no one buyer is able to influence the market price in any way. The buyers should not have any kind of organisation so that they compete for the market supply only on an individual basis.

3. Existence of homogeneous products:

The sellers are expected to sell completely identical products. There should not be any differentiation of products by sellers by way of quality,variety,colour,design,packing or other selling conditions of the product. Thus, the buyers have no basis to attach themselves to one seller or the other, and purchasing a seller's product on any basis other than price.

4. Free Entry and Exist of firms:

There is absolutely no restriction on entry of new firms in the industry or the exit of the firms in the industry. This condition should be satisfied for long period equilibrium of the industry.

For pure competition, the above conditions are necessary. For a perfect market, some more conditions are to be fulfilled.

5. Perfect knowledge of market conditions:

Perfect knowledge of market conditions are conditions are necessary for both buyers and sellers. Sellers must know the prices quoted by other sellers in the market , and similarly the buyers should know the price being charged by other sellers.

6. Goods and services

The goods and service as well as resources are to be perfectly mobile between firms. This will guarantee that all the firms in the competitive industry have identical cost conditions.

7. All the firms should enjoy easy access to the market. There should be absence of any transport costs of the product from one part of the market to the other.

8. There should be absence of government or artificial restrictions on the working of the firms. There must be no restraint upon the independence of any buyers or sellers either by custom, contract or collusion.

From the analysis of the above conditions, it can be seen that perfect competition probably does not exist. The term denotes the extreme freedom from control over price. Thus, perfect competition could be a mere concept, a standard available to economic theory to measure the varying degrees of imperfection."A perfect competition is a myth"

PRICING UNDER PERFECT COMPETITION

price under perfect competition is determined by the laws of supply and demand. The action and the inter- action of the forces of demand and supply determine price under perfect competition. Prices will be fixed at a point where the supply and demand are at an equilibrium, and this equilibrium will change by changes in the forces of supply and demand. The demand side is governed by the law of demand based on marginal utility of the commodity to the buyers; and the supply side is governed by the cost of production. So to say, the inter-action of marginal supply and marginal demand decide the price and this is called equilibrium price and at which point the buyers and sellers are satisfied and the demand and supply are equal.

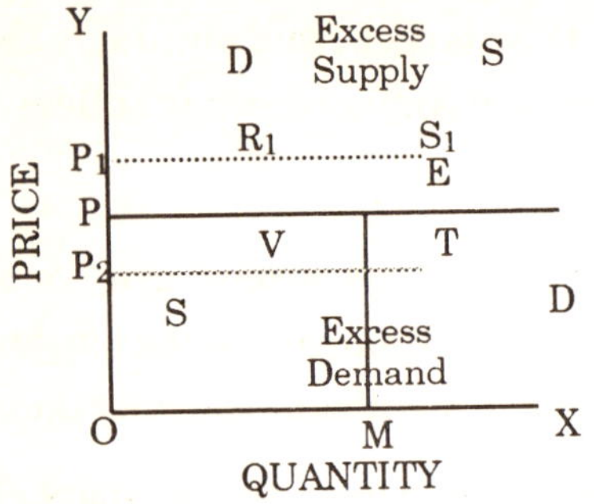

DD is the demand curve sloping down and SS is the supply curve sloping up ward . They intersect at E, the equilibrium point. The corresponding price is OP and the quantity is OM. At the OP price, the industry is prepared to supply OM quantity and at that price, the market is prepared to take one. Suppose the price increases above the equilibrium price to OP1, the demand is only P1,R1, while the supply is P1, S1 which the buyers will not take of the market at price OP1. In order to dispose off this excess, sellers will complete and bringthe price to OP. Similarly if price falls to OP2, there is an excess demand VT, and the price will be pushed up and equilibrium price will prevail in the market. The inter-action of demand and supply and the resultant price is called the equilibrium price. If there is any change in demand or supply or both, the equilibrium price will also change. In perfect competition, the firms have to take up the equilibrium price determined by the industry. No individual seller or buyer has any control over price. Any single firm in a purely competitive situation has to adjust its production and sales policy to the given market price. In perfect competition marginal revenue is equal to the average revenue, because every unit is sold at the same market price, irrespective of the quantity sold. For equilibrium of the perfectly competitive industry, long-run average costs include normal profit for a firm.

B. MONOPOLISTIC COMPETITION (Pricing under imperfect competition)

1. The monopolistic competition is defined by several economists as follows:

According to Joe. S. Baix "monopolistic competition is found in the industry where there is a large number of small sellers, selling differentiated but close substitute products".

Prof. H.N. Liobhafsky writes "monopolistic competition has today come to mean a state of affairs in which there is a large number of sellers selling non- homogeneous or slightly differentiated products and in which freedom of entry exists".

Prof. Lift witch describes "monopolistic competition as "IT is a market situation in which there are many sellers of a particular product but the product of each seller is in someway differentiated in the minds of consumers from the product of every other sellers". Under monopolistic competition, a firm has some freedom to fix its price and it has a price policy.

Monopolistic competition is one of the subdivisions of imperfect competition. It has a large number of small unorganised sellers in the market and a large number of unorganised buyers. It is product differentiations by sellers that differentiates pure competition from monopolistic competition. The products of different sellers are close substitutes, but not complete substitutes, as in monopoly. That is to say, that there are various monopolits under imperfect competition competing with each other. They do not produce identical products, and they are different in some ways, but not all together. The product of different sellers have a high cross of elasticity of demand. It is this product differentiation that introduces an impurity in the pure competition.

2. Characteristics features of monopolistic competition:

Every economist till the days of Prof. Marshall analysed economic problems on the assumption of either perfect competition or Monopoly. Since then, the market situation is considered under conditions of monopolistic competition. The number of buyers and sellers is large, but they are broken up into groups, and each group is linked to a given product. This is due to product differentiation and imperfect knowledge of the market.

a) Large number of buyers and sellers:

In every heterogeneous group, there is homogeneity, which creates competition among these buyers. Unlike monopoly there is no absolute monopolists in monopolistic competition. The price determined in the market is influenced by the competition among the buyers belonging to a seller or a product and also sellers producing to a seller or a product and also sellers producing close substitutes. Each firm acts independently without caring for any effect which its action may have upon those of its competitors.

b) Buyers attached to sellers or products:

Unlike perfect competition, buyers in monopolistic competition are not susceptible to price and price variations only. They have their own preferences, which may be due to actual differences in products or fancied differences in products. The actual differences may be in colour, taste, smell, brands, names or labels. The fancied differences exist not in products but in the behaviour of the sellers. The sellers may be more courteous, polite, may attend to the buyers inperson, more personally attentive, may attend to buyers in person, more personally attentive, may provide credit facilities, may arrange home deliveries, may be known for his honesty and dealings etc., On these grounds, the buyers get divided and attach themselves to different sellers or different products.

c) Un-restricted Entry:

Entry into industry is unrestricted. The new firms are able to commence production of very close substitutes for the existing brands of the product even though they cannot make items, which are exactly identical in the eyes of the buyers, to existing brands.

d) Lack of perfect knowledge of the market:

Under monopolistic competition, the buyers and sellers have lack of perfect knowledge of the market conditions. There are innumerable products, each being a close substitute of other. The buyers invariably purchase products out of few varieties available for sale near their home. They remain attached to a particular seller or a product. Likewise, the sellers being unable to determine the exact preference of buyers fail to make benefit. Much of the selling cost is simply meant to create imaginary superiority in the minds of consumers. The products may really be the same but consumer may come to know a particular brand name more than others. This divides the whole market in-to sub-markets, where individual firms have monopolistic conditions.

e) Product Differentiation:

Product differentiation is the '"villan of the piece" in monopolistic condition, like price discrimination under monopoly. This creates problems both for the buyers as well as the sellers. These differences may be actual or fancied.

Actual differences may depend upon differences in taste, smell, colour, brands, names of packing etc., Fancied differences arises due to the behaviour of the sellers and various facilities provided by the sellers. These may include courteous behaviour, special attention given to buyers, free gifts and samples, reduction in price on bulk purchase, seasonal concessions, credit facilities, home delivery of product etc. Though these are selling drives, they are capable of influencing the demand of buyers. Thus, product differentiation and selling costs go together. The larger the variety available, the greater should be the appeal to the buyers. Product differentiation is more important for a seller than to a buyer. Larger the number of commodities (varieties of) introduced by the seller to the market, greater will be the opportunity for the sellers to attract and appropriate the buyers. A firm in order to maximise output, will have to work out the demand price and cost of each variety. The selection and production of a given product will depend upon the calculations made by the firm.

f) Selling costs:

Every firm through different types of expenditure on salesmanship and advertisement tries to promote its own product among the consumers. The effect of these advertisement expenditure or selling costs may be to attach particular consumers to particular brands. Selling costs are in the nature of costs which have to be covered along with production costs.

The term 'selling cost' is used by Prof. Chamberlain in his book momopolistic competition. It implies the actual cost incurred by the producer of a product in selling it. In marketing, one of the items of expenditure is on advertisement. He says "that selling cost is a cost incurred in order to alter the position or shape of the demand curve for a product". This includes cost of advertisement, window dressing, salaries of salesman, home delivery service, gifts, and cost of other methods employed by sellers to boost up sales.

The demand for a commodity is based more on the utility which the consumer derives from its marginal unit than so much on its price. If this utility is more, the consumers will not be reluctant to pay a slightly higher price. "Utility, not price in the market, is a determinant of demand". Product differentiation is the root giving rise to advertisement in the industry. The producer has to face two problems. Firstly, he finds that there are other producers producing either the same product or very close substitutes. Secondly, the buyers have their own value judgments and prefer a particular commodity only. Selling costs assume their importance on account of the above facts.

g) Group Equilibrium:

In monopolistic competition, the entry and existence of competitive firms do not create an industry, because an industry is a production unit comprising of several firms producing same or identical commodities. These several firms constitute not an industry, but a group, because they are not producing identical products. Therefore, it is not possible to draw an average revenue and average cost curve for the graph.

The different methods of competing rivals, other than price like after sales service, a gift scheme, an undeclared discount etc., are secret ways of attaching more customers to a particular brand. Thus, each seller acts independently basing his policies on his estimate of his demand and cost conditions and also considering the policies of other firms as given and not affected by his policies. Since an individual seller is only a part of the total market, his price and output do not seriously affect the market.

The situation under monopolistic competition ranges all the way from a close approach to perfect competition to a close approach to monopoly. In the short-run, the seller of a slightly differentiated product, competing with many rivals, has only a limited range within which he can control the price of the product he sells. With a slight reduction in his price he can attract all the customers he can handle, because differentiated products are good substitutes for each other and their cross elasticities are high. Like other sellers, he will maximise his profits by an input output adjustment based on a comparison of marginal costs with marginal revenue.

In the long-run adjustment, a group of firms for a particular industry may be at an output level, which will yield each of them a monopoly profit. If all firms drop their price the increase in sales is much smaller than anticipated. The firm sees not potential profit available to it by cutting prices. If the number of firms in the industry is more than the equilibrium number, price cuts are made as before until all firms are making considerably less than normal profit, or vice-versa. Firms with reputed brands can charge higher prices for their products. Even an offering for sale an unknown brand at a lower price can bring about an increase in the sale of substantial quantity.

Under monopolistic competition the average revenue curve is relatively elastic, because any slight change in the price of the product can bring about a very large change in total sales. The Average Revenue Curve, therefore slopes downwards, and the Marginal Revenue is less than Average Revenue depending upon their relationship.

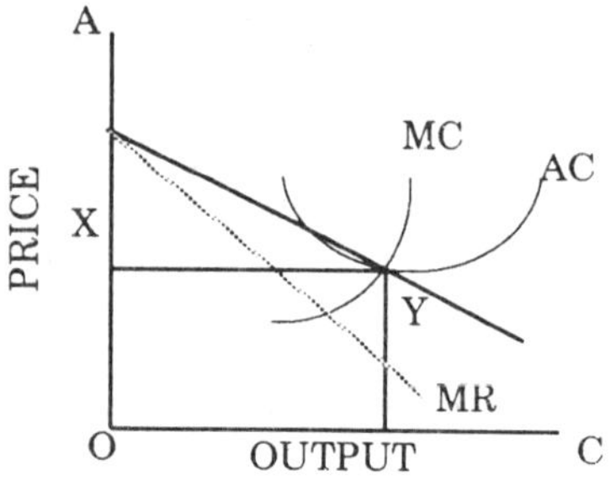

The firm under monopolistic competition reaches the point of equilibrium when Marginal Revenue (MR) is equal to Marginal Cost (MC) MR=MC; and average Revenue (AR) is equal to Average cost (AC). AR=AC.

In the long run, the firm earns only normal profit. The point X indicates MR=MC and the point Y indicates AR=AC.

PRICE FIXATION

Under monopolistic competition, a firm is "Price-Maker" unlike in perfect competition where a firm is a "price- taker". The firm has to determine a suitable price for its product, which yields maximum total profit. Under monopolistic competition, the firm has to attain equilibrium with three independent variables namely, price, output, and selling costs.

There are some negative points in monopolistic competition. It is argued that firms through immoral and unsocial methods try to accumulate more profits, that too by exploiting the consumers. Since the firms can exit from the market freely unrestricted, they can create frequent unemployment in the productive sectors. The expenditure involved for advertisement, salesmanship, window dressing etc., are ultimately to be borne by the consumers. The cross transport expenditure will have an impact on the consumers only. The little scope for specialisation in the production of a product might affect efficiency and quality under monopolistic competition.

The degree of market imperfection today are so large, that many types of imperfect competition have set in. Neither pure competition nor monopoly is in vogue today; and monopolistic competition in one order of form or the other is prevailing.

C. MONOPOLY

Normally, when total supply and total sales are controlled by one seller, the situation is said to be one of monopoly. monopoly means absence of competition. Under monopoly the cross elasticity is zero. The demand for a commodity depends on the prices of related goods, which are substitutes and complements. The monopolist is said to be the king of the market. He rules the market with his price.

a) Advantages of Monopoly:

1) A Monopoly is a combination of several producers and they agree to produce a given output and to charge a given price. Thus, there is a community of interests among these producers. Since it has the benefit of large scale production, it enjoys the fruits of internal and external economies, as it has large resources at its disposal. It can have the benefit of scientific and technological progress and carry out industrial research and innovation. Thus, it can reduce the cost and reap maximum benefits in the form of profits.

2) Monopoly avoids cut-throat competition and its attendant evils. There is co-operation among several producers in fixing output and price. There is production planning leading to elimination of wastages.

3) The monopolist purchases infrastructure on a large scale and there by possess strong bargaining powers to purchase commodities at low prices. This enables him to reduce cost of production leading to higher profits.

4) A monopolist enjoys the benefit of large sca;e marketing. The capital and resources at his disposal are very large, and, therefore, can indulge in public marketing technique. He can indulge in huge advertisement and affect the consumer's choice. He can dictate terms to retailers and earn huge profits.

5) A monopolist by employing factors of production on a large scale can help in the industrialisation of the country. For examples, the "Managing Agents", who supplied initiative, enterprise, promotion and risk capital in India during the British Rule, were mainly responsible for the industrialisation of India. But, they took more profits in different styles.

Through complex division of labour, specialisation, extensive use of machines,industrilisation of the country could be promoted.

b) Disadvantages of Monopoly:

1. The greatest sufferer under monopoly is the consumer.

At the time of selling the commodity, a monopolist can charge higher prices. Since the bargaining powers are with him, he pays less to the owners of raw material and to the labourers less wages and thereby affect the consumers demand. Under monopoly, the consumers lose their economic sovereignty and are not able to exercise free choice of the commodity. Since the monopolist is a large scale producer, he does not bother about the wishes of the people. He manufacturer only such designs and varieties which give him maximum profit. Thus, we find consumers exploitation.

2) **Effects on Small Producers:**

Small scale producers also bear the brunt of Monopoly. A monopolist carries on severe competition against the small producers and weed them out of the market. He may even deliberately fix low price, and kill the very enthusiasm of the small producers. Since, he has large resources he can meet any financial situation.

3) **Effects of Government:**

A monopolist through his decisions can create artificial scarcities of commodities in the market resulting in greater inflationary conditions. He can throw out labourer out of jobs aggravating unemployment. Inflation and unemployment are always a problem to the government. Many great powers of the world are influenced by business magnets. Concentration of wealth leads to concentration of economic power. Thus, they are capable of influencing the economic policies of the State. The ending of the 'Managing Agency' system was due to this problem. The Government of India amended the Indian companies Act, 1932 and introduced the 1956 Act to remove the evils of the system.

4) **Effects on the Country:**

Monopoly is very harmful to the economic development of the country. The monopolist always thinks of personal gains and not much interested in the general economic welfare and development of the country. Thus, production in monopoly is profit - oriented and not welfare-oriented. Quite often the allocation and utilisation of resources do not conform to national interests.

During the twenties of this century, extensive legislations were passed by U.S.A. Germany, India, etc., to check the growth of monopoly powers. Today in every country there is some type of antimonopoly legislations. There is need for a public policy against monopolies and that should be strictly adhered to. The public policy could be either controls and regulations or a policy of total abolition of monopolies. The government may also check the size of monopolies and reduce their output by encouraging competition in the market. The government should be vigilant against indiscipline and esploitation by the monopolists.

C) Price Determination under Monopoly:

As and when the price falls, the demand increases. A monopolist can sell more commodities by fixing a lower price. The total revenue (TR) of the monopolist can be arrived at by multiplying the quantity (q) of a commodity and its price(p). (TR=qp). In monopoly the Average Revenue is equal to price AR = p. With a fall in price, both average revenue and marginal revenue decline, but marginal revenue declines at a faster rate and it is double the rate of decline of average revenue. The average revenue cannot be zero, but the marginal revenue can be zero or negative.

A monopolist can follow an independent price policy for the commodity, where as under perfect competition price is determined by the equilibrium of the forces of demand and supply. Under monopoly, supply is not free to adjust itself to demand, because supply is controlled by monopolist. The monopolist while fixing the price for the products is faced with two alternatives namely,

a) he may fix the price for the product of the supply and output is fixed by the conditions of demand prevailing in the market; or

b) he may fix the output or supply of the product and leave the price to be determined by the conditions of demand prevailing in the market.

A monopolist cannot fix both price and output. Invariably he prefers to fix the output and leave the price to be determined by the conditions of demand. The ultimate objective of the monopolist is to maximise profit, and therefore, he is not much interested to fix either the supply (output) or the price.

If the demand of his product is elastic, he cannot fix a high price and if the demand is less elastic, he can charge a higher price. If the product is produced under conditions of increasing costs (or diminishing returns), it will be to his advantage to charge higher price and keep the sales at lower level. Or on the other hand, if the product is produced under conditions of diminishing costs (or increasing returns), it is advantageous to the monopolist to keep the output at lower level and charge higher price. He always produces till MR is greater than MC, because his profits increases as the MR is higher than MC. He stops producing when MR=MC. At the point of equilibrium he stops producing the output, since it is equilibrium output giving him maximum monopoly net profits.

D. OLIGOPOLY

Oligopolist enjoys the monopoly power, but the oligopoly firm is not a monopoly, because it is not the only firm constituting the industry. Oliography is the form of imperfect competition, where sellers are few in number and each seller is of a giant size, who can affect the market price either by increasing or decreasing his output. Each seller has to be conscious of the reactions of his rivals, since there are a few firms in the industry, with or without product differentiation.

The demand curve of oligopoly is indeterminate. The demand curve of a seller relate to different quantities that could be sold at different prices charged. In oligopoly there exists two opposing attitudes among sellers simultaneously all the time. Under oligopoly all the firms co-operate and take a united action. Thus, all of them can maximise the joint profits, so that each can get a greater share. This type of co-operation or collusion is possible under monopoly because of the smaller number of firms. Under oligopoly, the industry is dominated by a few firms, who are producing an identical product, or producing close substitutes, but not perfect substitutes. An oligopoly situation may exists in any industry, when economies of scale or advantages of large scale production exist and a few firms will be in a situation to supply all or much of the total industry output. For example, Steel industry and cement industry have reached this stage. Need for heavy investment of capital in some industries might create a oligopoly situations. Generally in an oligopoly market, there are a few well established firms with products which are popular and which possess large demand. Thus, other firms may not enter the field due to the popularity of the oligopolistic firms.

Price determination under oligopoly

Price determination under oligopoly may be of any one of the three types explained below:

1. **Independent pricing:**

In an oligopoly industry, each firm follows an independent price and output policy imperfectly evaluating the reactions of its rivals. The price determined by each seller independently could be a monopoly price in the event the products differ. But generally firms do not produce homogeneous products and their cost of production invariably differs. Firms may not have a determinate demand curve and therefore, the price and output will be indeterminate. The result would be price instability; price-wars between rival firms may face stagnant price and the rival firms may not be willing to change the price when once they are satisfied leading to price rigidity. Modern economists are of the opinion that independent price setting may not continue for long in oligopoly. All the firms tend to enlarge their size of business and lower their cost in an attempt to capture a large share of the market for themselves. A large firm may even seek a position of price leadership.

2. Oligopoly Pricing Under Collusion:

In economic terminology, collusion refers to "coming close together to achieve an end". When oligopoly firms follow independent price and output policies collusion in the forms of insecurity, uncertainty and antagonism are the result. "If competitors of oligopoly firms co- operate in pricing their products, they are said to have resorted to collusion". In countries where restraints of trade are illegal, countries collusion is open and official. Collusion may be by agreement or by understanding among the rival firms. Collusion by written agreements may be in the form of Cartel, Rings or Pools, where the output, price, sharing of profits are determined by agreements on an agreed basis.

When rival oligopoly firms enter into perfect collusion, price and output will be set at such a level as to secure maximum industry profits.

3. Oligopoly pricing under price leadership:

According to Prof.Arthur Burns "If changes are usually or always inaugurated by the same firm and usually or always followed with similar price changes by other sellers, price competition may be said to involve price leadership". If most of the firms ; or all the firms in the industry offer to sell at a price fixed by one of the members, price leadership is said to exist and operate.

Price leadership differs from industry to industry relating to the duration of leadership and loyalty to the leadership by the firms under oligopoly conditions. Generally the largest firm in the industry takes this leadership. Price leadership may be through formal or informal agreements between rivals with regard to price fixation.

There are many types of price leadership :

a) The price leadership of the dominant firm, in which case one of the firms in the oligopoly industry produces considerably a large portion of the industry's total output and is in a position to dominate the market with the monopolist power. The small firms, which contribute only a small portion accept and follow the policies dictated by the dominant firm.

b) Very old, well experienced and highly respected firm takes the price leadership. This firm is in a position to gauge the market conditions, in view of its experience, related demand, costs, competition etc., and lay down the price policy, which is accepted by other firms. This type is known as parametric price leadership.

c) The third type is the aggressive price leadership, in which the dominant firm in the industry may follow legal and at times illegal methods to weed out all its rivals form the market. The dominant firm follows price-war- or cut-throat competition to weed out the rivals. It may even go to the extent of selling its products below the cost of production and the only aim being to remove other rivals from the market. "I do not mind losing my one eye, but the opponent to lose both the eyes" will be the policy.

When once the price leader fixes his price for the product, the others follow suit in fixing their price either slightly low or high to distinguish their products and to accommodate for market variations. This is done by the smaller firms to avoid cut-throat competition and to continue the position of supernormal profits.

A dominant firm can remove its rivals either through price-wars or cut-throat competition and assert itself as a monopoly. This may lead to complications and the government may interfere to control the situation. As for the small firms, the price fixed by the dominant firm becomes a constant price and they produce and sell their output which equates its marginal cost with the price. The marginal cost of the small firm becomes its supply curve.

OLIGOPOLY AND PRICE RIGIDITY

Price rigidity is an important character of oligopoly. Though there is change in the conditions that influence demand and supply, price continues to stay fixed. An oligopoly firm would like to continue the existing price and output policies so long it gets its profits, and not prepared to play with the price line. Even though there is a decline in demand, an oligopoly firm maintains the same price, but resorts to more selling pressures to maintain its present sales. The oligopoly firm would not like to change prices, since it has already spent a considerable amount on advertisements etc., to build up a line of customers, who are already conversant with the price and products. The price that the oligopoly firm has arrived at has been the result of debates, discussions, conflicts, conference and manouvers among the rival and as such, it would not like to meddle with the price again. Under the oligopoly price collusion, the price has already been set at a lower level and that price has been yielding sufficient profit and as such the firm will not be willing to change the price unless there are drastic changes in the supply and demand conditions.

Summarisation (points at a glance)

Pricing policies - Perfect competition

1. *Perfect competition is a state of market where all the potential sellers and buyers are aware of the prices offered by other buyers and sellers for the identical products offered for exchange. Thus, there will be one ruling price all over the market.*

2. *The features of perfect completion are, -*

   a) *the presence of large number of buyers and sellers,*

   b) *Homogenous products or identical,*

   c) *Free entry and free exit of the firms,*

   d) *Perfect knowledge of market conditions,*

   e) *Uniform price through out the market,*

   f) *Perfect mobility of factors,*

   g) *Absence of selling and transportation cost,*

   h) *Firms get normal profits, and*

   i) *Large number of firms in the industry.*

   Under perfect competition, prices are determined by the action and the inter-action of the forces of demand and supply. Most of the adjustments to changes in supply will be through adjustments in the quantity purchased, if the demand is highly elastic. If the demand is in elastic, the adjustment will take place in price.

3. *The rules of the price-game.*

   a) *If demand rises, prices go up or vice-versa.*

   b) *If supply rises, prices godown or vice-versa.*

   c) *Given a shift in demand curve, price will rise less or fall less, if supply curve is inelastic.*

d) *Given a shift in supply curve, price will rise less or fall less, if demand curve is elastic, price will rise or fall more, if the demand curve is inelastic.*

e) *If both demand and supply increase, sales are bound to increase, but price may or may not rise.*

f) *An increase in demand with a simultaneous decrease in supply will rise price and increase sales, if the new demand price is higher than its new supply price.*

g) *If demand rises, price goes up but sales will increase. If supply rises, prices go down, but sales will increase.*

h) *If both demand and supply increase, sales are bound to increase, but price may or may not rice.*

4. *Time element in price fixation, - In a very short period, supply remains inelastic and prices are governed by the changes in demand. In short period, demand analysis plays more important role that the supply in price determination. In a long run, prices are determined on the basis of cost of production and the state of supply. In the long period, prices are governed by changes in consumer behaviour and cost of production.*

   If average variable costs are covered by the sale price, the firm will decide to continue its business operation, otherwise the firm may decide to shut down.

Price Fixation under Monopoly

1. *Monopoly is a situation, where only one seller control the whole of the supply o the product that has no close substitute. Natural factors, legal factors, cost factor, market factor, large investment, tariff policy and protection and public rights are the factors responsible for the emergence of monopoly.*

2. *In monopoly, average revenue is equal to price (AR=price). Price under monopoly is fixed in either of the two ways, namely,-*

   a) *fixing the price first and allow the supply to be determined by the forces of demand; and*

   b) *fixing the output first and leave the price to be determined by the conditions of demand.*

   The monopolists also consider the elasticity of demand. The charging of higher price by monopolist depends upon elasticity of demand for goods, feat of substitutes, new eutrants and government control on prices and output.

3. *Under simple monopoly, the monopolist charges ordinary price in all the markets, but in discriminating monopoly, they charge different prices in different markets, These price discriminations may be in the form of personal discrimination, trade discrimination and geographical discrimination. The object of price discrimination is to -*

   a) *maximise the monopoly revenue;*

   b) *to dispose of surplus stock;*

   c) *to drive out from business his rival from the market;*

   d) *to develop a new market; and*

   e) *to utilise the un-utilised capacity of the plant and machinery.*

   Market segmentation, market sealing and multiple - demand elasticities are the necessary conditions or price discrimination. In the interest of society price discrimination is beneficial.

4. *Monopoly has certain negative repercussions, it leads to higher prices; wrong allocation of economic resources; discourages technical progress; increases instability in the*

economy leads to unfair business practices and bring about rampant political and economic corruption. Thus, it is necessary to control monopoly through Anto-monopoly legislation (MRTP Act in India); maintenance of fair competition; price and out put control measures; through publicity and propaganda; Purchaser's Association; collective bargaining; consumer's forum and public ownership or monopolies, etc.

But monopoly has certain benefits, if properly controlled. It can help the economy to face depression; it can face foreign competition due to its large financial resources; it can help in enlarging markets and in a case of public utilise if is a great boon.

5. ***Oligopoly :-*** *This is a situation where a few sellers (more than two) are in the market to sell identical products. Oligopoly could be of various types. It could be closed or open oligopoly on the basis of competition; it could be pure differentiated oligopoly based on the nature of product, it could be partial or full oligopoly and it could be organised or un-organised oligopoly.*

6. ***Under oligopoly :-*** *Price is determined through pricing under collusion. An oligopolists is indeterminate and follows at times very aggressive or defensive marketing methods.*

7. *Price is always determined and fixed by the price leader firm and other firms follow the price or adjust their prices accordingly. The price leader should take into account the reactions of rival, the entry of powerful competitors into the market and the doubtful loyalty of the followers.*

MONOPOLISTIC COMPETITION

Monopolistic competition, also known as imperfect competition, is a situation where there is a large number of firms, the commodity or service is not homogeneous, the role of transport costs makes competition imperfect. Ignorance of the buyers is also the cause. Since each firm sells close substitutes, the output and price policies of an individual firm is partially dependent on the output and price policies of its rivals. A firm under imperfect competition can reach the point of equilibrium when its MR=MC. During short period, there can be only partial equilibrium but in the long period there will be general equilibrium and every firm will be earning only normal profits, neither more or less.

1. *Selling costs play an important role in the case of imperfect competition. These costs include costs on advertisement, publicity and salesmanship, and the cost of free distribution of subsidiary products or service since they form part of advertisement. A firm under imperfect competition has to incur total selling costs, whenever it wants to sell larger output at the same price or same output at the higher price.*

2. *Pricing method could be either full cost pricing or going rate pricing. Full cost pricing (cost plus method) is set to cover both fixed cost and variable cost. The going rate pricing is adjusted to the general pricing structure in the industry.*

3. *Price discrimination is a practice adopted by seller to boost his sale by charging different prices for the same commodity to individual buyers or group of buyers. The objectives of price discrimination are -*

   a) *to create new market for goods;*

   b) *to destroy competition;*

   c) *to dispose of essential surpluses to earn monopoly profits;*

d) to boost sale by charging lower prices;

e) to make use of unutilised capacity.

Price discrimination can operate effectively under conditions o consumer's ignorance, purchasers irrationality, nature of goods, tariff value, government laws and differences in the elasticity of demand.

CHAPTER - **6**

PRICING OF PRODUCTS

1. INTRODUCTION

"Production and Profits go together".

Modern production has to face extreme competitive situations in the market today. Every producer produces commodities not only to meet domestic demand but also to export commodities to international market, where they have to face competitive markets, competitive goods and competitive prices. In the context of this situation, product improvement, sales promotion and pricing of products are very important activities to be analysed and skillfully handled. While analysing these problems, which are interdependent and mutually influential, a systematic and scientific approach would be necessary. Pricing is not an end in itself, but a means to an end, in the same way as "Production is a means to consumption and consumption is the end of production". The multi- product firm, and an independent manufacturer in the competitive position have to analyse this problem of pricing the product through a systematic approach. A logical classification of pricing problems and an explicit conception of pricing objectives, pricing theory, pricing research and a pricing policy would be necessary to arrive at an eventful decision on the subject.

Products may have to be priced under different situations and Products of lasting distinctiveness, whose life is pretty long and which have no acceptable substitutes. There are products where a long-run monopoly position could be held. In the case of such monopoly products, pricing will have to be on different style. The problem is to find out the price and the rate of output (determined by the price) that will maximise profits to the monopolist. Monopoly pricing raises tough problems. The monopolist has a far wider discretion in fixing prices.

Pricing problem starts when a company finds a new product entering the market and making inroads and enjoying protection. The seller in this case has to resort to product differentiation. Thus, pricing the product involves a good deal of strategy and skill on the part of the company.

2. PRICING POLICIES

Formulating the pricing policy and setting the price are the most important aspects of management decision- making. Any business firm would like to realise maximum revenue through the source of price. Price is a tool through which market could be expanded.

The external factors like the elasticity of supply and demand,the extent of competition in the market, the goodwill built up by the company,the market trends, the buyers purchasing power and the government policy govern prices. The internal factors are the cost of production, the management policy,selling costs etc. Setting prices is a complex problem and there is no definite formula to guide the management to pin down a particular market conditions, and other varied factors have to be considered. Business objectives, the competitive position of the company, promotional and product policies,the response to price, and the entry of non-business groups in the determination of prices are views to be kept in mind while formulating the price policy.

A. OBJECTIVES OF PRICING POLICY.

Pricing strategy and decision are apart of general strategy; and while setting the prices, the firm may aim at one or more of the following objectives:

1. Maximisation of profits for the entire product line. Production stands for profit. Any firm would like to maximise its profits and firm exists to achieve this goal. The profit incentive is always if, there, whether is public sector or private sector. The only difference between the two is the degree and margin profits is like a bait to production. How can a firm exist without profit. If the firm to maximise profits adapts various methods, economies and measures to maintain this.

2. Promotion of the long range welfare of the firm. The firm would like to maintain its status and further its welfare measures. In order to weed out unhealthy competitors from the production process and to maintain its position in the market, the firm has to resort to the promotion of long range welfare through price mechanism. The price strategy adapted by the firm should be such that it should not only discourage competitors entering the field but also guarantee the firm's continued existence in the market.

3. Adaptation of prices to fit the diverse competitive situations faced by different products. Many firms involve themselves in the production of products which are either very identical or very close substitutes. Hence, the firm has, if it has to exist in the market, to adapt various methods in the fixation of price to meet the challenges. Product differentiation and price discrimination are some of the methods followed, though they are not healthy. The problems of risk, uncertainty and survival are ever present in the market.

4. Flexibility to vary prices to meet changes in economic conditions affecting the various consumer industries. The economic environment in a country is not always constant. The national and international forces have an impact on the economic conditions, and they in turn affect market

conditions and which in turn affect the price line. The price policy of a firm cannot be rigid or conservative and it has to be flexible capable of adaptation and accommodation to the changing market circumstances. The price policy should suit the requirement of the economic - situation. This flexibility to vary prices also affects the customers and industries. A rigid price policy is not only harmful to the firm but it affects the other customer industries also.

5. Frequent change of price policy and price decision are not conducive to the health of the firm. Oscillations in price affect the other economic variables like savings, investments, production, budgeting etc. Price stability leads to economic stability. As far as possible prices should be established in the interest of the firm. The margin of profit the firm maintains should be also stabilised. Frequent change of margins on profits would be harmful to the firm. It should fix up a definite margin. A constant margin would promote business and attracts more customers. Stability in price and stability in margin should be the twin objectives of a firm.

Besides the above strategy-objectives, which are general in nature, Dr.Kotler has listed the following additional objectives.

6. **Market Penetration:** The firm should not indulge itself in superficial business. It should aim at capturing the large share of the market;that is market penetration. At times, the firm has to set a low price for its product to stimulate market growth. It should establish firmly its root in the market and to gain this, it may have to resort to fixing lower prices, of course, without sacrificing the quality of the product, and capture the business and build a reputed customer line.

7. **Market Skimming:** The firm has to understand the trend of the market and it may even charge higher prices initially to take advantage of the higher purchasing power of the buyers, who value its commodity very high. But this should not lead to exploitation of the buyers,lest the firm may gradually lose the entire business.

8. **Early cost Recovery:** Certain firms set a price for their products in such a way that thereby recover the cash early to meet their tight money conditions or they may be uncertain about the future market conditions. There are two ways of doing this: under monopoly conditions, they may increase the price and resort to early cash recovery or in the other way, they may even lower the price of the product in view of uncertain market conditions and make cash recovery as early as possible.

9. **Satisfaction:** The firm feels satisfied if the rate of return (on investment)is considerably good, though a higher price may produce even better returns. Some firms feel satisfied on a balanced return on investments through a price policy. That is to say, that the firm is not too avaricious to get higher returns through a higher price policy. It is just satisfied with a sound price policy.

10. **Product Line Promotion:** Here the firms set price which would enhance the sales of the entire line of products. Almost every firm has several items in its product line. The problem of product-line pricing is to find the proper relationship among the prices of members of a product group. Production pricing may refer to products physically distinct and also physically the same, but sold under different conditions. This gives the seller an opportunity to charge different prices.

In managerial economics, product line pricing policy plays a very important role, because most of the firms produce more than one product, that is they are "Multi- Product oriented" firms. According to prof.Jole Dean "The problem of product line pricing is to find out the proper relation among the prices of a member group. The essential economic feature of the product line is the cross elasticity of demand that exists among parts of the sellers output"

Under product line pricing policy, cost of a product does not form the direct determinant of price. Price of products should reflect demand elasticities and competition rather than cost. The role of cost should be to identify the price-output combination that is most profitable. But practically, the firms fix prices in such a way that they are proportional to full cost.

Since many products undergo "Life Cycle", the prices must be systematically related to "the stage of the market and competitive development"of individual product. While estimating competitive development ,the management should take into account:

1) The number of competitors;

2) The extent of company's market share; and

3) The degree of similarity of competitive product and the the price adjusted accordingly.

The relevant concept of cost applicable in product line pricing is incremental cost. The margin between incremental costs and price differ from product to product depending on demand conditions. According to Prof.J.Dean "a product that cannot be priced equal to average cost must be dropped".

The standard cost accounting procedure considering technological advancement and economies of scale should be the basis for projecting "Long -term cost" as against "Short-term cost".

B. PRICING POLICIES:

1. Cost plus Pricing.

Business firms mostly employ cost plus pricing or full cost as the pricing method. The cost-plus pricing method envisages a process under which many varieties of costs are involved namely,- estimation of average variable costs of producing and marketing a particular product, adding a percentage markup, or margin for profits. The charge of indirect cost or overhead costs is determined by allocating these costs among the firm's products on the basis of their average variable costs of planned production. But this type of method is very much criticized on the ground that this technique fail to examine demand conditions and its emphasis is on accounting cost, rather than marginal cost. Under this method, the price is set to cover the costs (Material, Labour and over -heads) and a predetermined percentage of profits. The percentage of profit added on differs from industry to industry, firm to firm and from product to product.

Most firms use Standard or "Normal" cost concept. First, the per-unit direct cost is estimated, then allocating the firm's expected indirect expenses or over -head, then assuming a "Standard" or "normal" output level. The resulting standard cost per-unit then used for price determination, irrespective of short term variations in actual unit costs. The use of historical accounting costs as the basis for the cost- plus pricing method gives rise to several problems explained below:

a) firms fail to properly adjust the historical cost data to expected price changes for key input factors.

b) the unadjusted historical costs have little affect on decision making;

c) to get a correct picture, the firm should use estimates of future costs;

d) the accounting costs rarely reflect through economic cost

e) For optimal decision making, the concept of opportunity cost must be employed,

f) Incremental costs, rather than full costs, should be used for optimisation in pricing decisions.

The price policy of a firm would depend upon the elasticity of demand. If the demand is in-elastic, it would not be profitable for the firm to reduce its price. The price reduction for expanding sales would be profitable for product with highly elastic demand. Though in the long run, all costs have to be covered; in the short-run direct costs are more relevant for management decision. In a single firm, all costs are direct with respect to the product. Problem are highly complex in a multi-product firm. The selling price must cover all direct costs, both manufacturing and non- manufacturing, both variable costs and fixed costs to a product; and finally it should include the profit margin.

2. Cynical pricing

Fluctuations in inventory capital outlay, national income and in employment influence pricing decisions of a firm. The prices of agricultural products, certain raw-materials and finished goods are subject to cyclical fluctuations. But the prices of other raw-materials and products of 'Price-leaders' are not subject to fluctuation. This is because, the price leaders are reluctant to change their prices frequently and they are willing to limit price cuts even during periods of declining demand, nor they are prepared to increase prices when demand indicates an upward trend. This inflexibility in price could be assigned to cyclical changes in the conditions of demand, costs, competition and profits.

Producers are always under the impression that the demand for their products is highly elastic, any change in price would not lead to increase in demand.

Since industrial pricing is done under conditions of oligopoly, even the price leader has to maintain stability in prices to avoid competition.

The variable cost per unit tends to remain relatively constant over long periods. Full costs to appear cyclically rigid.

The price leaders and many firms, who enjoy latitude in profit making are satisfied with reasonable profits rather than profit maximisation and thus during periods of business cycle they do not alter the price level.

3. Price Policy and consumer Psychology:

The responsiveness and sensitivity to price changes differ from consumer to consumer. Under certain circumstances, the behaviour of an individual may not remain constant and may not be adherent to the law of demand. The consumer behavior is never constant but ever changing. Likes and dislikes, tastes, fashions, imitation, habits of a consumer is subject to change. The actions and reactions of a consumer to the same price are not constant. Endogeneous factors and exogeneous factors influence the income of the consumers and their by the price line. The psychological factors have a tremendous impact on consumers' behaviour and their responsiveness and sensitivity to the same price are different at different periods. To consumers price is an indicator of quality, because price is an easy means of product measurement and product satisfaction. Prices are generally increased during boom periods and not during periods of depression. The main problem for a firm is one of adjustment of prices to changes in costs. Prices are also to be revised to maintain constant returns on capital investment. Appraising decision involves planning into the future and as such it has to depend upon estimate revenues,expenses and capital outlays,and not on historical costs.

Pricing is the most important single consideration in international marketing. Export pricing decision should be based on the total understanding of the varied marketing situations;which change from country to country,product to product and from time to time. The concept of marginal pricing is very useful in respect of export pricing."export prices are set on the basis of what the traffic can bear and are often unrelated integrally to domestic prices or even to costs of manufacture".

C. PRICE DISCRIMINATION

1. Introduction:

Price discrimination is also known as differential pricing. Some times a monopolist charges different prices for the same or for the different buyers at the same time or at different times. It is profitable to monopolist to do so. According to prof.J.S.Bain"price discrimination refers strictly to the practice by seller of charging of different price for different buyers of the same good".Mrs.Joan Robinson has described price discrimination as "the act of selling the same article produced under single control at a different price to the different buyers".The price discrimination not only increases profits to the monopolist,but also the total output. Price discrimination is important to the monopolist just like the product differentiation to imperfect competition.

2. Kinds of Price Discrimination:

there are three classes of price discrimination adapted by the monopolist.

a) the seller bifurcates the buyers according to their income or purchasing power. Factors like geographic location, individual tastes, kinds of uses of the product, etc., contribute for charging different prices. A doctor may charge a higher price for the rich people and lower price for the poor people. So long the demand elasticities among buyers are unequal it is advantages to the monopolist to charge different prices. He can follow market segmentation process, that is by dividing the total market into homogeneous sub-groups based on economic criterion or based on demand elasticity concept.

b) The monopolist can enforce price discrimination based on locational factor. He can charge higher prices at home and lower prices in foreign markets. (This is also called dumping)

c) He may charge lower prices for bulk purchases and higher prices for individual units. A discrimination is also possible depending upon the timing of the use of product. For Ex:Railways can charge different freight rates for different types of haulage. Telephone rates for trunk-calls are different in a day as compared to night; more on week days and less on sundays.

3. Conditions of price discrimination:

There are several conditions and price discrimination needs some conditions in the market for its effectiveness and operation.

a) Existence of monopoly conditions in the market is necessary for the effectiveness of price discrimination besides absence of competition in the market. In that case, a monopolist can rule the market with his price, since he is the king of trade.

b) **Market segmentation-** The division of the market into sub-markets. The market is distinctly divisible into various sub-markets in view of varieties of products and these products could be exchanged.

c) The expenditure in sub-dividing the market should not be more than the expected profit increase because of price discrimination. At times the monopolist has to incur some expenditure for keeping the sub-markets seperate, so that he can charge different prices in different markets. The consumers are also prevented from transferring the products from one sub-market to the other sub-market.

d) **Multiple Demand Elasticities:** If price discrimination in different markets is to be profitable, the elasticity of demand for the product of the monopolist should be different in different markets. If the price elasticity of demand is the same in all sub-markets though they are seperated, there is no use in discriminating the price. This is because of the fact that the monopolist can expect to increase his profit through price discrimination only if he restricts his output in the market with lower elasticity of demand and transfer the output (product) to that market to sell more where elasticity is higher. Mrs. Joan Robinson observes that "the sub-markets will be arranged in ascending order of their elasticities, the highest price being charged in the least elastic market".

e) **Product differentiation:** It is another factor, which is very important for imperfect competition, that has a bearing on price discrimination. Monopolist's market consists of rich and poor consumers. He can charge a higher price for the rich people for the same commodity by packing the same commodity in deluxe packing. For ex: the normal coffee drink supplied in hotel (restaurant) could be charged a higher price by supplying the same stuff in a fashionable cup and saucer as special coffee. Thus, he can collect a higher price for the same commodity from the affluent class.

f) **Legal sanction:** Some times the government permits the public utility service like Railways to charge different rates to different consumers; and this is possible because, the railways are owned by the government sector only. (Eg. of monopoly). In Railways the first 50 KM will have a different rate.

Price discrimination is done only, when elasticity of demand for the product is different for different buyers. The degree of discrimination is not uniform. It varies from product to product and consumer to consumer. We have a "perfect discriminator". (in the terminology of Mrs. Joan Robinson) when the monopolist fixes a price for the product knowing the amount of money each consumer is willing to pay and he knows the consumer surplus and that surplus he takes it way by changing a higher price for the product.

There is limited discrimination also, where the change differs depending upon the income. For example, A doctor can charge a higher rate to people with higher incomes and lower to others. The schedule of rates charged by railways could be regarded as second degree discrimination, the monopolist divides the consumer into different groups or classes on the basis of the elasticity of their demand for the product and charge different prices to different class of buyers.

4. Techniques of price discrimination:

The technique of price discrimination is derived towards achieving certain objectives. They are -

a) To appropriate the consumers surplus through price discrimination by charging different prices for the same commodity to different sectors of people. A consumer enjoys a surplus satisfaction when he gets a commodity at a lower price, while he was prepared to pay a higher price for the commodity rather than go without it. Thus he has a surplus money. This surplus is taken away by the monopolist through price discrimination.

b) To develop a new market for the commodity. Since market segmentation is one of the conditions of price discrimination, he takes advantages of the same.

c) To destroy competition. Monopoly is opposite to competition, the other extreme. Through price discrimination, the monopolist will try to destroy competition.

d) To make maximum use of the installed capacity of productive enterprise. Price discrimination helps the monopolist to increase the output to the maximum through the capacity utilisation of the infrastructure. When there is optimum utilisation of the inputs, the total output will increase and there by the monopolist is at an advantageous position to control the market with his price.

e) To earn monopoly profits. Monopoly stands for profits and profit earning is the main goal of a monopolist. The discriminatory monopoly firm can secure higher profits than the simple monopoly firms.

f) Through the policy of cut-throat competition and dumping, the discriminatory monopoly firm can acquire more powers, which will help the monopolist to rule the market with his price.

Price discrimination is generally through market segmentation. The total market for the commodity could be divided into different groups based on segmentation by income; quality of purchase, classification of consumers; Geographical location like national and international markets through variations of dumpting charges; segmentation by time (seasons) and age (in USA senior citizens get maximum privileges and benefits) and by trade marks, parents and brands etc. Through all these sources, a monopolist can charge discriminatory prices and make profits.

5. Arguments in favour of price discrimination:

Price discrimination becomes necessary in public utilities, like Railways, P and T, Telephones etc., which stand for service. "Rob the rich, relieve the poor". This is possible not only through optimum output but also with higher monopoly powers. Even the poor and average consumer get better satisfaction through lower prices. The monopolist may even share his profits with the work force, who are responsible for his affluence. From the point of view of dumping also, price discrimination is advantageous.

6. Price and output determination:

Both ordinary monopolist and discriminating monopolist have the same equilibrium and cost. But from the point of view of revenues, the analysis differs. This discriminating monopolist is in equilibrium, when he produces profit maximising-output, because, his combined marginal revenue from different markets of his product equals his marginal cost.

For equilibrium of a discriminating monopolist:

a) marginal cost of total output must be equal to his combined marginal revenue

b) marginal revenue in all the sub-markets must be equal to combined marginal revenue;

c) total output will be determined where his marginal cost intersects (equals) his combined marginal revenue from the various sub-markets;

d) The total output will be distributed for sale in the various markets according to their price elasticities;

e) greater the elasticity of demand for the product in a market, greater the proportion of output sold and greater will be the profits and vice-versa.

CHAPTER - 7

NATURE OF PROFITS

Profit is said to be a reward for organisation, just like rent to land, wages to labour and interest to capital. Profits are the primary measure of the success of the organisation as also the individuals firm's performance. Profit is said to be an excess of income over cost of production. Profit has always been a centre of controversy. In the real world, incomes do not turn out as expected. Some economists argue that profit is a residue after the payment of rent, wages and interest to the infrastructure for its sacrifice in the productive process. A business always faces a number of uncertainties and risks,- technical, market, consumer demand etc. A business man to earn profits has to successfully manage the risk. The greater the risk and uncertainty, higher will be the profits. In a dynamic society profits vary from year to year. Some opine that profit is a functional income and some others as non-functional income. An entrepreneur has to organize and coordinate the various factors of production and he earns profit for undertaking this function. Since the organiser, who is the captain of the industry shoulders risks and responsibilities, he should be paid and that payment could be termed as profit. Prof. Schumpeter says that profit to the entrepreneur is a payment for innovation while Prof. F.H. Knight argues that profit is payment to entrepreneur for bearing risks and responsibilities.

Prof. J.M. Keynes has expressed the view that profits resulted from the favorable movements of the general price level and thus a non-functional income. Mrs. Joan Robinson and Prof. Chamberlain attribute profits to imperfect competition and monopoly - the non- functional income.

1. Gross profit and net profit

A business man analyses profit as income available to him after the payment made to contractual-hired factors, like taxes, depreciation charges, insurance charges. That is to say, the excess of revenue receipt over explicit payment and charges.

a) Gross profit = Total Revenue --- Explicit costs

Net profit, also called as pure profit or economic profit, is the residual balance of income after making payments to all contractual and non-contractual payments to factors of production. The implicit costs have to be deducted from the gross profit to arrive at Net Profit, which could be positive or negative.

b) Normal Profit and supernormal Profit

Normal profits refer to that portion of profit which is absolutely necessary for the business to remain in operation. That is the minimum necessary to induce the business to remain and operate. Normal profit forms part of the average cost. The organiser obtains normal profit when average revenue is equal to average cost (AR=AC)

Super-normal profit or abnormal profit could be treated as any return above the normal profit. It is the residual surplus after paying for explicit costs, implicit costs and normal profit. When average revenue or price is more than the average cost, the entrepreneur gets super-normal profits. The existence of this profit is not obligatory to the firm to remain in business like normal profits.

2. ACCOUNTING PROFIT AND ECONOMIC PROFIT

Accounting profit is the revenue obtained during the period minus the cost and expenses incurred to produce the goods responsible for getting the revenue.

Accounting profit = Total Revenue - The cost involved in producing and selling.

This theory is heavily discounted on the ground that it does not take into consideration other expenses like the entrepreneurs wages, rental incomes on self-owned land and interest on self-capital (Also called as imputed cost)

The Economic profits refers to those items that take into consideration both explicit costs and implicit costs. The economists point out, that economic profits are more important than accounting profits since they alone reflect the true profitability position of the business enterprise.

Economic profit = Total Revenue - Explicit

Costs+imputed costs.

OR

Economic profit=Accounting cost-Imputed cost.

B. THEORIES OF PROFIT

The theories of profits could be analysed and explained as follows:

1. Profit as the reward for risk bearing and uncertainties;
2. Profit as the consequence of frictions and imperfections in the economy (Dynamic theory of profits);
3. Profit as the reward for successful innovation; and
4. Profit as a payment for organising other factors of production.

Thus, there are several view points in explaining theories of profits.

To some economists profits are nothing different from rent. "Rent is a differential surplus". So also profit arises since some entrepreneurs have more ability over others in the field of production. While rent refers to land, profit refers to production. A superior entrepreneur enjoys more talent as compared to a marginal entrepreneur. Prof. Senior and Prof. Mill treated rent and profit on the same level and this was responsible for developing a full-fledged theory of profit by the American economist Prof.F. Walker. His theory is called the "Rent Theory of Profit".

Prof. Walker's concept of profit is synonymous with Prof.Ricardo's theory of rent. Rent arises due to the fact that not all pieces of land have the same fertility and productivity; like-wise profit arises due to differential factors in talent and ability of the entrepreneur, who is supposed to be the captain of industry. This position ensures the emergence of differences in industrial revenue profit, just like the differences in agricultural revenue-rent. Prof. Walker treats profit as "rent of ability".

1. Risk and Uncertainty Theory of Profits:

This theory envisages that rent is a reward paid to organisation for undertaking risks. People generally do not want to shoulder risks, but some who are prepared to venture in spite of risks involved should be rewarded and the rewards payment is profit. Higher the risk, higher will be the reward. Since business operates under conditions of uncertainty, the risk premium , in the form of profit is to be paid. Risks are not confined only to owners who receive profits and even non-entrepreneurial risks are also important, like the risk of vocational specialisation. According to Prof. Hawley risk-bearing is the special function of an entrepreneur and it leads to the emergence of profit. Greater the risk, greater will be the expected gain to induce entrepreneur and to start the business. Most of the business are speculative and reward is necessary to the risk-bearer. In Prof. Hawley's concept., enterprise is the only real productive factor, the land, labour, and capital are subordinate factors and mere means of production. Prof. F.H. Knight contends that risk is an inherent factor in any business and they are of two kinds, insurable risks and non- insurable risks. In the case of insurable risks, one can predict the event and it could be subject to insurance. This insurance premium becomes a part of the cost of production, and enters into price. But business risks are non-insurable and these risk are necessarily to be borne by the entrepreneur himself. They include risk of competition,technological risks, business cycle risks and risks arising from governmental action such as tax policy, price control, import and export restrictions, etc. The above risks are not insurable. Prof.Knight advanced the theory that pure economic profit is related to uncertainty. The foreseen risks are insurable. The only unforeseen risks are non-insurable and they are responsible for the emergence of profit. According to him, it is uncertainty-bearing rather than risk-bearing that earns profit for the entrepreneur.

2. Profit as a reward for market imperfection and frictions in Economy:

(DYNAMIC THEORY OF PROFIT)

In a static economy neither demand nor supply changes. The demand for a commodity depends upon the size of population,incomes,consumer's tastes, substitutes of commodities, price and the price of related goods. In a static equilibrium, the supply of the commodity do not change. When demand and supply do not change, the price as well as the cost of production remain constant.

So to say, in a static equilibrium the price of the product will be equal to the average total unit cost of production including normal profit. But this static equilibrium concept is only theoretical in character.

In a dynamic world, things move on changing and every thing is uncertain. In a dynamic economy all factors that influence demand and supply change continuously resulting in profit or loss. The demand for a commodity or service may increase due to many factors like population, rise in incomes, non-availability of substitutes, changes in tastes etc. Such a demand may increase price of the product and the cost of production remaining constant, profit will arise. Similarly the supply position may also increase due to improvements in transport facilities, introduction of new production processes, reduction in the cost of rawmaterials, etc.,

According to Prof.Clark, profits belong essentially to economic dynamics and not to economic statics, where the economy is frictionless and full competition pervades. In a static economy, pure profit's would be eliminated as fast as it could be created.

A war, an inflation, a business depression are all factors in a modern economy which lead to profit or losses. During inflation, prices and costs go up but prices increasing at a faster rate than costs resulting in larger margins of profit to producers and merchants, During a depression the opposite trend prevails. These consequences are common to all firms and industries beyond the control and influence of any one.

At times individual firms introduce dynamic changes through inventions of science and technology;introduction of new process of production; introduction of new commodity and changes in advertisements and salesmanship. These changes are the causes for the emergence of profit. Some argue that profit is the result of disequilibrium and imperfect competition in the market. Especially the monopoly powers prevailing in the market help producers of companies to accrue profits. They raise prices by restricting output and the economy cannot adjust itself immediately to changes in costs and demand. Their concept of profit is due to the enhanced earnings of a permanent monopoly and which is market imperfection.

3. Innovation Theory of Profits:

Prof.J.A.Schumpeter's theory of profits is almost akin to the theory of profits enunciated by prof.J.B.Clark, Prof.Schumpeter in his innovation theory attributed profits to dynamic changes in the productive process due to the introduction of modern science and technology of production techniques. Risk plays no part in this theory and profits are solely attributed to dynamic development. Innovation may bring about changes in methods of consumer tastes increasing national output more than an increase in costs. The increased net output is the profit out of the innovation. New organization, new promotion, new raw- materials, new markets or new products constitute innovation. Through advertising and research laboratories innovation is built in to the competitive system. It may also be argued that profit is the cause for innovation. According to Schumpeter profit ia both the cause as well as the effect of innovations and thus it is the cause and effect of economic progress also. Profit accrues not to the innovator, nor to the financier but to the entrepreneur who introduces it into the productive process. When innovation becomes obsolete profit disappears and innovation is always subject to competition. Innovational profits have a tendency to appear, disappear and reappear as the result of emergence of new and more clever innovation.

4. Profit is a reward for organising other factors of production:

A proportionate combination of the various infrastructure,-men, material, money, machinery, marketing is quite indispensable to produce the desired output. Entrepreneur takes this responsibility to coordinate these infrastructure to produce products. He not only takes unforeseen risks but also n the midst of uncertainties he combines the factors of production to produce output. A disproportionate combination of factors only increases cost of production and reduces profits. It is here that the entrepreneural skill and wisdom play a very important part. In owner-managed firms, part of the profit goes to manager's skill. In large corporations, the responsibility of organising the infrastructure, and their efficient and effective utilisation to the optimum point fully rests with the salaried managers, and as such the companies profit is to be treated as a payment for organising and directing activities.

All profits in a sense are complementary, since many factors, like risk, uncertainty, innovation and monopoly powers etc., affect every business activity in profit earning.

In general it could be argued that under perfect competition, when the price is equal to the average and marginal costs, the entrepreneur gets only "normal profits" and not supernormal profits.

Under imperfect competition,- which includes monopoly, duopoly, oligopoly and monopolistic competition,- the entrepreneur by exercising control over the supply and price of his product and by creating artificial scarcity in the availability of products can earn supernormal profits.

In the real world there is imperfect competition. No single theory is capable of explaining the cause for the emergence of profit. All the theories are inter- related. Innovations cause dynamic changes leading to economic progress. Uncertainty is the hallmark of dynamic changes, and innovation is uncertainty tied up with risk. Thus all the causes of profit are inter- related and inter-dependent. The result is that profit is always uncertain, profits are non-calculable and cannot be accurately estimated.

Prof. peter drucker has enunciated very three important functions of profit namely, 1. profit can measure the business performance and its soundness and effectiveness 2. profit is the premium that covers the cost of staying in business and the indicator of that covers the coast of staying in business and the indicator of the general efficiency of firm ; 3. and profits can guarantee the supply of future capital necessary for innovation and expansion of the business enterprise. thus, profit is a very important tool for the business enterprise for its continued existence and to cater to the needs of the community.

3. PROFIT MEASUREMENT

It is rather difficult to measure the amount of profit earned by a firm during a given period, since a portion of profits earned will have to be attributed to previous period and subsequent period. The true profitability position of any investment cannot be fully determined untill the ownership of the investment is fully determined. Thus, there is only arbitrariness in the determination of measurement of profit. Accountants use the term "business income " instead of profits; while the economists do not agree with them on the ground that it is a conventional accounting method. The accounting method is based on -

1. inclusiveness of coast ;
2. Depreciation ;
3. valuation of stock ;
4. Treatment of deferred expenses ; and
5. Capital gains and losses.

Under this method the values involved is so large compared to trading profits and any small variation in the value can bring about large variations in the determined profit. Accountants measure business incomes by finding the difference between the opening value of the assets and the closing value of assets in balance. Profit is regarded by him as the revenue released during the period minus the costs and expenses incurred in producing that revenue.

To the economist, now income is essentially a speculation about the future. The economists balance sheet is an attempt to aggregate the future earning of the firm's properties now on hand. An economists's balance sheet derives entirely from income expectation's, while an accountants balance sheet is a basic tool for computing accounting income.

Though both start with widely different views in measuring income, they arrive at same estimates but only in a stationery economy. But in the real world of business cycles and technological revolutions, the estimates of both, Accountant and Economists are widely different, and both are important for the management. From the managerial point of view, economic profits are more important than accounting profits, since they reflect the true position. From the overall business point of view, the accounting conventions used in arriving at profit are also important.

4. DEPRECIATION

With the passage of time and use, the equipment, machinery and buildings wear out and in course of time they become useless from the business point of view. They only have scrap-value. To measure the true income of a business, a charge is made by the accountant against the annual income of the business and this charge is termed as Depreciation, and it is usually provided in equal amounts over the life of the asset. The provision of depreciation enables the firm to provide for replacement of the asset by the time it is declared a scrap. The depreciation charges vary from company to company. In heavy industries like Iron and steel, Air Transport, Railways, Aluminum industries, etc., heavy depreciation charges are provided; whereas in the case of banks, Insurance companies, financial institutions etc., the depreciation charges are relatively lower. Depreciation acts as an instrument for stimulating capital formation and directing investments in the national interest.

For the purpose of reporting business profits to the share-holders and income-tax authorities different methods of measuring depreciation are followed. It is an important method of capital formation.

The commonly accepted methods of depreciation are:

A. Straight Line Method:

Under this method an asset is supposed to wear evenly during its normal life and depreciation is provided uniformely on the assumption that the asset depreciates more rapidly at some stages of its life, than at others. Assuming that there is no scrap value ,the annual depreciation is worked out by dividing the initial value of the asset by the number of years estimated. If the asset has scrap-value,it is deducted from the initial cost and then divided by the estimated life in years.

For example: If the initial cost of the asset is Rs.5000/- with a scrap value of Rs.500/- and estimated life of 5 years, the amount of annual value of depreciation would be-

$$\text{Rs. } 5000 - \frac{500}{5} = \frac{4500}{5} = \text{Rs. } 900\text{/per Year.}$$

This method is very simple, provided the asset is not prone to premature retirement due to obsolescence or accidents.

The depreciation charge is made against annual income and set apart for being credited to depreciation Fund. This method does not take into consideration the fact that the cost of repairs is likely to be higher in the later years of the life of the asset due to heavy wear.

From the economists point of view, there are two methods of charging depreciation namely,-the opportunity cost of equipment,that is, the most profitable alternative use of the asset that is foregone by putting the asset to its present use; and secondly the exhaustion of year's worth of limited valuable

life of the asset to be the basis of depreciation charges, and this is measured by the replacement value of the equipment that will produce comparable earnings. Both these economic concepts are important to management, since the opportunity cost is required for operation problem of profit-making, whereas the second is required to find out the replacement of eroded earnings ability, which help financial problems of preserving and administering capital.

B. Reducing Balance Method:

According to this method, depreciation is provided at a uniform rate on the written down value of the asset at the commencement of the year. For Example: if the value of the asset is Rs.2000/- at the beginning of the year and the rate of depreciation is 20percent, the first year depreciation will be Rs.400/- and the written down value of the asset in the beginning of the second year would be Rs.1600/- and the written down value in the 3rd year. Rs.1280/- and so on. Under this method even after 5 years the written down value will never be zero and as such the asset is supposed to have some scrap value.

The formula could be as follows:

$$D = 100 \frac{\overline{1 - x}}{\frac{S}{C}} \quad 1 - n\frac{S}{c}$$

D = stands for percentage of depreciation

S = stands for Residual value of the asset

c = stands for Initial cost of the asset

n = stands for Estimated life of the asset in years

From this method, it could be seen that the written down value at the close of the 5th year is equal to the scrap value of the asset.

C. Sum of the year's Digits method:

This method is similar to declining balance method, that is to provide for more or less uniform total cost of operation of the asset. But this method differs from the declining Balance method in that, the book value remains constant while the annual rate of depreciation changes. For example: the expected life periods are 5,4,3,2, and1, which will be 15 that serves as a common denominator of the numerators 5,4,3,2, and 1. Thus, the annual rates are 5/5,4/5,3/15,2/15 and 1/15 respectively, If it is assumed that the original value of the asset is Rs.1000/- and scrap value as Rs.100/- and the expected life of the asset is 5 years; the base is Rs.1000 -100 =Rs.900/-

Age of asset	Varying rate of Depn	Annual Depn	Accumulated Depn	Book value
1.	5/15	300	300	700
2.	4/15	240	540	460
3.	3/15	180	720	280
4.	2/15	120	840	160
5.	1/15	60	900	100

Either of these two methods DBM and SYDM will be found useful as well as equitable.

1. Valuation of Stock:

The methods of valuation of stock could be:

a) First in first out method (FIO) which assumes that the units purchased first are issued first.

b) Last in First Out Method (LIFO) which assumes the units purchased last are issued first.

c) Weighted Average Method (WAM) which assumes that the goods purchased are intermixed and units are issued at a cost which is an average of the cost of each purchase, weighted by the quantity purchase at that cost. Even the closing stock is valued at the average cost.

5. Treatment of Capital Gains and losses:

Some conservative companies, which are traditionally bound have a tendency not to include capital gains in the current profits and would like to write off capital losses from the current profits of the year in which the loss takes place. In case of unrealised capital gains, they should not be included in the profits. In case of revaluation of property, if there is gain, it is usually transferred to capital reserve. Capital gains and losses may be defined as other real goods. All the assets that constitute the value of the firm are sucessptible to windfall changes. For example, Value of the cash depreciation in inflation,inventory is subject to fire etc., lead to capital losses, and they may be written off out of retained earnings. Thus, the amount of profit would also be affected by the treatment of capital gains and losses.

Treatment of Deferred expenses:
(Amortization of long term intangible assets)

These assets could be classified into two categories:

1. Those having a limited life for example patents, licenses, etc.

2. Those having no such limited life for example trade marks, goodwill preliminary expenses, et.

With regard to first item, there is no difference of opinion on the question of writing off these assets during their life time. The justification is based on the grounds of conservation.

In the case of intangible assets with no limited life, there is a difference of opinion whether the assets could be written off, then what should be the period of their amortization. For example: Goodwill, There is a view that is should be written off immediately upon or after acquisition because goodwill is a fancy asset that has no place in the balance sheet.

6. Profit maximisation and planning:

In the modern dynamic world the attitudes and policies of business firms are entirely different. The economic theory makes an assumption that the maximisation of profits is the sole objective of a business firm. Today profit maximisation refer to the long run periods; to managements rather than to owner's income; to include non-functional income; to restrain competition; to maintain management control, et. of late there seems to be realisation on the part of management and economic theorists that firms do not always aim at profit maximisation in relation to marginal cost and revenue, but set standards and targets of reasonable profits for the following considerations:

a) To attain industry leadership;

b) To forestall potential competition;

c) To prevent governmental intervention and restraints;

d) To maintain and foster consumer good will;

e) To control wage increases;

f) To avoid risks threatening the survival of the business firms and

g) To maintain the liquidity of the business firm.

Modern business firms feel that they have a social responsibility and an obligation to society and therefore they are even prepared to sacrifice profits during the short run periods. The executives want to limit profit in order to maximise their own benefits either by not-diluting control over the industry or by the desire to maintain pleasant working conditions. Today firms set "Profit Standards" through a percentage on sales or a reasonable return on investments. To discourage potential competitors, return on investments seems to be a relevant profit standard, if all new firms have similar cost standards. From the owner's point of view return on capital is the best method for profit standard because the ratio of profits to sales vary very widely among firms. Now the problem is how to set the standard and what is the criteria behind it.

Capital formation is by attracting investments (profit is a bait to attract capital along with the interest rates) and also by ploughing back the earning of profits. Therefore, the criteria to be set depends upon the mode applied to achieve the above.

it is necessary to set different standards for different companies and purposes, since they give widely varying results-depending on market conditions. The business firms pursue variety of profit policies to achieve different goals like longrun survival; to maintain safety margins; to introduce leisure as a variable; to maintain financial control of the firm; to maintain liquidity; to earn a satisfactory return or to maximise sales subject to profit constraints, etc.

7. Profit Planning :

A sound and healthy business should always aim at consistent profit in the midst of risk and uncertainties, which are the result of dynamic nature of consumer needs, peculiar nature of competition and uncontrollable nature of costs. Thus planning for profit is absolutely necessary, which demands a thorough understanding of the relationship among output, cost and price; and it is the "break-even analysis" that can explain this relationship clearly. Through break even analysis it is possible to derive managerial actions to maintain and increase profitability.

8. Break-even Analysis :

Break-even point may be defined as that level of sales at which total revenue equals total costs and the net income is equal to zero. The break even point is the "No Profit No Loss point". Breakeven analysis requires the study of revenues and costs of a firm in relation to its volume of sales at which the firms costs and revenue will be equal. The breakeven point may be determined either in terms of physical units or in money terms, that is sales value in rupees. The formula for calculating the breakeven point is very simple and as follows:

$$BEP = \frac{\text{Fixed Costs}}{\text{Selling price - Variable costs per unit}}$$

$$\text{ForEx: } \frac{\text{Fixed Costs Rs. 10,000}}{\text{Selling price Rs. 5 per unit - variable cost per unit Rs. 3}}$$

$$\text{Therefore BEP} = \frac{\text{Rs. 10000}}{(5-3)} = \text{5000 units.}$$

The conclusion that could be drawn from the above example is that sales volume of 5000 units will be the accurate point at which the manufacturing unit would not make any loss or profit.

The breakeven analysis could be used for -

a) maintaining safety margins;

b) determining the volume necessary to reach the profit target;

c) changing price;

d) changing costs;

e) determining whether to expand the capacity or not;

f) finding out the effect of alternative prices; and

g) choosing promotion-mix, etc.

The breakeven analysis is useful to management as it presents a microscopic pictures of the profit structure of a business enterprise.

The break-even analysis is based on certain assumptions as detailed below:

1. All costs are either perfectly variable or absolutely fixed over the entire period of production; but this assumption may not hold good in practice;
2. The volume of production and the volume of sales are equal; but in reality they differ;
3. All revenue is perfectly variable with the physical volume of production and this assumption is not valid.
4. The assumption of stable product-mix is unrealistic.

a) Importance of Break-even Analysis :

1. It can high light the areas of economic strength and weakness in the firm and also it can point out the leverage that can improve the profitability of the firm;
2. It can help the business firm to examine the profit vulnerability and make change in business conditions;
3. It helps the management to determine the 'safety margin' and to decide the level of sales that can generate profit to the management;
4. It helps to determine the new quantity or the new selling price;
5. It helps the management to identify the actual production capacity necessary for balanced development;
6. It is useful in deciding the questions of product planning.
7. It can help management to decide whether to buy a particular component from outside or to manufacture the same locally.

8. It can also be used to compare different ways of doing jobs.

9. The break-even analysis can also contribute its share in determining the production planning that could give the management a reasonable profit and fixed costs.

b) Drawbacks of Break-even Analysis:

It will be useful only in situations relatively stable and slow moving rather than volatile and erratic ones. In conditions when proper managerial accounting techniques and procedures are maintained, the BEA will be useful. In a particular period costs are affected not by the output of that period but due to past output or a preparation for future output. As such the BEA cannot pin down that cost is the result of output of a particular period. It is difficult to deal with selling costs under the frame work of BEA, because changes in selling costs are a cause to bring out changes in output and not the result of output sales. In the real world perfect competition is very rare and as such it is necessary to make calculations at different time periods. The relationship among cost, revenue and volume (output) is realistic only over narrow ranges of output and for long range BEA is not effective. If too many products and too many plants are grouped together in a productive process, the BEA cannot identify which is good or which is bad, since all are grouped together. The BEA assumes that profits are the result of output but ignores that other factors like technological changes, improved management and variations in the proportions of fixed factors are also possible for profits.

Inspite of these limitations, the Break-even Analysis is very useful as a guide to decision making, which is a very important tool in the management process under the present conditions of dynamic changes in the productive process.

c) Cost Control and Profits:

Costs always have a tendency to increase resulting in increasing profits. Cost control methods are important to stem this tendency. The management should search for better and more economical methods to control cost. The increase in profits are not always specific expenses and by the economical and efficient use of money resources cost could be controlled, and this will help not only to improve profitability but also competitiveness. Cost control also helps in reducing prices and a reduction in price leads to higher competitiveness. Ratio analysis, value analyses and standard costs and budgets are various instruments of cost control. Materials, labour and overheads are the three important items that can help in controlling costs.

A diagram on Break-even Analysis:

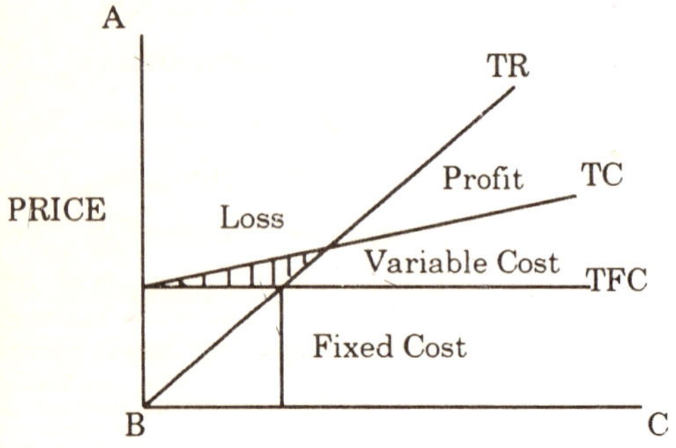

TR = Total Revenue
TC = Total cost
TFC= Total fixed cost.

The intersecting point of TR and TC is known as the break even point.

To management, the use fullness of break-even analysis lies in the fact that it represents a microscopic picture of the profit structure of a business enterprise. It is possible through breakeven analysis to obtain managerial actions to maintain and increase profitability.

Summarisation (points of a glance)

PROFITS

1. *The entrepreneur in the productive process has to bear risks and responsibilities and profit is the ultimate result of this risk. Larger the risk and uncertainties in business, the greater the opportunities for larger profits, and they may be gross profit or net profit. Total revenue from sales minus explicit costs is the gross profit and gross profit minus implicit costs is the net profit. Normal profit is what is normally expected in business, and profit in exceed of normal profit is super-normal profit.*

2. *Profit is the result of ability,-innovation and the reward for risk bearing and uncertainty. According Prof. P. Drucker, profit measures performance; it is a premium paid to cover costs of staying in business and profit ensures the supply of future capital. The revenue realised during the period minus the costs and expenditure incurred to produce that revenue is accounting profit. Deduction of imputed costs from revenue is economic profit which is normally preferred by management.*

3. *Every business equipment like plant and machinery is subject to wear and tear with the passage of time and constant use. Depreciation is a charge on profits and hence the level of profit depends upon the method followed.*

4. *The inventory valuation method could be -*

   a) *FIFO, that is first in first out. Units received are issued first; and*

   b) *LIFO, that is last in first out, Last units received are issued first; and*

   c) *Weighted Average method. Under this method, units are disposed of at average cost as they are mixed up and individual cost of units cannot be judged seperately.*

5. *Capital gains should not be included in current profits, so also the losses should not be written off. Ammortization process should be adopted for long term intangible assets. Those having limited life, like patents, permits, etc., should be written off during or before the life time of the assets. Those having no limited life, such as good will, copy right, etc., should be written off as early as possible after their acquisition.*

6. *Profit maximisation cannot be always the aim of a firm; because the firm has certain obligations and responsibilities to the society, to consumers, to workers and to the government. To attain industry leadership, to forestall the potential competition; to prevent government intervention; to maintain consumer goodwill; to restrain demand for wage increase, to avoid risk and to maintain the liquidity of the firm, the management or firm should not consider profit as the only objective.*

7. *To increase the profit performance of management, it is necessary for the firm to increase the volume of sales, to increase the selling price; to reduce the variable expenses per unit; and to reduce the fixed costs; to utilise the available potentialities of the firm to the optimum extent; to eliminate the infrastructural wastages; to effectively and efficiently manage the organisation and to always maintain cordial and harmonious human relationship between labour and management.*

1. Break-even analysis:

a) The break-even analysis involves the study of revenue from sales is equal to total cost, fixed and variable cost, is called break-even pint. This point is very important for taking managerial decision. The break- even point could be determined in terms of physical units, interms of sales value and as a percentage of full capacity and these are based on certain assumptions.

b) *The break-even analysis is usefull to management as it provides safety margin; helps to fix up the volume required to attain target profit; helps to change price and costs; to expand capacity of the firm or otherwise; to choose promotion mix and to indicate the effects of alternative prices.*

CHAPTER - 8

NATIONAL INCOME ANALYSIS

1. MEANING

The economic theory could be studied under two parts, - namely - Micro Economic Theory and Macro Economic Theory, the major two branches. The micro-economics is concerned with the output of perticular goods and services by individual firms or industries, by single house holds and the unit of study refers to the part rather than the whole. The macro economics relates to the theory of income, employment and money. It studies the over-all averages and aggregates of the system. It deals with the functioning of the economy as a whole.

The micro economics seeks to explain how the single firm decides the sale price for a particular product, the amount of output that will maximise its profits and determination of the low cost combination of infrastructure to produce the output. The Micro economics with the given total output, total employment and total spending for goods and services, try to investigate the process of allocation of output and employment among various individual firms and industries and to determine how the prices of products of these individual firms are established. In the analysis of economic processes that determine the nations wealth, one has to consider both micro and macro aspects.

When labour and capital of a country acting on its natural resources produce annually a certain amount of goods and services, which could be called the gross national product (GNP) and this GNP in terms of money is national income. The national Income of country could be defined as the total market value of all final goods and services produced in the economy in a year. The National Income measures the value of annual output and it is a monetary measure. In order to accurately realise the changes in physical output, the figure for national income is adjusted for price changes. While calculating national income accurately, all goods and services produced in any given year should be counted "only once". National income includes only the market value of all final goods and ignores the transactions of intermediary goods.

National income presents a total value of production; it represents a total receipts and total expenditure. It is obvious that every expenditure is at the same time a receipt. The sum of all incomes of the people of a country is called national income. In the productive process, land, labour capital and organisation are pooled together proportionately to produce output. Each factor is exploited to the optimum point to get the maximum benefit. The total output, thus produced is national income in money terms. As such, it is necessary to reward the various factors for their sacrifice. Land gets rent, labour gets wages, the capitalist gets interest and the entrepreneur gets profits. Thus the national income is distributed to these various factors. The total income obtained as rent, wages, interest and profits are the national income of that country. The total value of all the goods produced by various productive firms or business in a year is known as social or national product. (The gross national product is defined as the total market value of all final goods and services produced in a year). The GNP measures the market value of annual output. GNP is a monetary measure, and the figures for gross national product is adjusted for price changes. Final goods are those goods which are being purchased for final use and not for resale or for further processing.

The gross national product at market price could be obtained by adding up -

1) personal consumption expenditure;
2) gross domestic private investment;
3) export-imports or net foreign investment; and
4) government purchases.

2. NET NATIONAL PRODUCT OR NATIONAL INCOME AT MARKET PRICES

During the production of gross national product of a year, equipment, machinery, etc., are consumed. The capital goods are subject to wear out resulting in the reduction of value due to consumption in the production value. The fall in value of capital due to wear and tear is called depreciation. When depreciation is deducted from GNP we get net national product (NNP)

GNP - Depreciation = NNP
OR GNP=NNP+Depreciation.

3. NATIONAL INCOME AT FACTOR COST

National Income at factor cost means the aggregate of all incomes earned by source suppliers of land,labour,capital and enterepreneurial system which add upto an year's net production. The difference between National income and net national product arises from the fact that indirect taxes and subsidies cause market prices of output to be different from the factor incomes resulting from it. The national income(or national income of factor cost) is equal to net national product minus indirect taxes plus subsidies

That is N.I. or NIFC (National income at factor cost) = NNP-Indirect taxes + subsidies (National income at market prices

4. PERSONAL INCOME AND DISPOSABLE INCOME

Personal Income is the aggregate of all incomes actually received by all individuals during a given year. In calculating personal income,corporate profits, social security contributions and corporate income tax are deducted from National Income and transfer payment; corporate dividends and interest payed by consumers and government are added. The three types of income which are earned but not-received are to be subtracted from National Income and Incomes received but not currently earned are to be added. Payment made to government as personal taxes, like Income Tax and personal property taxes, from personal income is called disposable income, which can be either consumed or saved.

Disposable Income = Consumption + Savings

GNP = Consumption goods + Producers goods + Exportable goods.

5. METHODS OF MEASURING NATIONAL INCOME

National Income is the total money value of different goods and services produced in an economy during a perticular period of time. There are three methods of measuring national income.

a) Product method or value added method:

Under this method, National Income is measured on the basis of net output of each product or the value added by each product. The economy is divided into various sectors like agriculture, industry, mining, fishing etc., and the National Income is measured by adding the income of each sector. The outputs of various products under each sector is measured interms of values and added upto get the total value under each sector. Then the values of all the sectors are totaled up to get the Nationals Income.

b) Income Method:

Under this method the National Income is measured on the basis of income accrued by the factors of production in the economy. The contribution of each sector is measured by estimating the total number of employees at different levels and categories of employees and the salaries of each worker or employee. The grand total of all the income from different sectors gives us the national income.

c) Expenditure Method:

Under this method the national income is measured on the basis of expenditure. In an economy there are four types of expenditures, namely, - (1) consumption expenditure; (2) Investment expenditure; (3) Government expenditure; (4) Net imports.

Consumption expenditure is spent on consumer goods. Investment expenditure is spent on producers goods. The government spents on commodities and services. People also spend on imports. The aggregate of all different types of expenditure gives national income.

It is not sufficient to use any one method since each method has its own limitations. At least any two methods will have to be applied. In India the income method and products method are applied to measure the National Income.

$$Y = C+I+G+M$$

Y = National Income

C = Consumption expenditure

G = Government expenditure

I = Investment expenditure

M = Expenditure on imports

6. DIFFICULTIES IN THE MEASUREMENT OF NATIONAL INCOME

The difficulties are both conceptual and statistical in nature. The first problem relates to the treatment of non-monetary transactions such as services of housewives and farm output consumed at home. The next problem relates to the treatment of Income arising out of activities of the foreign firms in a country. The question is whether they should form a part of the national income of the country in which they are located or should it be brought under the national income of the country owing the firm. On this issue, the international Monetary fund is of the view, that the profits earned should go to the parent country, while the production and income generated from the enterprise should go to the country, where production takes place.

In under developed countries, the problem is still more difficult, since in the agricultural sector the farm produce is consumed at the farm itself and does not come to the market. The illiteracy prevailing in the rural areas make it difficult to assess the quantity produced and its value. The lack of differentiation in economic functioning of an individual makes the task of estimate more difficult. Agriculture being an unorganised sector, the incomes from agriculture have to be estimated by a guess work, making national income unreliable. The statistical data available are inadequate, not-comprehensive, in accurate and not reliable, and they are a handicap in measuring national income in these countries.

Inputs = Land. Labour, capital organisation = Output(GDP)

It is thus clear that it is composed of four main categories of expenditure, namely, -

a) personal consumption expenditure;
b) gross domestic private investment;
c) net exports of goods and services; and
d) government purchase of goods and services.

The GNP for any given period is therefore equal to the sum of these four types of expenditures, and it varies with their total.

In conclusion, we may summarise, as follows:

1. Expenditure for output create money income for the nation. Money income must vary with the level of expenditure.

2. The income flow is a circular flow involving flows of expenditure into the market for output, into income receipts, back again into the market for output.

3. Saving and investment play crucial roles in the flow of income. Saving can be reinjected as spending for output only through investment spending. Private saving can be re-injected into demand for output by government purchases in excess of its disposable income.

4. The nation could be at equilibrium and balanced growth if it can succeed in saving only an amount just equal to investment expenditure for output.

5. The government can directly affect the flow of incomes by changing its rate of expenditure for output, the amount of its tax collections at each level of Y (national income) and its rate of transfer payments.

CONSUMPTION AND SAVING

Y = GNP

Y = National Income

c = Personal consumption expenditure for output.

S_p = Personal saving

S_b = Gross business saving = capital Consumption allowances + Undistributed corporate profits.

S = Total savings = Sp + Sb = Y - c

I = Gross private investment = Gross private domestic investment + Net foreign investment

Yh = Personal or Household disposable income

The above are stated at annual rates.

Assuming that there are no Government economic activities, we can have the following accounting identities:

Y = c+i

YH = Y-Sb

Sp = YH-C

S = (Sb+Sp)=Y-c

Both consumption and saving are positive functions of the level of income. That is, at levels of income, the private sectors will both consume more and save more and vice versa. The income and output can be at an equilibrium level only if investment demand is exactly equal to the supply of saving.

CHAPTER - 9

BUSINESS CYCLES
(Economic Fluctuations)

1. INTRODUCTION

Prof. Samuelson observed that "Business conditions rarely stand still. Prosperity may be followed by panic or crash. National Income, employment and production fall. Price and profits decline, and men are thrown out of work. Eventually the bottom is reached and revival begins. The recovery may be slow or fast. It may be incomplete or it may be strong as to lead to a new boom. The new prosperity may represent a long,sustained plateau of brisk business demand and plentiful jobs, buoyant prices and increased living standards or it may represent a quick, inflationary flaring up of prices and speculation to be followed by another disastrous slumps. Such in brief was the so called Business Cycles. That used to characterize the industrial nations of the world for the last century and a half at least-ever since the elaborate interdependent money economy begin to replace a relatively self-sufficient pre-commercial society".(Samuelson, "Economics" 1970)

The economic progress of capitalistic economies has been marked by occasional fluctuations in the tempo of economic activity in the investment, in output, in income and in employment. The ideal equilibrium among the various economic magnitudes is never realised in practice. The dynamic magnitudes is never realised in practice. The dynamic forces operating in the economy create various kinds of business or economic fluctuations. Some fluctuations are sudden, isolated and discontinuous. Some are continuous for long periods in the same direction, while some others are rhythmic and recurring in nature. These economic fluctuations could be classified as follows:

a) Secular trends;

b) Seasonal Trends;

c) Cyclical Trends;

d) Random trends;

Thus, business cycles or economic fluctuations are periodical, universal and have an international application. Prof.Hicks says"preriodicity and synchronism are the virtures of a Business Cycle". Regularity is its feature. Though business cycles are not so serious today as in the past, still people are afraid of these trends and fluctuations. They are not uniform and standardised. Some are mild while some others are serve and deep. In the field of "Macro Economics", they occupy a very important place seriously disturbing investments, employment, income and savings. In managerial economics, it is very important since long-term planning and forecasting inter-act with business cycle.

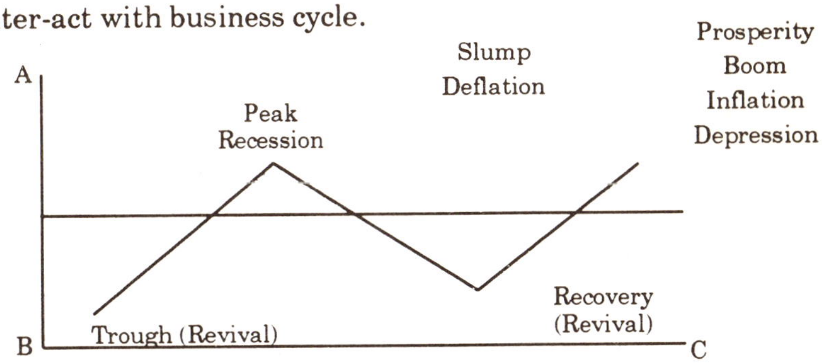

During expansion or boom period, we have high level of employment,production, income, money wages and profits; and where as in recession, the reverse happens. According to Prof Estey, the average duration of a major cycle is 40 to 50 months. The minor cycles have duration 6to8 years. The first clue for the business cycle is reflected in the capital goods sector of the economy. Since the great depression of thirties, major economic fluctuation has not taken place and it could be attributed to keynesian prescription, namely,- (C+I+G=GNP) consumption, investment and government expenditure would be equal to gross national product. According to Dr.J.M.Keynes, GNP is in equilibrium, when total savings and total investment are equal. When total outlay (expenditure) is less then total income, the GNP will fall resulting in either recession or depression. When total investment, exceeds savings, there will be boom or prosperity equilibrium in GNP.

When I is greater than S, there will be inflation and when S is grater the I, there will be deflation and when S=I, the prices will be normal.

Since business cycles are inherent in the very process of growth of the economy, it is always dangerous. The government should take immediate proper measures to counter act the dangers of business cycle so that the economy is not thrown out of gear. Inflation breeds inflation in its several phases, like creeping inflation, crawling inflation, walking inflation, running inflation, and hyper inflation. Recession is the most dangerous period, since it creates economic chaos and confusion in the economy. If inflation is bad, deflation is worse. If inflation is replaced by deflation, it is as good as exchanging a known devil with an unknown devil. During the period of hectic inflation, consumers go to the market with bags full of money, and return home with pockets full of commodities and this is because of rocketing prices in the market. Deflation is a very bad period of economic dislocation and distortions. Though prices are very low, people will have very little purchasing power. Due to the absence of profits during deflation, the investors will have no incentives or inducements to make investments., Thus, both the periods are dangerous and it will be the responsibility of the government to take steps to prevent the occurence of these economic fluctuations.

2. THEORIES OF BUSINESS CYCLES

There are several theories available to explain the causes, course and effect of business cycles. These theories throw ample light on the behaviors of the cycles.

a) Psychological Theory

b) Over Production theory

c) Over Savings theory

d) Monetary theory

e) Keynesian theory

f) Climatic theory

g) Auckley's theory of Dynamic

h) Credit theory, etc.

a) Psychological Theory

Prof.A.C.Pigon is the propounder of this theory and he says that 'Psychological behavior' of businessmen are the cause for business cycle. The waves of optimism and pessimism dominate the business community. they suffer from "Mass psychology" and the 'sheep instinct' in a business man is mainly responsible for bringing about economic fluctuation. A businessman is tossed like a ball between the courts of optimism and pessimism. When they are optimistic, they expand business providing more investments and employment leading to more income and more output. "When they are pessimistic, investment contraction takes place leading to unemployment, production and price distortions. Booms and depressions are the result of these behaviors. This theory fails to explain the root causes of business cycles.

b) Over production Theory

This theory is contributed by socialist-oriented economists, who argue that over production which is inherent in the economic system is the sole cause for business cycles. Each firm in a competitive mood produce maximum and flood the markets with commodities, without studying the demand conditions prevailing in the market. This will lead to sudden fall in prices of goods, which in turn force them to back out from productions creating unemployment, low income, lower price and depression. Many firms collapse in the market bringing about slump conditions. Even this theory fails to explain the causes for business cycles.

c) *Over saving Theory*

Prof. Douglas and Prof. Hobson are the authors of this theory. This theory is also known as "under- consumption theory". Extreme inequality in incomes create less purchasing power in the working class, who are both producers and consumers, and who are in majority. The supply being more than demand in the market due to low purchasing power in the hands of majority of people leads to low consumption and imperfect adjustment between supply and demand causing economic fluctuations. This theory is not comprehensive enough to explain the causes of business cycles.

d) *Innovation Theory*

This theory is subscribed by Mr. Joseph Sehumpeter and he says that 'waves of Research and development in the field of science and technology and their innovation and introduction into the productive field bring about new and better products into the market and there by collapse of demand for old products. Innovation refers to refined way of utilising the existing resources with the application of new scientific methods, raw materials, etc. Innovation is a Universal phenomenon having a tremendous international application. Business men inject more money into production and more income, leading to higher consumption and higher employment. When full employment is reached, more investment would only result in higher prices. Dr. Keynes says, more monetary expansion, beyond the point of full employment of resources, would only lead to high prices beyond demand when the rate of interest is raised by banks, borrowing are discouraged, investment is reduced leading to downward swing of business, because prices begin to fall due to lack of demand. This theory assumes full-employment level, which is not correct. Often innovations may be financed from internal-financing rather than from borrowing from banks.

e) *Monetary Theory*

This theory is associated with the names of Prof. Hawtrey and Prof. Hayek. Hawtrey says that "Business cycle is purely a monetary phenomenon". Elasticity of money supply is the sole cause for economic fluctuations. An increase or decrease in money supply together with bank credit bring about prosperity or depression. An any increase in bank rate by the central bank can bring about reduction in money supply, since banks borrow less from the central bank otherwise they have to pay a higher rate on their borrowings. If the borrowing rate is low then the lending rate by commercial banks will have to be lower to their customers and constituents. This leads to monetary contraction as against monetary expansion. Even this theory cannot be a complete theory to explain the cause for cyclical fluctuations. Even when the bank rate is low, borrowers may not borrow more loans, if the market is not very encouraging. The great economic recovery of thirties was due to pumping more money into circulation via-public work programmes rather than through Bank Rate Policy.

Dr. Hayek advocated "over-investment" in the industrial sector, when there is low interest rate, as a factor, responsible to bring about stability in the economic system. In this theory, the non-monetary factors responsible for cyclical fluctuations have been left out.

f) *Dr.J.R. Hicks Theory*

Dr. J.R. Hicks contributed a theory based on "autonomous investments" caused by changes in investment. Hicks has written a book seperately on "Trade Cycles" explaining his own view point on economic fluctuations. "Autonomous investment is short-lived".

g) *Keynesian Theory*

Dr. Keyne's contribution to economic thought and analysis has been one of immortal concepts. His approach has been on a 'Macro-level', unlike others, who discussed economic fluctuations in a micro- level on the ground that the failure of one industry could bring about an all round collapse of the entire economy. Most of the economist relied on natural process for adjustment of economic fluctuations because "supply creates its own demand". This myth was exploded by Dr. Keyness by negatively arguing on the belief that there is 'automatic adjustment between supply and demand in the economy. His contribution to business cycle is substantial.

According to him, so long there is economic inequality and disparties in wealth there will be deficiency in aggregate demand for goods and services due to lack of "effective demand". The lack of effective demand is due to unemployment and low incomes. When the prospective yield is less than the cost of capital, total investments lags behind total or aggregate savings. When savings are higher than investments, incomes get reduced, due to lower investments and lower employment (because expenditure of some people is the income of some other people), the profits start falling. Since production responds to rate of profit only in a market economy, a chain reaction is created bringing about recession followed by depression.

When depression is the result of excess of aggregate savings over aggregate investments, prosperity will also set in when investments exceed savings. This will happen when the government enters the field, when there is depression, and starts pumping money into the market through "public works programme" providing greater employment opportunities, resulting in increased income and more consumption.

Thus ,when consumer goods industries are stimulated, the capital good industries also expand their activities resulting in higher investments, more employment and a period of prosperity. Dr. Keynes emphasised on government intervention to fight back depression,because the government has sources and resources to supply funds. His anti-cyclical weapon is "compensatory fiscal policy", that is taxing more and spending less (by government) during prosperity and taxing less and spending more during depression periods. He also advocated the balancing of budget over a number of years and he had no belief in annual budgets. He was against cutting wage rates to stimulate production, because if wage rate is cut, aggregate demand would reduce leading to lower production, and lower employment.·the entire keynisian theory revolves around the following concepts;namely,

1. Propensity to consume;
2. Effective demand;
3. Marginal efficiency of capital;
4. Prospective yield;
5. Savings; and
6. Investments;

h) *Climatic Theory*

Prof.Jevons, a Sweedish economist of the Mathematical school, is the propounder of this theory. According to him the natural factors like climate, environment, Geographical location and rainfall, etc. have an influence on business cycles. Excessive rainfall or failure of rainfall cause economic fluctuations. They have an impact on vegetation and food production, which will have a tremendous effect on supply and demand. The action and the interaction of the forces of supply and demand have in influence on price and there by on business cycles. Even this theory is not sufficient enough to explain the root cause for economic fluctuations.

i) *Theory of Dynamic change*

This is the contribution of Prof.Auckley, former chairman of council of Economic Advisors, U.S.A. In the light of this theory, the earlier theories have been relegated to the background. Dynamic changes attempt to synthesize micro and macro view of equilibrium. Any disturbance in the equilibrium point would create distortions, disturbance and dislocations in the economic system. Macro Economic Equilibrium may be stable in the short and long periods. In the practical world, this equilibrium is always dynamic, due to continuous constant changes in the economy. He stressed on the point of harmonius blending of Micro Economics and Macro Economics, if real equilibrium concept is to be achieved. Quantity theory of money (Irving Fisher's Equation) explained as a demand theory by Lord Keynes and Gunnar Myrdal as the basis for Macro Economic Equilibrium. Savings and investments must be in equilibrium (S=I) as well as the demand and supply of money. Monetary and Fiscal policies should be synthesized to achieve equilibrium in the economy. Monetary changes bring about changes in output, pricing, employment, income,savings, and investments. It is necessary to control the volume of money, stabilise taxation levels and Government expenditure. In conclusion, it may be observed that price control is at the basis of integrated economic development and stability.

3. EFFECTS OF TRENDS

a) Secular Trends:

A persistent movement continuing in the same direction over a long period of time is called secular Trend. A long period of secular trend generally encompasses within it a number of business cycles. In the study of economic fluctuations and business forecasting, secular trends are the best, since they have an impact on long term forces making for change. In the total economy, secular movements reflect changes in population growth, technology, accumulation of capital, propensity to consume and saving which cause changes over a long term.

b) Seasonal Trends:

Seasonal fluctuations refer to the periodic movements in business activity that take place due to changing seasons within the period of a calendar year. These fluctuations are observed in various business and economic phenomena like prices of industrial products, agricultural commodities, bank clearings, interest rates etc. Social customs are also the causes for seasonal variations in economic activities. Seasonal variations do not present any serious social or economic problems, since they are predictable well in advance.

c) Cyclical Trends:

Economic activity moves continuously through alternations of rise and fall and they are called cyclical fluctuations, which are wave like fluctuations of economic activity characterised by recurring phases of expansion and contractions. Cycles are rhythmic and irregular, but they have stipulated pattern, but difficult to predict.

d) Random Trends:

The random trends are non-recurring and irregular operating in the economy in bringing about revolutionary and sporadic changes. Floods, earthquakes, storms, famines, strikes, tornedos etc. are very good examples. Most of these factors are accidental in character. They are unpredictable, non-measurable and non-periodic. All these trends are interrealted and inter - woven, cyclical fluctuations have attracted major attention of the economists, since their impact is very severe.

These business cycles are an alteration of periods of prosperity and depression of good and bad trade. Prof. Gordon observes that "business cycles consists of recurring alternative of expansion and contraction in aggregate economic activity,the alternating movements in each direction being self-reinforcing and pervading virtually ali parts of the economy". The statistic of output, income and employment throw light on the occurrence of these fluctuations.

4. FEATURE OF BUSINESS CYCLES:

a) A business cycle is a wave like movement and characterised by prosperity and depression (Expansion and contraction). The prosperity is followed by depression.

b) They are recurrent in nature. They are rhythmic and have a recognised pattern. Dr.Hicks says "Periodicity and Synchronism are the virtues of a business cycle.

c) they have a cumulative self-reinforcing nature of the movement in expansion and contraction. Each feeds on itself and gain momentum. Inflation breeds inflation and deflation breeds deflation.

d) They contain self-generating forces and they cannot have an eternal boom or depression. These forces tend to terminate at one end.

e) They affect every segment of the economy and all pervasive. Through the mechanism of international trade and inter-national economic relationship, they become universal with international application.

f) Dr.Keynes points out that a trade cycle is characterised by the presence of a crisis. That is to say the peak and the trough are not symmetrical;in other words, a business cycle is relatively narrow at its peak and broad at its trough. During fluctuations prices and production move in the same direction.

g) The cyclical fluctuations are more prominent in capital goods industry than an consumer's goods industry. Prof. Haberler points out that MV increases during prosperity and decreases during depression. There are dissimilarities between cycles in different countries and in different periods.

h) Prof. Samuelson observes that "No two business cycles are quite the same; yet they are recognisable as belonging to the same family".

The business cycles are caused by endogeneous forces (factors within the economic system) and exogeneous (factors outside the economic system) forces, and therefore they vary in length and effectiveness. But still they have uniform pattern, as revealed in their effects.

5. THE PHASES OF A CYCLE:

A business cycle could be studied under four inter- related recurring phases.

a) Inflationary phase, also called as prosperity, boom or period of monetary expansion.

b) Recession phase, that is a period of monetary confusion, chaos and complexities;

c) Deflationary phase, also known as Depression, slump or period of monetary contractions; and

d) Recovery phase, also called a period of revival.

a) Prosperity Phase:

During this phase, the following features could be observed Large volume of production and trade; large volume of employment and mobility of labour vertically and horizontally; rising prices; rising structure of interest rates leading to bullish tendency in the stock exchange, expansion of credit and bank borrowings; growing real investments; rise in wages, incomes and profits; business optimism; and growing confidence among the business community. The variable income group dominate the society, while the fixed income group is suppressed and compressed under the heels of inflations. Rocketing and meteoric rising prices, a sellers and producers market. Expansion is cumulative due to the cooperation of dynamic forces. Increase in effective demand, higher investment, higher production stimulating employment. Thus, prosperity reaches the peak. Inflation breeds inflation.

At this stage, economic bottlenecks start appearing creating forces of self-destruction and business calculations go wrong. Over optimism leads to over- pessimism gradually and recessionary trends start operating.

b) Recessionary phase:

Where prosperity ends recession starts. Recession is generally for a short period. This recession is first reflected in a stock market. During this period, businessmen lose their confidence. Diffidence breeds diffidence. Investments gradually decline and production of capital goods fall. People would like to have greater liquidity and such as the banks are forced to curtail the credit expansion to increase their liquidity ratio. Layoff of workers starts resulting in greater unemployment. Income reduce and savings are affected. The aggregate effective demand reduces. Prices and profits fall. Prof. Lee remarks that "A recession, once starts, tends to build upon itself much as forest fire, once under way, tends to create its own draft and give internal impetus to its destructive ability". Thus, recession is a period of ulter confusion and chaos.

c) Depression phase:

If prosperity is bad, depression is worse. One cannot with stand the on slaught of hyper-inflation, but during depression, the conditions of economy is highly deplorable. The resources become idle; the level of unemployment increases; the real income is consumed entirely; the savings, which are necessary of investments, decline rapidly because the incomes are less. The resources remain unused; absence of capacity utilisation; the volume of production shrinks, over all prices fall; wages and profits decline; the effective demand and aggregate expenditure fall; general contraction of credit; bank reserves increase; stock market crash and every where pessimism prevades. The structure of interest rates declines and all construction work comes to a stand still. Depression is short-lived and gradually the economic activity gathers momentum giving room for economic recovery. While controlling inflation, the economists and the statesman should not try to introduce deflation as a remedy. If so, as keyness says "It is curing the disease by killing the patient". So maximum care should be taken to see that one is not replaced by the other.

d) Recovery phase:

Recovery normally starts with the revival of demand for capital goods. During the periods of recovery, the government expenditure should increase enormously, since the private investments are very shy. The economy requires an electric kick or a shock theraphy. A spark is necessary to ignite the whole economy, and that is to be done by the government. During the period of revival, level of employment, output, income and general demand slowly increase. Stock markets become sensitive and bullish atmosphere prevails in the stock exchange. Bank loans and demand for credit start slowly increasing. Then recovery starts breeding on itself leading to a self generating economy. Employment, output and income indicate an up-ward swing. Recovery gradually merges with prosperity and the cycle repeats itself. These cycles may be minor or a major one. Prof. Lee observes thus, ;just as there may be a number of earth tremors before a major earthquake, so the economy will ordinarily experience a variable number of minor cycles between major cycle movements". Economists are only concerned with cycles.

6. STABILISATION PROCESS - REMEDIAL MEASURE:

The stabilization process could be brought under three different heads:

a) Monetary Measures;

b) Fiscal Measure; and

c) Non-monetary and non fiscal measures.

a) Monetary Measures:

The most commonly advocated measure is through the operation of monetary policy. This policy consists of measure through banking and credit system. The Central Bank of the country and the commercial banks have to take necessary steps to combat inflation and flight back deflation. The volume of credit has a direct bearing on the price line and so it is necessary to regulate the volume of credit to stabilise the economic activity. Since the second world war, the importance of debt management as a contra cyclical programme has increased.

The commercial banks motivated by profit, expand credit and this credit creation has a tremendous impact on price situation resulting in inflation. Credit expansion leads to an increase in investment potential, expenditure increases in terms of money bringing about inflationary situation. Thus, the central bank of the country has to interfere to control the credit capacity of commercial banks. The quantity of money in circulation has to be regulated, since monetary expansion leads to inflation, credit inflation leads to capital and investment inflation, and they inturn lead to price inflation and profit inflation.

The central bank, which provides funds to commercial banks either as advances or by re-discounting the bills of commercial banks, has to take stringent measures to curb the tendency of the commercial banks to resort to the central bank for monetary accomdations. The central bank has in its armoury quantitative techniques or traditional weapons like Bank rate policy, open market operations and variable Reserve Ratio method to control the credit activities of commercial banks and the total volume of money in the market. During inflation, Bank Rate is increased discouraging commercial banks from borrowing money and the reverse during depression, Under open market operation method, the central bank enters the open market (securities market) and sells government securities to withdraw money from the market. This results in the inflow of money into the government leading to monetary contraction. The investors with draw money from their banks to reinvest them in the government securities. During depression, the Central Bank follows the opposite course, that is instead of selling, it starts buying securities releasing cash into the market.

Under the variable Reverse Ratio method, the central bank varies the reserve ratios to be maintained by the commercial banks with the central bank. During inflation, the central bank increases the Reverse Ratio and tighten the liquidity position of the commercial Banks and vice-versa during depression.

Besides these quantitative techniques, certain qualitative or selective controls are also applied. They are credit rationing, Moral-suasion and direct action method intended to control the behavior of the commercial banks with regard to credit portfolio. The monetary policy is flexible enough to bring the results, but monetary policy alone cannot achieve the desired objectives without the help of fiscal policies. They should co-exist.

b) Fiscal Measures:

The Fiscal measures or techniques have assumed great importance as a tool of economic stability since 1930's under the influence of Keynesian Economics. The Fiscal Measures are applied by the government, unlike the monetary measures, which are by the Central Bank. The Fiscal measures embrace taxation policy and the expenditure has a tremendous impact on price. The taxation policy pursued by the government has a lasting effect on the finances of the state. The level of public expenditure and the incidence and effects of taxation have a bearing on the economy. Taxation aims at withdrawing money from the private economy, while expenditure determines the channels by which the government funds are pumped in to the economy. Through multiplier effect, the government spending has influence on aggregate demand, incomes etc. Taxation reduces consumption and investments reducing the disposable income and saving also. A deficit budget encourages private spending, while a surplus budget produces a deflationary trend. Thus, the fiscal policy has both quantitative and qualitative aspects. Manipulation of the taxation structure, budgetary adjustments, export-import policy and guide lines on government expenditure etc., are some of the fiscal methods that could be applied to contain inflation or to fight back deflationary trends. Some economists are of the view that there could be built-in flexibility or automatic stabilisers within the fiscal policy to avoid administrative delay and minimisation of errors in the implementation process. Besides automatic stabilisers, discretory policies are also necessary depending upon the circumstances.

In a free enterprises economy, fiscal policy is a more suitable device. Both monetary policy and fiscal policy must work together to achieve economic stability. Monetary policy is more effective during inflation, while the fiscal policy can bring positive results during depression. The monetary devices could be employed as complements to the fiscal devices to avoid economic fluctuations.

c) *Non-Monetary and Non-Fiscal Measure:*

Under these measures, direct control is considered as a good device. This is applied by the government, which forbids certain kinds of investment or economic activity. These controls may be more discriminatory than the other policies. But direct controls are criticised on the ground that they suppress individual initiative, inhibit innovations, freeze activity and breed speculation. Its implementation requires honest, efficient, administration and to be used under extraordinary circumstances.

Public co-operation in the form of avoiding tax- evasion, black-marketing, hoarding, exporting without permits etc., are also necessary. A sound public policy and price support policy would be of great advantage. Unemployment insurance scheme is also suggested as a remedial method. Without the co- operation of the people, no measure will succeed. People should develop economic and national consciousness.

In conclusion, there is no fool proof method for solving the problem of trade cycle. All measures should be co-ordinated and implemented. No single method would succeed in isolation. Cyclical fluctuations are inherent characteristic features of capitalistic societies. Certain fluctuations are beneficial to economic growth. Dr. J.M. Keynes observes "the right remedy for the trade cycles is not to be found in abolishing booms and thus keeping us permanently in a semislump; but in abolishing slumps and thus keeping us permanently in a quasi-boom". Anti-cyclical or contra cyclical weapons should be used by the authorities at the right time and in right measure (quantity)

The depression should be fought back seriously to avoid its evil effects on the economy. Tight measure should be taken to avoid negative results. "The operation is successful, but the patient died". This should not be the case.

Summarisation

Business Cycles (Trade Cycles)

a) *A business cycle is a period of business prosperity and full-employment alternating with a period of adversity and increasing unemployment. It has several stages. (analysed as inflation, recession, deflation and recovery periods)*

The under consumption theory of Prof. Hobson, the over-investment theory and the Keynesian theory of savings and investment are the most important theories. The evil effects of business cycles could be mitigated through fixed investment policy, cyclical pricing; besides monetary, financial and other measures.

These business cycles are international in character. With the development of international institution like the world bank; the international monetary fund, international trade organisation; world food organisation and other international financial institutions; the development of communications and transport. etc., the nations of come nearer and together. As a consequence of this, these cyclical fluctuations have become universal with international implications. As such, they require an in-depth study and analysis. "A preventive measure is always better and preferred to cultivate measure.

* * * *

PART - B

CHAPTER - 10

MANAGEMENT SCIENCE

1. Introduction

Co-ordination of individual efforts is essential to achieve the desired objectives and that is through management. Management is a multi-purpose organ that manages a business and manages managers and manages worker and work. The need for an environment to perform effectively and efficiently requires no special emphasis; and it is the responsibility of every manager to provide this environment. Many influences both inside and outside the organisation are to be judiciously considered by managers. Most of the business failures are the result of inexperienced or unqualified management. When highly developed and organised societies have realised the importance of management, it is no exaggeration when the importance of management is emphasised for underdeveloped countries which are continuously plagued by the problems of poverty, unemployment and economic distress. Here comes the role of managers to contribute substantially their might for alleviating there social evils in large measures. Peter Drucker observes "the achievement of business management enables us to-day to promise the abolition of the grinding poverty that has been mankinds lot through the ages .... management provides the invigorating force that brings to life what would otherwise be only potentialities".

If Japan, U.S.A. and some of the European countries have achieved progress and development, it is because of sound and efficient management of the available resources and not simply the existence of bounty of nature. A reasonable, rational, systematic and scientific management of resources alone would bring plenty and prosperity. This is more so for underdeveloped countries.

2. Definitions:

The following are some of the important definitions of "Management".

According to Prof. Harold Koontz "Management is the art of getting things through and with people in formally organised groups. It is the art of creating an environment in which people can perform as individuals and yet co-operate towards attainment of group goals. It is the art of removing blocks to such performance a way of optimising efficiency in reaching goals".

Kimball and Kimball observe that "Management embraces all duties and functions that pertain to the initiation of an enterprise, its financing, the establishment, the outlining of the general form of organisation, under which the enterprise is to operate and the selection of the principal officers".

The French Writer Prof. Henry Fayol has attempted a functional approach to management science. According to him "to manage is to forecast and to plan, to organise, to command, to co-ordinate and to control".

Prof. Peter Drucker justifies this functional approach to management.

The human approach to management received accredition and support by Professors Elton Mayo and P.J. Roethlisberger, while during twenties and thirties the human approach to management received a set back infavour of automation approach to human resource.

According to the President of an Americal Corporation "we do not build automobiles, aeroplanes, refrigerators, radios, we build men and the men build the products".

"Management may be defined as the art of securing maximum results with a minimum of effort so as to secure maximum prosperity and happiness for both employer and employee and give the best possible service to the public" Prof. John F. Mee.

Mr. Stanley Vance observes that "Management is simply the process of decision making, and control over the action of human beings for the express purpose of attaining pre-determined goals".

Prof. Lawrence Appley observes that "Management is the development of people and not the direction of things .... Management is personal administration". He further states that "Management is the accomplishment of results through the efforts of other people".

The observation of Mr. George Terry is as follows, "Management is a distinct process consisting of planning, organising, actuating and controlling".

Prof. Ross Moore says that "Management means decision making".

According to E.A. Chiles that "Management is Trusteeship". This is because that the professional manager has to act as a trustee safeguarding the best interest of the owners of business, the employees, the customers, and the general public.

From these few definition, one could draw a conclusion that Management has primarily a twin objective, namely customers satisfaction and maintenance of employee morale through proper decision making and scientific management. Management is a critical ingredient in a nations growth. According to Prof. Peter Drucker, "Objectives are essential in all key areas of management where performance and results directly contribute to the growth and survival of the business for enabling managers to organise and explain the scope of business; to verify the objectives of business operations; to predict the employee behaviour, loyalty and devotion to duty; to evaluate the soundness of decisions and subsequently improve the performance".

In conclusion, it could be summarised that management consists of forecasting, decision making, planning, organising, co-ordinating and controlling the multi purpose and multidimensional activities of a business enterprise with the ulterior motive to serve the public in the best possible way.

3. Management as a Science and Art

"Science could be defined as a particular branch of knowledge or study, a recognised department of learning". It is an organised theoritical knowledge empirically derived, critically tested and generalised into theories, laws and principles. Even Management makes use of similar tools and processes in its application to streamline the administrative functions. The experienced practical knowledge of managers are abundantly utilised in the discharge of managerial functions and thus Management could be treated as science.

Management application is governed by the aptitudes and skills possessed by the managers. Imagination, insight and creativity are highly personalised characters of managers. Art is creative since it embraces the creation of objects and events. Management has to achieve concrete results through systematic skills in every department of production. Creativity, skill, personality development are the ingredients of arts and every manager has his own way of approach to problems. "Even in the most exact of exact sciences - physics - there are areas where, scientific knowledge must be replaced with speculation and hypothesis. "Akin to medicine or engineering management is both a science and art. Scientific truths are axiomatic principles internationally and universally accepted, but to appreciate and enjoy the fruits of this truth, one should have an artistic and aesthetic knowledge. So also management, which is highly personalised and creative, and the product of experience discharges both the functions of science and art.

4. Management VS Administration.

The words 'Management and Administration' are used in a productive enterprise without making any distinction what so ever. It was Prof. Oliver Sheldon who raised this terminological conflict in 1923. He opined that administration is a decision-making function, while management involves execution. One school of thought considers that Management and Administration are one and the same with minute distinction. Prof. McFarland observes that in government agencies administration is preferred over management; where as business administration refers to the activities of high level management. Some opine that administration is involved in policy making, while management is shouldered with the responsibility of execution of this policy to achieve the pre-determined objectives.

Authors like Henry Fayol, Koontz, Odonnel etc are of the view that Administration and management are synonymous involving the same functions, principles and objectives. According to Prof. Newman "administration is the guidance, leadership and control of efforts of a group of individuals towards common goal". Henry Fayol, while addressing the second international congress of administrative science, emphasised "All undertakings require planning, organisation, command, co-ordination and control and they have to observe the same general principles in order to function properly".

According to O.Sheldon, Spriegel, Zausberg and others administration is above management, involving different functions. While administration is policy making, management, being a tool of administration, should implement the policies laid down by management to achieve the desired results.

Prof. Brech observes that Management is comprehensive having within its orbit administration. That is to say, that administration is an integral part of Management. Planning, integration, programming, organising, disecting are all the responsibilities of management achieved through high-level, middle-level and low level establishments.

If one analyses the theories, principles,processes and objectives of both management and administration, one can observe the same set of functions and theories. One can find the difference only conceptually and theoritically and with no difference practically. If management is supplementary to administration, then administration is complementary to management.

5. Management as a profession.

Prof. Kenneth Andrews, after making an in-depth study of the problems of professional management, observes that there are five basic criteria which determine and decide that Management as a profession. Then what is profession? Profession has different connotations. Specialised skills which contribute to the betterment of society or community and in the larger interests these economic skills achieved are not measured in terms of money. A profession involves the actual application of expertised knowledge in the selected problem areas that are governed by a set of well disciplined code and conduct aimed at social responsibilities. Recognised profession and business management have common features. Both aim at accelerating ethics in business to achieve the pre-determined goals.

Professionalisation in management could be viewed from three angles, namely from the point of view of (a) owner-Managers, who risk their investments, (b) Practical concept where previous experience counts in making them practicing manager and lastly, (c) those who enjoy are gift of organisation and self- salesmanship operating through a body concept. According to Prof. K. Andrews knowledge, competent application, social responsibility, self-control and community action are the basis for determining Management as a profession.

The increasing complexities in modern business, the goal and role of industrialisation to solve the twin problems of poverty and unemployment; the need for leadership, honesty and integrity to up-hold the business ethics; the advent of industrial democracy and the problems in the process of its implementation, the man-power management; the profit motive inherent in a business enterprise and the social audit and accounting have made management highly professional in character.

The optimum utilisation of men, material, money and technology for economic development and growth have become indispensable in this competitive world. The professional Management has to play a vital role in this direction.

6. Evolution of Management Thought

"Scientific management is a new philosophy of industrial regeneration". Scientific management is an integral part of "Rationalisation". The impact of systematic Management was felt only after the industrial Revolution. The development of Management theory in a systematic way started making its impact in the highly industrialised twentieth century with substantial contributions made by theoreticians and practitioners in U.S.A., Europe and England. In U.S.A. this concept originated from industrial manager in order to avoid wastage and inefficiency in the productive process; while in England and Europe the aim for developing this concept was to crystalise the vital functions of business to achieve managerial performance effectively and efficiently. The tremendous increase in the size of the market; the complexity in the nature of consumer needs; the growth of large scale industries to produce more to meet the needs of international trade; for rational decisions rather than decisions based on traditions and intuitions etc. are some of the contributory factors mainly responsible for the evolution of management concept.

Various experts in the field of Economics, Psychology, Sociology, Management science etc. have made substantial contributions in this field, besides these people, public administrators, Business managers, Behaviouralists and systems scientists have also contributed their share in the field.

Prof. Charles Babbage (1729-1871) stressed the need for accurate data and rigid investigation in the management of enterprises.

Prof. Jameswatt and M.R.Boulton (1770-1848) emphasised a market research, forecasting, production planning and planned machinery lay out as important tools in the management process.

Prof. Robert Owen (1771-1868) stressed an improved human relation in the industry to influence the worker's performance and congenial environment in the industry.

Prof. H.R.Towne elaborated an important management technique resulting in "gain-sharing"system, under which gains in the industry were awarded to the departments on the basis of relative efficiency and performances.

Prof. H.Emerson (1853-1931) popularised scientific management and expounded the concept of standard time, standard costs, preventable wastes etc.

Prof. F.A.Halsy, (1856-1935) invented the incentive system of wage payments. His "premium plan of paying labour"aimed at eliminating rate-cutting. It guaranteed daily or hourly rate for fixed quantity of work based on performance. (Modern Deed-based wage system.)

Mary Parket Follet (1868-1933), political and social philosopher, explained the need for psychological insight into the human relationships within industrial groups. She said that conflicts in the industry could be harnessed not through domination or compromise but through integration allowing the parties themselves to examine together to arrive and achieve their conflicting desires.

Prof. F.B.Gilbreth (1868-1924) emphasised on "Motion study" as an important tool for managers to increase productivity. He stressed on the need for welfare measures in the organisation both for individuals and groups to keep the wheels of industry moving.

The concept of Management developed very fast since the time of Henry Fayol and Frederic Taylor (1856-1915). Taylor is supposed to be the father of "SCIENTIFIC MANAGEMENT". According to him "scientific Management is the art of knowing exactly what you want to do and then seeing that how they do it in the best and cheapest way". Born in U.S.A. in 1856 and graduating in physics and Mathematics form Harvard university, he joined Bethlehem steel company, where he gained rich experience in managing activities. He was for functionalisation. He perceived several new functions for executives; namely

a) Replacement of rule-of-thumb method by scientific determination of each element of worker's work;

b) specific way of selecting of employees and their proper training;

c) Co-operating management and labour to accomplish work in accordance with scientific method; and

d) a more equal division of responsibility between managers and workers.

He adapted differential piece rate plan to motivate workers for higher efficiency. Taylor , based on his experience and experiments published the following articles namely

a) A piece rate system
b) Shop management
c) Art of cutting metals.

After integrating his ideas and collaborating the facts, he published a classic titled "The Principles of Scientific Management" in 1911; which covered the followings concepts;

1) Seperation of planning and doing;
2) Functional Foremanship;
3) Job analysis;
4) Time study;
5) Motion study;
6) Fatigue study;
7) Standardisation
8) Scientific selection and training
9) Financial incentives
10) Economy, and
11) bilateral Mental Revolution.

Taylor's emphasis was not on general management but on management at the shop level. However, his concept was not free from criticisms. He was branded as utilitarian and impersonal and stressed more on specialisation. His concept promoted industrial autocracy and concept like job analysis and fatigue study were treated as abstract elements not subject to scientific measurement. Inspite of these criticisms, his theory has left profound foot-prints in the management science and the basis for further development of the concept.

Henry Fayol born in 1841 graduated in 1860 as Mining Engineer. As Managing Director of a coal company, he was responsible for its all round development at the time of retirement.

Both Taylor and Fayol has similar ideas about management science. Their approach to problem of personnel and its management was based on and aimed at the smooth functioning and success of the industry. While Taylor's approach in the operation of the industry was from bottom to top; Henry Fayol's approach worked downwards. Taylor did not emphasise on managerial organisation and processes, where as Fayol laid more stress on this aspect. He studied the functions and principles of Management in a systematic manner. He is supposed to be the father of modern "Operational Management Theory". He published in 1916 his famous book in French titled "Administration industrial -el-general". and was translated to English in 1929, four years after his death. He discussed organisational function from manager's point of view. According to his theory all industrial activities could be divided into six groups;

1. Technological activities
2. Commercial activities
3. Financial activities
4. Security activities
5. Accounting activities
6. Managerial activities

The above activities relate to production, buying, selling, exchange , capital formation and its optimum use, protection of property and person, statistics, planning, organisation, command, co-ordination and control.

So to say, the above activities are so comprehensive that all organisation functions are brought under its umbrella.

These activities satisfy the basic requirements of industrial growth. Men, Money, Material, Marketing and management, are the most important ingredients for industrial organisation, growth and development.

Prof. Fayol's approach in studying Management could be analyzed in three parts; namely

a) Managerial qualities and training;

b) General principles of Management; and

c) Elements of Management

While identifying the qualities of manger, he elaborated that physical, mental, moral, educational, technical and expertise and experience are the distinguishing features between a manager and a layman.

In the analysis of general principles of Management, Prof.Fayol narrated 14 basic principles of management and they are

1) Division of work;

2) Authority and responsibility

3) Discipline that is respect for agreements

4) Unity of command

5) Unity of direction.

6) Subordination of individual interest to general interest;

7) Remuneration of personnel

8) Centralisation

9) Scalar chain, that is "a chain of superiors ranging from the ultimate authority to the lowest ranks". This process though very lengthy, still no one should depart from the line of authority.

10) Order both in respect of human and material;

11) Equity which is necessary to promote and evoke devotion to duty,loyalty, sensitivity, responsiveness and justice.

12) Stability of tenure of personnel.

13) Initiative; and lastly

14) Expirit -de-Corps; this principle envisages 'union of strength'. That is to say "Each for all and all for each"concept.

Henry Fayol holds the strong view that

a) Planning
b) Organisation
c) Commanding
d) Co-ordinating, and
e) Controlling

are the main elements of management functions. According to him the above factors are an indispensable ingredients for the conduct of business in any type of organisation. He emphasised that management is universal and applicable to other forms of concepts like politics, religion, military and small, medium and large scale sectors also. The management principle are versatile and not highly rigid or conservative in character.

The views of Taylor and Fayol are complementary and the problem of personnel management is the master-key to industrial productivity and progress. In their attempt to find solutions to managerial problems, they stressed upon scientific method and approach. If Taylor could be regarded as a "Management Engineer", Fayol was a "Management Philosopher", The managerial revolution that took place after the forties of the twentieth century could be attributed to the contributions made by the two intellectual giants. If Taylor has introduced scientific plant management, Fayol laid the foundation of the pattern of theory and process of management. Their concept is a new philosophy of industrial regeneration and management.

7. Functions of Management. (Management Process)

There seems to be no unanimity as regards functions of management. At best the following six functions could be recognised as major functions;

1) **Planning,** a crucial function which determines objective; selection of the course of action; policies; procedures; methodology adopted; rules, strategy and budget.

2) **Organisation,** which includes determination of activities; grouping of activities; departmentalisation, and delegation of authority and responsibility.

3) **Staffing,** consisting of selection of the rightman for the right job; training of personnel; promotion; retirement; appraisal of staff and determination of remuneration.

4) **Direction,** which includes teaching and coaching; instruction; ordering and supervision.

5) **Motivation** to employees to do their jobs willingly to achieve the common goals of the enterprise.

6) **Controlling** the activities of the enterprise so that the events are according to plan already envisaged, controlling also includes setting up of standards; appraisal of performance and corrective measures.

Prof. Earnest Dale includes 'innovation' as another function of management. He says that "innovation may encompass any new procedure that contribute towards corporate objectives".

In view of growing responsibility of business to society, the function of representation has assured greater importance. The success of business projects entirely depends upon the application of techniques of management.

While specialisation is important in scientific discipline, professionalisation in management to guarantee quick solutions to the problems of poverty and unemployment. Profit no longer stands as a motivating element in the productive process. Prof. Galbraith observes that "it is in the field of management and administration not economics, where the most interesting problems of the future will be encountered and where the most serious dangers will be faced".

It is management's responsibility to-day, in this competitive world, to achieve maximum output from the minimum inputs and to assure the minimum standards of living to the people at large.

Summarisation (Points at a glance)

1. Management process could be classified under planning, Organising, Staffing, Direction, Leading, Controlling, Innovation, Motivation and Representation.
2. Management requires Judgement, Common-sense, Knowledge and analytical power besides academic discipline and techniques.
3. Management draws inspiration from an indepth study of economics, sociology, psychology and political science in the management of an organisation.
4. The ultimate object of management is to create a surplus and a balanced input-output-ratio without sacrificing quality.
5. Modern management is under the stress and strain of dynamic forces, and, as such, it requires constant research and vigilance against these forces.

6. To-day management besides earning profits, has a social responsibility to discharge. It is answerable to the society in general and the shareholders in particular.

7. The environmental influences are severe so and tremendous, that modern managers operating in a pluralistic society have to represent and respond to the needs of the society in which they live in.

8. Ethics in management has come to play an important role like ethics in industry. "If ethics is lost, the organisation is lost". To-day 'management ethics' is a very important concept and it should exists in all the three levels of management (top level, middle level and low level management). The management has a right and privilege and so also duties and responsibilities. Ethical standards improve the morality of the industry and gives management a position of prestige and dignity in the productive empire.

9. The management has to face various limits in its operations. The economic environment prevailing in the country influences the revenues, plans, objectives and the financial resources of the corporation.

   Secondly, the Federal and State laws limit the scope of management. For Ex: the Anti-trust law in U.S.A., and the anti-pollution laws existing in the developed and developing countries are a limitation.

   Thirdly, the trade-union laws are severe today, that they even interfere with the location of the plant and on decision making policies of the management.

   Fourthly, the technological limitations have an impact on the location of plant, the size of the plant and the capital requirements of the productive process.

10. The innovation of scientific management has made the industry more efficient, but it has failed still to bring about a "mental revolution" (As envisaged by Frederick W. Taylor) between management and labour, who are working for an identical goal.

11. The Taylor system envisaged seperation of planning and doing, functional foremanship, time study of the elements of job, motion study to perform a job and a differential piece work of payment to make labour more effective and result-oriented.

12. Prof. Harrington Emerson's contribution attempted to persuade higher management to be more scientific in its planning and control activities.

13. Mr. Elton Mayo's contribution was towards the organisation of workers into a homogeneous groups that created a "sense of belongingness" often lacking in a dynamic world.

14. Prof. Hawthorne emphasised on the point of productivity and morale in industry and further stressed the need for nonfinancial incentives, which can practically improve the trust-worthiness of the workers.

15. Prof. Henry Fayol stressed the need for the administrators to recognise unity of command, unity of direction, responsibility equal to authority, etc.

16. The organisation of an institution is based on certain theories, and there are three theories enunciated namely,-the classical theory, which primarily emphasised on the work related to the findings of psychology and sociology, secondly, the Behavioral theory, which is primarily concerned with the people who make up the organisation and believed in the rational ways of dividing the work; and thirdly the system theory, which believes in

the interaction of many variables and that exist in an organisational system.

17. Thus, management has a very great responsibility to bring together the various infrastructure in the productive process; their proportionate application to keep down the cost of production; optimum utilisation of these infrastructure, namely, - (men,material, money, machinery,marketing and also otherwise analysed as programme, purpose, policy, principles and people) in the best interest of the industry.

CHAPTER - 11

PLANNING

1. Introduction

"Planning is the very essence of Economic life". It is one of the major functions of management process". "To plan is to survive". Some view planning is decision making to achieve a predetermined objective. It is the responsibility of top management in a business enterprise to predetermine and clearly establish the objectives, devise strategies and lay down policies.

"Planning is a road to prosperity". Prof.B.E. Goety observes that "Planning is fundamentally choosing and a planning problem arises only, when an alternative course of action is discovered."

The success of a plan largely depends upon the availability of comprehensive, reliable, adequate and accurate data and information and not on emotions and feelings. It becomes obligatory for the management, well in advance, to determine "what to produce; when to produce; where to produce; how to produce; how much to produce and why to produce". Especially in a competitive world, confronting free market economies with competitive goods and competitive price, it becomes a major problem for the management to forecast and decide about the products and prices.

The planning function determines organisational objectives and the policies, programmes, schedules, procedures and methods for achieving them. "Planning is essentially decision-making since it involves selecting among alternatives". Production is a means to consumption and consumption is the end of production. With alternative ends and with alternative means available, the problem of choice is always there.

Prof.George Terry observes that "planning is the selecting and relating of facts and the making and using of assumptions regarding the future in the visualization and formulation of proposed activities believed necessary to achieve desired results". With limited resources and unlimited wants, the problem of choice is ever present.

"Planning means systematically, scientifically, rationally and reasonably arranging and re-arranging the resources and exploiting those available resources to the optimum point". It is the major responsibility of management to see that the resources of the industry are subject to capacity utilisation to keep down the cost of production. It is an intellectual process based on facts, estimates and purpose. Planning has to bridge the gap between ends and resources. To minimise the problem of risk and survival, planning becomes absolutely necessary.

2. Nature of Planning

Planning is objective oriented. The very purpose of planning is to facilitate the management or the enterprise to fulfill the objectives by reaching the targets. Since under dynamic forces events change so fast and in a revolutionary fashion, managements have to be very alert and responsive and have to adjust themselves to the changing circumstances.

According to Prof.Geoty "Plans alone cannot make an enterprise successful. Action is required and the enterprise has to operate". Managerial planning seeks to achieve a consistent co-ordinated structure of operations focused on desired ends." In the absence of planning, there will be total chaos in the productive process.

Planning preceeds all other management functions. It helps organising, leading, motivating and controlling the management functions.

Planning is all pervasive in all types of management activities. Top management will be incharge of strategic planning, middle management looks after administrative planning, whole lower management concentrates on operational planning.

The process of planning should be adaptable to changing circumstances. It has to co-ordinate all managerial activities from top to bottom.

A planner has to recognise the various limiting factors like man power, materials, money, machinery and management and avail of their services economically and judiciously.

3. Importance of Planning

Planning improves the decision making process in the organisation with a clear and effective master plan, each department is aware of its duties and responsibilities to the company and to the corporate goal. The managers of various departments should have their own strategies and plan for a unified decision making frame work.

Planning is a continuous process, and as such it gives directions for the growth of the enterprise. Prof.Peter Drucker points out that "Planning cannot completely eliminate the risks and uncertainties of decisions." But planning can facilitate to identify the potential opportunities and threats and hold in minimising risks.

The performance of the company is very important for its progress. Planning helps in providing performance standards and determines targets to be achieved. To the investors in a company, the return on investments is very important and it creates confidence in the investing public.

Policies, programmes, principles and people are the basic ingredients for the growth of the company. Planning in all these directions are vital to tune the management to adopt and adjust itself with the changing environment. In a dynamic society, change also implies progress; and change is the essence of life. An enterprise and its environment are mutually interdependent and inter-acting with each other. A management through a comprehensive planning can anticipate and meet the challenge.

Planning has no substitute. All managerial functions including organising, staffing, directing, leading, motivating and controlling should support the planning process and in turn to be supported by the planning strategy. This concept of planning in the management process is called the primary of planning. The concept of efficiency is an implied factor in planning. "A Good plan should not only attain optional relationship between out put and input but also bring about the greatest deal of satisfaction to those who implement it". The planning activity provides sufficient safeguards against uncertainties, which are likely to change with the passage of time. Planning helps in the crystallisation of objectives, which will be the basis for the management activities to be performed. A proper integration of departmental objectives would help in attaining the overall objectivities. Planning helps in harnessing creativity and innovation of individual, which would create more effectiveness in the management of the company.

"Competition has become the hall-mark of modern business" and planning helps the industry to be more competitive and meet the challenges of a dynamic society. With the inroads of scientific and technological developments, new products are getting in to the market. Planning might greatly help in this direction in the identification of customer needs and suggest timely expansion of plant-capacity.

4. Limitations of planning

A plan is successful only when planning premises on which it is based are accurate and reliable. Factors of environment are uncontrollable and unpredictable. No plan can guarantee safeguards against risks or uncertainties. Since planning is a costly process, it may not be very useful to small and medium size concerns. Since planning is a time-consuming activity, it might delay action. The importance and benefits of planning out-weigh the limitations. If plans are simple, flexible, purposeful, well defined objectives, with democratic participation, planning would be a blessing and a boon to industry and business organisation.

Prof.L.F. Urwick observes that a good plan must have well defined objectives, because "management by objectives (MOB) is a method universally adopted for all levels of management; the planning process must be simple and easily understandable; highly flexible to suit the requirements of changing conditions; it should lay down good and balanced standards of performance; it should aim at optimum utilisation of resources and it should be pragmatic and highly developmental.

5. Types of plans

Planning could be classified in different ways. It could be either on the basis of time dimension or on the basis of functions of management. If it is on the basis of time dimension, it may be classified as short- term, medium-term and long-term plans. On the basis of functions of management, it may be Production planning, marketing planning, company planning etc. Planning is a primary function of management, because it is always directed towards efficiency. "A good plan should not only attain optional relationship between input and output, but should also bring the gréatest satisfaction to those who implement it". Planning is an integrated approach. All economic activities are monetary activities and planning is an economic activity and therefore a monetary activity. Planning is both a financial and a physical resources planning.

Short range planning confines to a maximum period of one year; while the long term planning extends upto 10 to 12 years and generally it is at the top of level management. Peter Drucker points out that "long range planning is the continuous process of making present entrepreneurial decisions systematically and with the best possible knowledge of their futurity, organising systematically the efforts needed to carry out these decisions and measuring the results of these decisions against the expectations through organised feed-back". Long range planning besides being risk taking in business, forecasting also. Still it is advocated on the ground that long term planning provides for a capital asset replacement; it ensures continuous flow of man power supply; it prevents hasty decisions; it provides a measuring rod to determine the performance of the company; it can predict the on coming competitions and it serves as a "review board" to judge the performance in the light of changing conditions."

In a broad sense, planning covers;

a) Purpose, mission or objectives;

b) Aims or objectives or goals;

c) Strategies adopted to achieve the goals;

d) Standards or desired performance to reach the goal;

e) Budgets envisaged to fulfill the targets;

f) Policies, procedures and programmes to be followed and realised;

g) Methods and rules to be strictly adhered to in the process of implementation.

One can also think of other detailed plans pertaining to each department under the scope of management like;

a) Sales planning.

b) Purchase planning.

c) Audit planning due to social responsibility of the management;

d) Production planning

e) Research & development planning

f) Man power planning etc etc

Objectives or Mission have to be crystallised for the enterprise as a whole, besides goals for each department also have to be planned or enunciated. The management should see that objectives determined within the capacity of the organisation and should have a purpose behind that.

Prof. Terry distinguishes the term strategic planning "with reference to fundamental issues, broad prospectives and long term periods" from tactical planning which deals with determining the most efficient use of the resources that have been allotted for achieving given and specific objectives. Plans specify direct goals and ordinary means to achieve them, where as strategies aim at counter acting the actions of the opponents.

Standards are performance evaluation and they help to measure the level of achievement desired. When ever there are deviations from the original plan, standards fixed earlier, help in identifying the deviations.

Budgets are important tools in the hands of management. It is a very good controlling device. Budgets could be expressed in financial terms or in units of products, machine hours etc. A correct budgeting helps the management to exercise proper control over all the departments and provide guidelines in the development of the departments.

Policies are general guidelines issued by the management to be followed strictly by the various departments. They are more or less based on the past experience and actions of the managers. They are laid down after experimentation and trial and so they are strict disciplines to be followed in the execution of work.

Procedures are more definite than policies. They define specific activities of the management to be followed in order to achieve the predetermined goals.

Managements lay down procedures to be followed by various departments in their a day to day operations; and they exist throughout the organisation. The follow up action of a procedure can bring longer and better results to management.

Programmes integrate policies and procedures that are necessary to achieve the anticipated goals. Programmes could be treated as "planned actions, integrated in to a unity and designed to bring about a stated objective".

Rules are laid down by management to be followed according to procedure and there is no scope for deviation and needs strict follow up.

Methods lay down the methodology to be adopted by management in the best manner in the performance of a task. It is micro in nature.

6. Planning premises

In a planning process assumptions are the basic factors on which planning has to take place. Environmental influences play a major role in determining the planning premises. these premises are varied both in content and degree depending upon organisation and industry. Some factors are external and some are internal. The growth and development of an organisation and industry would largely depend upon on these factors;

a) External premises

Just like the man who is the product of civilisation, so also a business organisation the product of environment.

Political stability, government controls; government Fiscal and monetary policies; population trends; employment levels; technological innovations; factor markets like land, labour capital and management are the most important factors determining the future progress of the industry and organisation. Forecasting and decision making are necessary in respect of these factors, since the supply of these factors are not constant and mostly depend upon environment.

Product market is an important factor since the entire success of the organisation and its results wholly depend on the responsiveness of the market and the elasticity of demand of the consumers. The market demand schedule is not constant, but ever changing. Price variations bring about changes in demand. The competitive nature of the markets changes with time and environment, thus the organisation has to be always alert and vigilant, sensitive and responsive to these changes.

b) Internal premises

Most of the economic theories are built upon postulates (assumptions) and the economic decisions for their correctness depend upon the correctness of assumptions. A business decision is an economic decision. Most of the external premises discussed above are interrelated and inter-dependent. Most of the factors of external premises are uncontrollable by the managements.

Every organisation would try to maximise its profits by maximising its sales portfolio and by optimum utilisation of the infrastructure. Here comes the need for sales forecasting at a given price. Most of the activities of the organisation are based on this very important factor. Both internal and external factors determine the selling at a particular level.

The basic policies of an organisation are inflexible and plans of an organisation are conditioned by basic policies.

Changes in basic policies result in higher costs and as such policies become a limiting factor to the management.

Formulations, adoption, execution and supervision are the main steps in the planning process. The organisation has to formulate plans within these limitations. Individuals hold positions in the organisation structure and they discharge managerial activities. The organisational functioning is disturbed by retirement, switch -over and other factors relating to individuals. Managers have to forecast the factors accurately in order to formulate accurate plans, since future cannot be foreseen with accuracy, it is obligatory on the part of managers to formulate plans based on different premises.

7. Decision making

It is a major managerial activity and a fundamental responsibility of the manager. while establishing objectives, laying down policies etc. decision making by management becomes essential. The organisational effectiveness is also influenced by decisions. Besides Directors, managers have to take decisions and these decisions have an impact on sub-ordinates as well as on the complex organisational processes.

Decision making may be defined as the selection based on some criteria among different alternatives. Peter Drucker observes that "Whatever a manager does, he does through making decisions". According to R.S. Davar "Decision making can be defined as the selection based on some criteria of one behaviour alternative from two or more possible alternatives". Decision making is the essence of management . To decide means to cut off or to come to a conclusion.

The selection is based on some criteria such as holding a major share of the market, reduction of costs, time saving devices, increase of quantity produced etc.

Choice is the essence of economic activity. One has to exercise choice at every stage of economic life. With limited resources and unlimited wants, the problem of choice has assumed great importance. To keep down the cost of production, the management is obliged to exercise choice in the selection of infrastructure to produce commodities at the nearest minimum cost. So also, the market being highly competitive with competitive goods and competitive prices, the question of selecting the market arises.

According to Dr.Saxena, decision involves the following characteristic features;

1. Decision is the end process preceded by deliberation and reasoning;
2. Rationality is another characteristic feature
3. Decision is the choice among alternatives.
4. Decision is aimed at achieving the objectives of the organisation;
5. It is a mental process where evaluation is necessary
6. It involves certain commitment.

Types of decisions

a) Organisational Decision

Organisational and personal decisions and this refers to individual decision taken by the executive on behalf of the organisation. The executive can take decision about himself which are personal decisions and which cannot be delegated to any one else.

b) Strategic Decisions

Routine and strategic decisions which are taken with reference to day to day operation of the organisation. They are mostly of repetitive nature and do not require much analysis and evaluation and can be taken quickly. They could be delegated to lower authority since they are within the broad context of policy. The strategic decisions affect organisational structures, objective, finances and facilities and as such they are non- repetitives in nature and they are taken at higher level of management.

c) Policy and operative decisions.

Top management takes policy decisions and they are important and do have long-term impact. These decisions involve location of plant, sale and purchase policies, volume of production , employment potential of the industry etc. and these decisions some times are embodied in manual, which becomes the basis for operative decision.

The operative decisions are taken by middle and lower levels and are applied to day to day operations, and they relate to supervision of actual operations.

d) Programmed and non-programmed decisions

Programmed decisions based on operations research are within the policy structure and they have a short run impact. These decisions are taken by lower level managers and relate to granting of leave and routine normal purchases.

Non-programmed decisions are very important for the organisation and they relate to items like introduction of anew product in the market, opening of a new branch at a new place etc.

e) Individual and group decisions

Individual decisions depend upon the person involved in making a decision. Group decisions are taken by a group constituted for the specific purpose or by standing committee and they are very important to the organisation. They have positive value.

The decision making requires a process through which a decision maker has to be emphatic, implicitly or explicitly. Identification of the problem and finding out all possible solutions to the problem to arrive at correct decision favourable to the industry is the major responsibility to the management. Proper diagnosis helps identification of the actual problem and the management should make an integrated and analytical approach. "Prevention is better than cure". The management should take preventive measures to avoid the problem. A through analysis is absolutely necessary to find out the sources of information to gain an insight to the problem.

The managers to get most satisfactory result of a decision must try to find out the various alternatives available. The next step is to evaluate the alternatives and select one that could give the best results. While selecting factors like risk, economy of efforts, timing and limiting factors should be considered. Experience, experimentation, research and analysis should be the basis for the selecting alternatives. While the selected alternative is put in to action, the effectiveness of action should be considered and right decisions help in effective action. A successful manager is one who modifies his decisions according to the subsequent march of the events, because a decision is based on some forecasts, which are by themselves are not absolutely correct.

Since decisions play a major role in the managerial task, it is necessary to maintain an organisation of managers at top, middle and lower levels. The soundness of decisions depend upon the information available to him, the techniques adopted and the sophistication of the decision maker.

The physical and psychological environment effect the nature of decisions. The expectation and behaviour of top management has an impact on the type of decisions. Mutual confidence among managers will result in self- confidence among managers. Proper timing of decision often constitutes part of a strategy. Group participation may be permitted and encouraged in decision making.

8. Planning, Forecasting and Control

Planning and control are twin managerial functions. Planning is a condition precedent for effective controlling. Peter Drucker says that "Planning is the continuous process of making present entrepreneurial decisions systematically and with the best possible knowledge of their futurity; organising systematically the efforts needed to carry out these decisions against the expectations through organised systematic feed back". Planning, action and control are inter-related and inter-dependent.

"Looking ahead is the essence of management" says Henry Fayol. This is the era of forecasting. This has become a MUST for all type of activities. "Business forecasting is the calculating of reasonable probabilities about the future, based on the analysis of all the latest relevant information with the aid of statistical and econometric techniques" observes Prof. Leo Burnes. Forecasting provides a logical base for determining in advance the nature of business operation related to future, and it forms the basis for managerial decisions about the material, personnel and other infrastructure. Forecasting promotes co-ordination, co-operation and team spirit. General business forecasting, sales forecasting and capital forecasting are of fundamental importance to the business management. Thus one can conclude that planning, forecasting and control are very essential for management to obtain the predetermined desired objectives.

Summarisation (points at a glance)

1. "Planning is the very essence of economic life". "To plan, is to survive", "planning is a road to economic prosperity", from these definitions it is clear that planning is absolutely necessary to survive in this competitive dynamic society.

2. The application of all the inputs (infrastructure) in to the productive process demands a planned process, (Man-power planning, material planning; investment planning; technological planning; marketing planning and lastly management planning) and this would bring maximum profits to the enterprise (a firm or industry).

3. The planning should be both strategic planning and functional planning. The strategic planning aims at and covers the objectives and means to achieve those objectives. The functional planning covers methods designed to increase efficiency of all the inputs to lead the firm or industry to the equilibrium point.

4. Business forecasting and decision making are the very important aspects of planning. Whatever may be the type of planning, these twin objectives are to be ever present. This is because, modern firms and industries produce goods also for international markets in anticipation of demand.

5. Planning involves selecting missions and objectives and means to achieve them. Constant control of planning process is necessary and planning and control are inter-related.

6. To achieve the pre-determined objectives of the firm or industry, the management has to systematically, scientifically, reasonably and rationally arrange and re-arrange the available infrastructure and exploit them to the optimum point. (that is capacity utilisation).

7. In the planning process, the management has to determine, what to produce, when to produce, why to produce, how to produce, how much to produce and to whom to produce; and decisions on these issues will have to be taken well in advance.

8. Choice is the essence of economic activity. A manager has to postulate about the existing and future environment; and he has to evaluate and choose the course to be followed to reach the target. Preparation of budget and its effective application is also his responsibility.

9. The long-range plans, where the gestation period is pretty long, are to be co-ordinated with short-range plans. The objectives in both the plans are verifiable at the end of the period and these objectives are in a hierarchical style from corporate level down to individual levels.

10. Management by objectives (MOB) has been the theme in practice today and performance appraisal and employee motivation are the responsibility of management. The management has to set goals both for line-managers and staff personnel and these goals are both qualitative and quantitative. The MOB also helps managers to analyse the structure of organisation, enforces commitment on the personnel to work for their goals and helps in developing effective controls.

    MBO emphasises on the philosophy of self-control and self-direction to subordinates. However much the plans are strictly made effective, the inflexibility persists and this is due to environmental changes.

11. Business policies and strategic policies provide direction to plans and the frame work to serve as a basis for managerial activities. The strategic planning indicates the working process and also the inter-relatedness of elements of the process. These policies have to be developed in the various sectors of management, such as growth, finance, personnel, organisation, marketing, public relations, cost, leadership, etc. These policies require deep penetration into the various levels of

administration, so that all the personnel should be aware of goals and their responsibilities.

12. The planning premises should include assumptions, forecasts, development of alternatives to meet contigency, provision for consistency and communications.
13. The objective of every plan should be to promote the achievement of the purpose of enterprise. These objectives should be very clear, meaningful, purposeful, verifiable, attainable, unambiguous and aim at the betterment of society.
14. The various levels of planning under each department in an organisation should be supporting and complementary to the major plan and ultimate objective should be reduction of cost of production. There is need for harmonisation and clear understanding among the various plans.
15. The success of the entrepreneurial planning depends upon its proper understanding, implementation, consistency and effectiveness.
16. Since a long gestation period is involved in longrun large projects of a business enterprise, the planning process should provide sufficient leverage and flexibility for adaptation and accommodation; of course not sacrificing the cost factor.
17. The planning is for an uncertain future and the business enterprise is always confronted with risks and survival. Thus, certain built-in safeguards are to be provided in the planning process itself toward of (prevent) any eventually that might arise in the process of implementation.

CHAPTER - 12

ORGANISATION

1. Nature, scope and meaning of organisation.

To work out the plan effectively, to attain the already pre-determined objective, the need for organisation arises in the management process. The various objectives of the enterprise have to be grouped together homogeneously and assigned to several departments controlled by managers, and to whom there has been delegation of authority. The managers should shoulder this responsibility and contribute their share in the attainment of pre-determined goals. A perfect organisation would help in the maximum exploitation of infrastructure to achieve the highest profit. With the expansion of the business in its multidimensional character, the responsibility of organisation and its impact increases.

Thus organisation contributes the foundation on which the super-structure of management is to be constructed. A few managers of brilliance from the nucleus with central authority and with delegation of authority to the decentralised sector to carry on the pre-planned objectives.

The word "Organisation" : is basically used in two broad ways. In one sense, organisation is treated as a dynamic process aimed at bringing together the different people to achieve the common objective; and in the other sense the organisation refers to the structure of relationships among individuals. It is viewed as an organisation with integrated parts for an effective group action.

Prof. Allen defines organisation as "the process of identifying and grouping the work to be performed, defining and delegating responsibility and authority, and establishing relationship for the purpose of enabling to work most effectively together for accomplishing objectives".

Prof. Koontz and Prof. O.Donnel observe organisation as "the establishment of authority relationships with provision for co-ordination between them, both vertically and horizontally in the enterprise structure".

From these definition it is clear that organisation is the corner stone of enterprise for the attainment of common purpose by an identifiable group of people. Prof. A.L. Fish rightly observes that "organisation is more than a chart; it is the mechanism through which management directs, co-ordinates and controls the business. It is the foundation of management". In short, one could conclude that organisation helps administration; co-ordinates the different agencies in the productive process; aims at optimum utilisation of technological infrastructure; encourages creativity, accountability and recognition of specialists and professional people.

In a nut-shell it could be said that organisation is a process by which the manager brings order out of chaos; removes conflicts between the people and establishes an environment suitable for team work.

2. Principles of organisation

The success of a business unit largely depends upon the strict observance and respect towards the following principles of organisation;

a. Unity of objectives:

Objectives of the organisation should be clearly defined for each department and there should be unity of objective so that there could be concentration of efforts. The mode of organisation structure should be well studied in the back-drop of pre-determined objectives.

b. Specialisation:

Efficient division of labour facilitates specialisation and each area of specialisation must be inter-related to the total integrated system through co-ordination of all departments and their activities.

c. Co-ordination:

Co-ordination is the orderly management of group effort to provide unity of action in the pursuit of common purpose. There should be balanced co-ordination in respect of authority - allocation, centrallisation and decentrallisation and lines of communication. It aims at higher efficiency and effectives. It should integrate the various management functions - planning, organisation, motivation and control.

d. Scalar principle or chain of command

The line of authority should be clearly defined. This line of authority invariably flows from the highest executive to the lowest managerial level and it should be an unbroken line. Every sub-ordinate must know his superior to whom he is answerable and from whom he should get guidance and direction. In the absence of this principle, there would be confusion and total chaos.

e. Responsibility and accountability

Each manager should enjoy enough responsibility to achieve the objective and target assigned to him. Besides this responsibility, the superior is accountable for the activities of his sub-ordinates and the subordinates are responsible to their superiors in the discharge of their duties. Responsibility and must be co-extensive in an organisation. Of late, this concept of accountability has assumed great importance in view public involvement either directly or indirectly.

f. Efficiency

This principles envisages that the organisation should achieve the target within a time bound programme at the minimum cost. "Maximum satisfaction with minimum effort" should be the ideal goal. Wastage of infrastructure adds to the loss and hence the ultimate objective should be maximum benefits with minimum cost. Efficiency at all levels is the basic need.

g. Span of management or control

Prof. V.A. Graciunas theory envisages a sub-ordinate-superior relationship and developed a mathematical formula that could lay down a principle regarding the number of sub-ordinates that a manager could efficiently control and obtain the maximum results. An average human brain can effectively direct three to six brains and no manager is over burdened with more sub- ordinates.

h. Delegation of authority (Decentralisation)

For an efficient and effective functioning of an organisation, the authority should be delegated to the competent level. Concentration or centralisation of authority is always dangerous and detrimental to the progress of organisation. The decision making power should be placed always nearer the scene of action. But while delegating powers to the lower authority, the manager or the chief executive should see that there is no misuse or abuse of such powers.

i. Communication and direction

The need for a continuous communication line downward and upward at different level of management is a must for efficient and effective result oriented organisation. A communication gap might either bring down production or result in the escalation of cost. The integration of activities inside the group would be hampered in the absence of communication and direction and common plan. The line authority should offer an ever present channel for the flow of communication at vertical and horizontal levels.

j. Exception Principle

"A good organisation is so arranged that only exceptionally complex problems are referred to the higher levels of management and the routine matters are dealt with by executives at lower level". Recurring decision should be handled in a routine manner by lower level managers. Matters concerning grave and important attention should be referred to superior authorities only.

k. Flexibility in action; definiteness in purpose; simplicity in approach, continuity of work, departmentalisation, sound leadership; personal ability etc. are some of the salient features that should be given priority and attention in an organisation for over all growth and development.

l. "Organisation is the foundation of management". Organisational deficiencies create inefficiencies, sound and well designed organisation improves company administration; gives impetus to diversification and growth and guarantees achievements and accomplishments as desired and anticipated. A sound organisation can ensure the following results namely;

1. Precise delegation;
2. Effective communication;
3. Equitable distribution of work;
4. Smooth administration and management;
5. Co-ordination and control;
6. Ethics in labour;
7. Higher managerial efficiency;
8. Elimination of inter-departmental rivalry and friction;
9. Optimum exploitation of available infrastructure;
10. Encouragement of creativity and sprit of innovation and motivation; and lastly
11. Adaptability and accommodation to the dynamic forces present within the industry and out-side.

Thus, a sound organisation can bring about an integrated development in the process of achieving the pre-determined goals by removing all managerial bottlenecks.

3. Departmentation

Prof. Koontz and Prof. O'Donnel define a department thus, "a distinct area, division, or branch of an enterprise over which a manager has authority for the performance of specified activities". Departments differ with respect to the basic patterns used to group activities. "Departmentation is the process of grouping activities in to units for purposes of administration.

To expand organisation and to get the maximum benefits of an enterprise, it is necessary to group activities and employees into departments. For every organisation or enterprise there are three fundamental functions to be undertaken, namely 1. production,2. Marketing and 3. Finance.

Units are formed around common functions. Thus, functional departmentation is the basis for organisational structure and the top management is the authority to take decision in this matter. A correct and sound departmentation in an organisation could be in the following ways, namely.

a. Functional departmentalisation:

The activities of organisation are grouped on the basis of functions to be performed, for example, Marketing, Finance, Production, research and development, materials, personnel, advertising, sales etc; and this happens to be the most common type of organisational structure. But this type of structure may not be applicable to organisation when they grow and expand. This type is more suitable for small and medium sized businesses.

b. Departmentation by Product.

Under this a reasonable degree of specialisation is required to get the maximum yield. This type has gained more popularity in recent years and the product lines are separated individually and each line is placed under the charge of special product executive to gain better advantages.

This type provides better customer service, since the salesman has more knowledge of the product. The top management can obtain more detailed information about the market conditions relating to specific product. Where product lines are diverse and complicated requiring specialised knowledge, this type is suitable. Even with regard to the determination of profitability of each product line, this type is useful.

But this product type suffers form certain disadvantages, namely it can create confusion to the customers in view of different products presented and also might result in cost escalation due to the maintenance of separate sales forces.

There is scope for duplication of costs. This product type of structure is advantageous to large enterprises, wholesalers and department stores.

c. Departmentation by Location

In the process of organising the sales efforts, departmentation by geographical or regional type structure would be more advantageous. The proximity to local conditions and the expertised knowledge of the manager and the staff with regard to customers and the prevailing competition of the region would be of great help. This type of departmentation helps the executive to demonstrate his ability and enjoy the benefits of favourable local conditions. Even this type of structure is not free from defects. This type increases overhead costs and demand higher costs co-ordination and more control from head quarters.

d. Departmentation by Customer

Since the customers belong to different classes having different preference and choice, this type of organisation structure envisages separate groups responsible for marketing programmes. This type is more favourable where the company is after better and favourable services to the customers. Even this type faces problems during periods of recession, when certain groups to customers disappear and when there are fluctuations in the activities of the enterprise.

e. Departmentation by Process.

This type is invariably motivated by the cost and economic considerations. Both direct and indirect cost is involved in forming a separate department. The organisation unit adopted in this type is determined by the pattern followed. The pattern may be serial. parallel, or unit assembly process. All the three patterns are followed usually to get the maximum benefits. This process has the advantage of specialisation, minimisation of the work movement, promotion of employees interest and reduction of cycle time. The disadvantage being that more time is required for training and the work has to be divided and routed through many employees to get the benefits of specialisation.

f. Departmentation by Project organization.

Under this system the responsibility for the total discharge of work is to be borne by the task force and each member of the task force is held responsible. The best available talent in the task force is utilized to complete the goal. When the objective is completed the task force is disbanded. Since each member is objective minded, there is scope for fuller utilisation of human resource. The main disadvantage under this system seems to be the feeling of frustration experienced due to the absence of an integrated whole and also the sense of insecurity felt by the seniors.

In conclusion it could be pointed out that departmentation is the last pillar of organisation structure. It provides sub-divisions of organisation for decision making purposes. It is based on division of labour and specialisation and enjoys all the advantages of decentralisation.

4. Span of Management

The term "span of Management" is made use of to describe the number of subordinates who could be directed and controlled by a superior authority. The main problem of deciding the span of management is to determine the number of individuals that could be placed under the management of one superior.

The problem is to determine the ideal span of management. The classical approach fixes the number between three and seven subordinates under each superior. Prof.U.Gracuis, a French Management consultant and Prof.W.W.Soujaneu- have contributed their share in suggesting solutions to this problem. Mr. Gracious has given a mathematical formula to find out the number of relationships; while Mr.Soujaneu observes that span of management cannot be a valid concept and that modern social science concepts have a better role than the traditional concepts. The number of subordinate may vary in the same organisation at different levels and at the same level in different departments.

There are various factors that can determine the span of management. Factors like:

1) the capacity of superiors, their ability, qualities, efficiency, effectiveness;

2) capacity of sub-ordinates, their efficiency, training and personality;

3) the nature of work and the knowledge of sub ordinates about the work to be discharged

4) the degree of decentralisation

5) delegation of authority

6) the extent of planning;

7) availability and utilisation of staff assistance;

8) the communication techniques and their effective utilisation and;

9) constant supervision are contributory factors. All these factors should be taken in totality while deciding span.

The efficiency of management lies in balancing span of control and levels of management.

5. Authority, Responsibility and Accountability

Efficient and effective organisation cannot be achieved by splitting the organisation in to smaller homogeneous segments, but the need is an integrated development to achieve the predetermined, anticipated objectives. This goal could be achieved not only through horizontal and vertical relationships, but also through the process of sharing authority caused by delegation.

The chief executive should redelegate his authority to the top management; and in turn the top management should redelegate its authority partly to managers and down to management hierarchy.

Then what is authority ? Prof. Henry Fayol observes that "authority is the right to give orders and power to extract obedience".

Pro. Simon defines that "authority is the power to make decision which guide the actions of another. It is a relationship between two individuals, one superior, the other sub-ordinate. The superior frames and transmits decisions with the expectation that these will be accepted by the sub-ordinate. The sub-ordinate executes such decisions and his conduct is determined by them".

The existence of right to authority and the delegation of this right by a superior to a manager, empowers the manager to regulate the behaviour and action of his subordinates. There is legitimacy in giving order, otherwise authority cannot be meaningful and operational. Authority gives right of decision - making which are to be carried out by his sub- ordinates. The objective behind authority is to influence the behaviour of the sub-ordinates to do things at right time so that organisational objectives are achieved. The use of authority is to govern the behaviour and attitude of sub-ordinates through the process of persuation, sanction, request, co-ercision, constraints, force etc. If authority is objective, its application is subjective.

6. Difference between power and authority.

Power is the ability or capacity to attain the goal, where as authority is the ability to command others to get things done. Authority has a sanction, where as power need not be sanctioned one. Prof. Sherweed says "that power is the capacity to secure dominance of one's values or goals and authority is the capacity to command in hierarchical sense". The use of power creates negative feelings in the persons on whom it is used. Power should not be concentrated in a single organisational unit. If organisation is to be effective, power should be balanced among different units to derive optimum benefits.

There seems to be different views regarding distribution of authority. Some opine that it should be from top to bottom and some others say the reverse. There are various theories available about the sources of authority.

a. The Formal Authority Theory:

This theory envisages that authority is at the top of the organisational hierarchy flowing from top to bottom through the process of delegation. From chief executive to production manager and to factory manager. The chief executive gets authority from board of Directors and they get it from share holders, who are the real owners of the organisation. The share holders in view of the institution of private property in the society and bear investment risks get this authority.

b. The Acceptance Theory

Prof. Charter Barnard of U.S.A. observes that the degree of effective authority possessed by a manager is measured by the willingness of sub-ordinates to accept it. The acceptance of an authority will depend upon relative consequences, both positive and negative. Two aspects are involved in this theory, namely the subjective aspect, the acceptance of communication or order as authorative, and the objective aspect, that is the character in the communication. This theory emphasises the leadership function of management. Managers require leadership as well as authority for effective functioning.

The main fault of this theory lines not only in conceiving authority without sanctions but also ignoring the effects of social institutions which confer power.

c. The Competence Theory

There is a feeling that authority is generated by personal competence. The theory believes that personal qualities of technical competence generate authority. Some individuals by the mere force of personality influence others by rendering timely sound advice. Their qualities may be technical competence or social prestige.

The specific limits of authority are due to sub- ordinates competency ; constraints and restraints of accepted plans and policies; Social constraints and other legal limits. Established policies and procedures should not be deviated.

In conclusion it may be said that one cannot over look that the fundamental source of authority is formal authority emerging from an institutional framework.

7. Responsibility:

The word responsibility is used by people in different senses. Actually responsibility can be defined as "the obligation of a sub-ordinate to perform a duty which has been assigned to him. The superior-subordinate relationship give rise to responsibility. This responsibility may be fulfilled by a single action or it could be a continuous obligation.

Prof. Norris Hurley says that "Responsibility is the duty to which a person is bound by reason of his status or task. Such responsibility implies compliance with directives of the person making the initial delegation".

Koontz and O'Donnel opine that "Responsibility is the obligation of a sub-ordinate, to whom duty has been assigned, to perform the duty".

Prof. G.R. Terry observes that "Responsibility is the obligation of an individual to carry out assigned activities to the best of one's ability".

The responsibility of subordinates to their superiors for performance is absolute; and superiors cannot escape responsibility for the organisation activities of their subordinates. Authority is the cement of organisation structure; where as the responsibility for actions cannot be greater than that implied by the authority delegated nor should it be less.

A significant cause of mismanagement is the granting of authority without exacting responsibility. Responsibility delegation is not the same as authority delegation. Superiors remain responsible for the proper exercise of authority by their subordinates.

Authority is the key to managerial job; and without authority there will be anarchy and chaos. Authority is the dynamic of management. Authority should be coextensive with responsibility. Responsibility and authority are complementary and responsibility cannot be delegated.

The concept of accountability is mostly used in defence organisation, of late this concept has gained greater importance in the sense that the managers and subordinates are accountable to or answerable for their actions to the higher competent authority. Social accounting and social responsibilities have increased enormously on the part of organisations and the subject of social audit is of primary importance. The organisation is answerable to the society for all its actions. Responsibility cannot be delegated at any stage. Prof. Keith Davis has observed that "Responsibility operates some what like the table of the magic pitcher in which the water level always remains the same, no matter how much water is poured out".

8. Delegation

The Chief Executive cannot perform all the activities in an organisation; he assigns some activities to his sub-ordinates and this is delegation of authority. This process of delegation and redelegation from superiors to sub-ordinates continues till the task is completed. In the management process the term delegation carry the meaning of granting of rights and approval to others to perform the duties as prescribed earlier. The person who delegates authority should be owner of authority. Thus, duties, authority and obligation are the three basic feature of delegation. It is always advisable to delegate the authority specifically in writing in order to avoid conflicts and duplication,delegation should be free from ambiguity,that is to say clarity and bravity are the essentials in the process. Since authority is of various types ,like technical authority, legal authority, operational authority, administrative authority etc.,it is necessary that the delegator grants specific authority.

Principle of Delegation

To make delegation more effective and operational, it is obligatory to observe the principles strictly. Following are the basic principles of delegation.

1. Responsibility and authority to be co-extensive and co-equal. Authority provides a person to take timely decision to obtain the results, where as responsibility creates an obligation on the person to perform the prescribed duties by using authority. Responsibility without authority has no meaning. Responsibility cannot be delegated. Both are interdependent, inter- connected and mutually beneficial. If the responsibility is not fixed accurately, the authority is undetermined. The responsibility of a subordinate manager is absolute towards his superior.

Delegation helps the manager to free himself from performing routine duties, which can be safely delegated to sub-ordinates. By doing so, the manager can concentrate his attention on more important matters.

Delegation can make sub-ordinates more responsible, responsive and duty bound. Through delegation, the organisation could be expanded and diversified, since there is continuity of work among sub-ordinates as compared to managers, who are subject to transfer and promotions frequently.

Delegation has the power of motivation among the sub-ordinates. The success of organisation depends upon the strict observance of the principles of delegation.

The inherent weakness of delegation of authority should be eliminated. By delegating authority to sub- ordinates,the executive cannot absolve himself from his responsibility and oblegation to the organisation; and therefore he should guide, direct and control the activities of sub-ordinates. Delegation does not mean abdication of responsibilities. Most failures of effective delegation could be attributed to inability or reluctance to apply them in practice.

When the manager feels that his services to the organisation are indispensable, he does not resort to the delegation of authority and this is highly incorrect. Some executives feel that their presence in every company meeting is essential and dominate the procedures. The attitude towards the sub-ordinate is very essential. In some cases executives feel that by delegating authority,sub-ordinate would become superiors in their performance and as such that their prominence is lost. The other factors like

1) Inability to direct

2) Lack of confidence in sub-ordinates

3) Absence of adequate control system

4) Desire of the executive for out-standing performance standards,

5) Tempermental aversion

6) The desire of dominance

7) Fear of incompetency etc

are the obstacles for effective delegation.

Authority should be pushed down in an organisation to the extent possible so that greater confidence is created in sub-ordinates. A good rule would be that "all authority not expressly reserved to higher management is granted to lower management". Prof. Allen says "just as a man's leg should be long enough to reach the ground, and no longer; enough responsibility and authority should be delegated to a position to enable the incumbent to accomplish whatever objectives are set for him". Trust in sub-ordinates should be the basis of delegation. It may be pointed out that inadequate and ineffective delegation is worse than no delegation. Johnson and Johnson believe that the best way to delegation is to pick up a good man and allow him full freedom to do his job.

9. Centralisation VS Decentralisation

Centralisation is the result of absence of delegation of authority. Centralisation is the withholding of authority at the control point. Authority that goes to reduce the sub-ordinates role in decision making is centralisation. If the organisation is very large and highly complicated, the management cannot by itself control the entire operation. If has to divide the organisation in to several convenient units capable of multiple decision centres; and this results in de- centralisation. De-centralisation is closely related to delegation. Centralisation and de-centralisation describe the manner in which decision-making authority is delegated among various levels of management in the organisation. There can be neither absolute centralisation nor absolute decentralisation in an organisation; and these two are extreme points in matters of distributing authority in the organisation structure.

Benefits of centralisation

A certain amount of centralised control is always necessary in an organisation, since total freedom and autonomy could be dangerous. Under centralisation the following advantages could be realised. It increases the prestige and power of the chief executive and thereby his importance. The policies, practices and decisions adopted could be more uniform. Centralisation results in lower costs and stricter control. Physical facilities required would be less and the services of highly qualified specialists, who are small in supply, could be availed of easily. Elaborate and extensive controlling procedures and practices will not be required under centralisation. The organisation could enjoy all the benefits of external economies also.

Benefits of decentralisation

The top executives under the decentralisation programme, can concentrate more on important decisions and operations by delegating to unit-managers the routine work.

Decentralisation facilitates managerial development, in respect of planning, organisation, staffing, motivating and controlling. It promotes employee co-ordination and enthusiasm. The unit-manager's efficiency could be evaluated interms of the return on investment and thereby it can foster competition among several units in the organisation. It is easy to identify the trouble spots in the organisation and necessary remedial measures could be applied to increase the efficiency of the organisation. In view of transferring greater decision-making power to managers, initiative is promoted leading to higher performance and motivation.

Decentralisation has certain negative points also. It increases costs and uneconomic use of resources. It involves in more number of capable executives to supervise and control the operational activities of managers to whom powers have been delegated.

As the size of the organisation increases, it becomes necessary to decentralise and divide the large organisation into a number of semi-autonomous units. When the organisation attains a certain point, dis- economies in the productive process set in necessitating a re-thinking of the policy of the organisation. Divisionalisation or decentralisation becomes necessary where the product lines are different. The success of decentralisation depends upon the availability of competent man-power. It is a good measure to provide training and development facilities to managers. Dynamic and competitive market conditions make decentralisation more important to bring effectiveness in organisation. Government regulations also control decentralisation. Lastly, the philosophy of top management and the nature of the growth of company itself promotes and determines decentralisation.

10. Functional authority

Koontz and O'Donnel have defined functional authority in the following terms, "Functional authority is the power which an individual or department may have delegated to it over specified processes, practices or other matters relating to activities undertaken by personnel in departments other than its own".

Due to several shortcomings like lack of special knowledge, lack of abilities to supervise processes, inadequate communications facilities, the delegation of functional authority becomes absolutely necessary. The functional authority is not limited to manager of a particular type of department, it may be extended to service departments, line staff departments also. A superior in the organisation delegates authority to the next in position in order to save time and to expedite the spread of information. The staff man demonstrates to line managers as to how the information should be used and put in to effect.

This authority is only for specified activities. It should be noted that excessive grant of functional authority may severely change the basis for line authority namely the unity of command. This authority is as binding as line authority, but this authority has no teeth to enforce discipline for violation. It should be established with prior approval among the departments affected. This authority is invariably delegated to a specialist. It is the right and power of one department to issue orders and instructions to another department in an organisation. The authority is feasible only in a large enterprise and there is always the fear of break of unity of command, which is so vital for an organisation to accomplish the predetermined objectives.

Summarisation (points at a glance)

ORGANISATION

1. Organisation generally refers to the job of bringing together or co-ordinating the various inputs together and effectively utilise them to achieve the common goal.

2. The various steps that include in organisation are formulating objectives, policies, programmes, fixation of standards, plans to achieve the ends, identification and classification of activities of the enterprise, grouping together various activities, delegation of authority, co-ordination of authority, etc.

3. In organisation, the term "span of management" is frequently used. This term denotes about the number of personnel that a manager can effectively and efficiently supervise. As regards the number of persons a manager can manage is determined by the authority delegated to the manager; the availability and effectiveness of communication techniques; and the standard of objective fixed, etc.

4. Organisation also deals with grouping of activities and man power into several departments. Departmentation is according to the function of enterprise and the equipment required. The new kinds of departmentation have increased due to product enlargement and project development.

5. Factors like job assignment; the way work to be done; the personnel involved; the technology supplied; and other factors determine the scope of management. If organisation has to succeed effectively, it is necessary to select a particular departmentation pattern and here lies the crux of the problem.

6. The relationship between line and staff is very important. In a line authority, the relationship is direct from supervisor to sub-ordinates; whereas the staff relationship constitutes rendering advice and counsel.

7. In organisation, functional authority is based on line authority and attributed to only selected processes, policies and practices. If functional authority is based on staff authority, there is danger of undermining the line authority due to lack of responsibility of staff and unity of command, which are very essential for the effective and efficient functioning of organisation.

8. In organisation, decentralisation of authority in decision-making is thought of , since it would promote

responsibility and job-consciousness. Centralisation refers to concentration of authority and defeats the policy of delegation of decision making. Delegation of authority and power is influenced and determined by the intellectual capacity and personal qualities of the person to whom it is delegated and who will be held responsible for the results.

9. Initiation of an enterprise may be more simple than an effective and efficient organisation because the need is to assign definite roles to various departments within the industry or firm so that they could contribute the maximum output with minimum cost.

10. Organisational planning involves identification of the needs of the personnel, removing the various staffing bottlenecks; elimination of duplication of work; establishment of proper communication lines, doing away with absolute methods and infuse or induct flexibility in organisational structure to absorb changes in environment.

11. In a huge enterprise, organisational conflicts could take place and these conflicts could be reduced by using organisation charts, bulletins, grapevine or informal. information that spread very fast among the personnel and even by building up an organisation culture.

12. No formal organisation chart or manual can give an entirely accurate picture of an organisation as it exists. The dynamics of organisation is the existence of informal organisation affecting from departmental heads down to the various sectors of the departments.

13. The quantum of specialisation differentiates a big organisation from a smaller one. As the firm grows in size, the activities are departmentalised. As and when there is further expansion of the firm or industry, the organisation

is divisionalised, so that the manager could concentrate more on planning, co-ordination and control.

14. The entire object of organising is to make the objectives meaningful, purposeful and creative. The organisation structure should be effective, efficient, should aim at limiting the span of management to achieve the cherished goals; and flexible to meet the changing environment.

15. Authority is the link-force of organisation structure to promote co-ordination. So long the line of authority (that is the scalar principle) is clear from the top management to subordinate position, better will be the responsibility for decision making.

16. The responsible individual in an organisation can contribute more toward achieving the objectives of the enterprise, provided the department has a clear cut policy relating to the results expected, work to be done and delegation of authority.

17. The organisation structure should adhere to the principle of balance of flexibility and principle of leadership. People in managerial positions should have good leadership qualities to guide the destiny of the organisation. The organisational structure should be in a position to absorb the advantages and benefits of both internal economies and external economies.

CHAPTER - 13

STAFFING

A. Nature and purpose

An organisation is both a social and technological device that helps the executive to achieve the goals, which are to-day highly complex and demanding very effective and efficient efforts. The executive single- handed cannot achieve this goal. The staffing process involves filling up of these positions by appropriate individuals which include selection, training and appraisal of the individuals in organisation. Staffing is a major managerial function. The staffing responsibility does not rest with one individual but it is on various individuals managing the organisation. The personnel department alone cannot be shouldered with this responsibility, because the staff recruited will have to work under guidance and discretion of managers under different sections. A recruiting system becomes necessary, whenever there is a need to expand human resources. Personnel planning constitutes the guidance system for the recruiting function. Every organisation has to develop three important plans, namely;

a) The Man-power planning;

b) The personnel development plan; and

c) The recruitment plan;

The man power planning is the basic need for the recruiting system. The managers at all levels have to bear the responsibility for the efficient execution of staffing function. The hierarchy starts from the board of directors selecting, developing and appraising the chief executive and in turn the chief executive exercise this function while selecting departmental heads and managers. The managers, while selecting their staffing follow this procedure. The managers take adequate interest while selecting the staff in order to obtain the best functioning of their departments and to prepare the subordinates to succeed them in future. In large organisation where staffing is a major function, the managers, who cannot be experts in all fields, take the help of personnel department, specially organised for the purpose, in the staffing process. The personnel department consisting of skilled, specialised officers appointed only for this purpose shoulder this responsibility.

In recent years, there has arisen an important sense of responsibility for staffing. The top level managers, in staffing policies and operations are involved. The staffing function includes man power planning; recruitment and selection; training and development and performance appraisal. The personnel department is invariably vested with this function, since managers have to concentrate on the production or manufacturing side and other important duties. However, their participation in this function is also necessary at various stages. According to Prof.Theor Haiman, "staffing function is concerned with the placement, growth and development of all those members of the organisation whose function is to get things done through the efforts of the individuals". In a growing concern, staffing activity is a continuous process. Peter Drucker assigns three responsibilities to management, namely:

a) Managing work;
b) Managing workers; and
c) Managing managers;

The staff function relates to the recruitment, selection, development training and compensation of subordinate managers. Prof.Apely says that "managers would be more skilled and more competent if they are carefully selected, specifically trained, continuously kept up-dated in their field of activity and knowledge and adequately rewarded etc."

The staffing function includes

1) Planning of executives;
2) Planning of managerial resources;
3) Administration of management development programmes;
4) Appraisal of executive performance; and the
5) Administration of executive compensation.

B) Manpower planning

The staffing process actually commences from Manpower planning. The primary objective of Man power planning is to provide adequately trained and qualified personnel to meet the needs of staffing. "Well trained, capable executives are required as professional managers to make decisions in many areas which will virtually affect the owners, the employees and the community in general". The chief executive who takes internal policy related matters shoulders the staffing responsibility. The organisations have to plan in advance the man-power requirement and the methodology to be adopted in recruitment and selection whether to promote from with in or secure managers from outside.

Prof.Geiser says that "Man power planning is the process by which a firm ensures that it has the right number of people and right kind of people, at the right place, at the right time, doing things for which they are economically most useful". Any definition of manpower planning should recognise the importance of:-

1. Effective utilisation;
2. Forecasting needs;
3. Developing appropriate policies;
4. Reviewing and controlling the total process etc.

The manpower planning should involve all the activities relating to human resources; it should adequately and accurately determine manpower needs well in advance; it should include an inventory of the existing manpower; it should study in-depth the demand and supply side; and make a detailed study regarding the environment in the enterprise for better working conditions.

The manpower planning should consider both short term and long term effects. In short term manpower planning the fundamental problem is to match the existing workers with existing jobs. The long term manpower planning considers all jobs and all persons at once and it is more concerned with future vacancies that is to say, it is perspective planning. The environment in which an organisation operates constantly changes and the job structure has to adjust itself to these changing circumstances. The first major step in long term manpower planning is to project manpower requirements of the organisation, which is beset with the problems of loss of manpower, the need for new manpower and the need to determine the abilities required to man the jobs. In the case of managerial cadre due to the lack of managerial talent, the recruitment, selection and training takes a long time. In the job analysis the major problem is that an executive job is non-repetitive in nature and all such jobs are different in content. The job analysis should clearly lay down, two things namely job description and job specification. The basic difference between the two is that job description describes in detail the contents of job, while the other describes the requirements of persons performing the jobs. The job specification is a major fool proof in the staffing process because it lays down the details of level of education, experience in years, intelligence level, trade, knowledge in terms of performance etc.

C. Manpower Inventory Analysis

The term inventory refers to the counting of tangible objects like raw materials, goods in process or finished products. Where as in the case of manpower inventory, the term involved are intangible items. It includes the appraising of present key personnel without reference to their positions in particular; and with reference to their abilities and aptitudes. The manpower inventory constitutes four steps namely;

1. Determination of personnel to be brought under inventory;
2. Details of background of information on each individual;
3. Detailed appraisal of each individual; and
4. Detailed study of individuals who have potential for development.

The process of procuring and developing managerial personnel is of no easy task. An executive inventory is more important than an operative inventory. The manpower inventory could include all the personnel inclusive of operative group who have potential for development.

When once the inventory is ready, detailed information about each individual is collected. The information to be collected should relate to age, education, experience, employment records, ranking and merit, health status, retirement data, psychological tests etc. These information will help the organisation for grouping together and could be used for manpower planning.

The next step is an appraisal of personnel included in the list. Various tests are conducted to find out the potential capabilities of individuals to determine their rating and performance and placement.

Such an inventory can help the management to find out :the right man for the right job". Through this inventory, it will be possible for the management to find out the existing and future gaps in managerial personnel and form the basis for recruitment, selection and training process. Well trained capable executives are required as professional managers to make decisions in many areas vital to the success of the modern complex organisation.

D. Training and Development

The efficiency and effective operation of any organisation directly depends on how best its members are trained. Good manager does not just turn up when needed; a great deal of development effort is needed. A managerial development programme should consider both organisational and human needs. Management is the process of individual growth towards the fuller utilisation of managerial capabilities. Immediately an individual is inducted into the organisation, the company will tailor a training schedule to make him an asset of the institution. Training is concerned with imparting specific skills for particular purposes. A person however capable and competent cannot contribute his best at a job unless he is systematically trained in the right direction.

Training brings about an improvement in the quality and quantity of output by increasing the skill of the personnel. A trained personnel can bring about a reduction in the cost of administration by economising the use of infrastructure . Training instills confidence in the worker to take decisions. It helps in bringing about healthy atmosphere and better co-ordination between different levels of management. Training can also help the selectors to recognise their weakness and mistakes.

Training and development are not synonymous terms. The term development is comprehensive and broadly refers to nature and direction of change caused in the personnel due to training and education. Education refers to personality development, socially, intellectually and physically. With the growth of organisation, the problems at supervisory levels have also increased necessiating for training to supervisory staff also. Now organisation have to undertake development programmes for middle and top level management also. Managers require more generalised education to handle managerial problems. Even non-managerial jobs require manual skills and technical procedures. As such, the contents and techniques of employee training and management development are different.

The management development programme should include a plan and an organisation to carry out the programme and a periodic appraisal relating to manager's performance.

The top management should support and patronise such programmes. Thus, training emphasises manual skills, while development emphasises philosophy needed for upward development.

E. Need and techniques training.

There are no two opinions as regards the need for training. Training is a means to reduce obsolescene in organisations. With the technological developments and its innovation in to the productive process, the need for training has enormously increased. Trained personnel is necessary to handle complex technological problems. Untrained human resource in a modern industry is not only a liability to the organisation but also results in a downward trend both in quality and quantity.

Morale is a major factor in the productive process. "Ethics is the science of morality". Higher the morale in the working class, higher will be the productivity. High morale results in greater enthusiasm and brings about greater co-ordination and participation in the organisation process. Job satisfaction increases morale in the employees. Trained employees can perform better quality work with more knowledge, skill and pride. Trained personnel require less supervision and demand more autonomy. Even the cost of the supervision reduces due to reduction in the supervisory staff. Training can reduce job accidents. Training leads to increased production and considerable savings in wastage and breakages having an impact on cost savings. There is scope for optimum utilization of machines with trained workers. Trained personnel can offer stability as well as flexibility to the organisation. Trained personnel is the greatest organisational asset. Training could be through lectures and guided conferences. The "case method of training" has been popularized by the Harvard Business school of USA. Theoretical training is different from "case studies" method. "SIMULATION" is one method of training and it is a form of vestibule training.

The in-basket technique is another form of simulation, when the worker is exposed to internal as well as external problems. "Role playing" is another form of simulation and it emphasises human relations problems. The technique of 'Role playing' helps the worker to create analytical ability and self consciousness as well as realistic imagination. The other methods of training namely 'Sensitivity training' and 'Laboratory training' are related to real problems existing in the training group itself; and they are more introspective and develop insight in to their actions. Prof.Drucker says "An institution that cannot produce its own mangers will die." The training programme can not be uniform to all levels of workers. Management group needs broad-based training, while other employees need specific job training.

The entire personnel of an organisation may be classified in to three levels, namely

1. Rank and file employee
2. Supervisory level; and
3. Management level

The first category requires training of technological nature and both pre-employment and on-job training. They also require refresher courses.

The second category, supervisory level incumbents are expected to know how to carry out approved programmes within the stipulated budgets to the requirement of their superiors. Their further career depends upon their skills and men of outstanding capacity are eligible to be promoted to middle-management cadres.

The third category incumbents do not have direct contact with working force. The management group could be classified in to middle - level management and top - level management group could be classified in to middle - level management and top - level management. The Middle management personnel need to know the theory of management as well as its application part also. They are generally supervisors who have several years of on- the-job practice. They are expected to know comprehensively the functions of managers because only through that media they can achieve the objectives expected of them.

The incumbents of top level management are normally functional managers aspiring after high management positions. They must have substantial background of the fundamental and techniques of management. In view of rapid development and the dynamic changes in the management theory and practice, there is need for frequent revision and up-dating of information relating to management concepts.

F. Performance Appraisal

The performance of sub-ordinates are appraised by managers and in turn the sub-ordinates form Judgment of their superiors, jobs and the operation of the company. Prof.Mac Farland observes that the bureaucratic - structured organisation attaches great importance to the official assignment superiors make of their subordinates; and the career and livelihood of employees largely depends upon these judgements. The managers ability to appraise others skills itself determines the judging capacity of managers.

Then what is a appraisal ? Appraisal is the evaluation of worth, quality and merit. The modern appraisal programme emphasises present performance and future goals. The performance appraisal should be systematic. The measuring rod applied for performance appraisal should be the same and uniform, so that the ratings obtained separately are comparable. The appraisals should be periodic according to plan. The appraisals should be unbiased, impartial and accurate and the outcome should be free from ambiguities.

A performance appraisal should serve the following objectives.

A systematic performance appraisal should provide information regarding promotions, salaries, lay-offs, transfers. It should guide employee development and provide opportunities for assessing employee's training in the organisation. When the employees are aware that they are subject to periodic appraisal, they develop positive and acceptable behaviour through psychological pressure. It is also necessary for strategic planning, motivation and communication. It is also absolutely necessary that appraisals are recorded for the use of organisation.

Appraisal approach could be of two types namely Trait approach and appraisal by results. These two approaches are interdependent. Ranking, man-to-man comparison, grading, graphic rating scales come under trait approach. This approach is commonly used in industry.

The success of the appraisal by results depends upon good job description, trust in the sub-ordinates, specification of definite goals etc., Management by objective should be the basis of appraisal. The appraisal system can not succeed without an appropriate basic philosophy for continuous support of all the managers. In conclusion, it may be said that appraisal of managerial ability based on performance against pre- selected verifiable objectives is the right step in the right direction.

Summarisation (Points at a glance)

STAFFING

1. The staffing function comprises of recruitment, selection, promotion, training, apprising and transfers. This is the most important and difficult task of management. The problem is whether to recruit people from outside or affect promotions within the industry or firm for higher jobs.

2. In the process of selection, verification of past records, interviews, written test and psychological tests are being conducted. But these processes would only help for eliminating the unfit person rather than for fresh

recruitments and this happens to be the opinion of some people.

3. In the larger sense, staffing also means filling up positions in the organisation structure. The first step is to find out the work for requirement etc., is being followed. The management has to find out "the right man for the right job".

4. In the case of posts of Managers, it is necessary to prepare a management inventory from the people available both within and outside. This is a hard task in the sense, the recruiting authority should evaluate the pros and cons of promoting people within the organisation or selecting from out-side.

5. The management while designing jobs, should consider the following points, namely,-

   a) The scope of the job;

   b) whether the job requires a full time or a part time incumbent;

   c) the challenges of the job;

   d) whether the job demands skilled people;

   e) whether there is co-ordination in the three wings of the job namely-content, function and relationship;

   f) It is necessary to ascertain whether the position could be designed for individuals or group.

6. The immediate superior of the candidate should be satisfied with the selection of personnel; because any erroneous selection would reflect the incompetancy of the manager. Frequent evaluation of the worker and integration of the new recruit with the already existing

personnel is absolutely necessary in the interest and promotion of the organisation.

7. Mere recruitment and placement may not be sufficient, but performance appraisal is essential for effective and efficient management. For Managers, the management by objective (MOB) approach is to be supplemented by appraisal of managers as managers. Periodic review of work, continuous monitoring and comprehensive appraisal are the best methods.

8. Management development programmes and organisation development programme are to be integrated to achieve the over all development of the organisation.

9. Job training, manager development training, job rotation, loyal and duty bound assistants to the positions, promotions etc., are all factors necessary for getting good results.

10. There are bound to be conflicts and differences and they are to be ironed out, managed and avoided. These conflicts could be eliminated through compromising; changing behaviors' bringing about structural changes; resolving the conflict at higher levels; altering the objectives, coordination of new methods and arranging work location, etc.

11. The organisation roles should be filled up with well qualified personnel, who are duty conscious and devoted loyalty.

12. To improve the managerial quality, it is necessary to define clearly the roles of organisation; precisely fixing the requirements of man power, using better techniques of manger appraisal and training; and establishing a harmonious relationship between worker and management.

13. It is necessary to clearly verify objectives and fix performance standards and against these the achievement of managers should be measured. These measuring rods are also to be applied to all the personnel and, if found deficient, opportunities should be given for correction and development.

14. The principle of self-development to the managerial staff is a must in a competitive and ever changing dynamic environment. Updating of information relating to managerial knowledge and technological developments could bring better results to organisation.

CHAPTER - 14

DIRECTION-LEADERSHIP-MOTIVATION

A. Introduction

Success of management is largely a matter of effective direction and correct leadership. Directing is the process around which all performance revolves. After planning, organising and staffing, the management has to start the function of directing. Without direction, human factors in the organisation become inactive resulting in physical factors becoming inoperative. The process of direction starts at the top and down to the bottom. In an organisation the manager as superior gives direction to sub-ordinates and receives direction from his superiors. Direction may be defined as a function of management providing instructions, guidance and inspiration to the human factor in the organisation. Prof. Koontz and Prof.O'Donnel observe that "Direction is a complex function of management that includes all those activities which are designed to encourage sub-ordinates to work effectively and efficiently in both the short and long run". Prof.Theo Haiman states that "Direction consists of the process and technique utilising issuing instruction and making certain that operations are carried out as originally planned. "A thorough analysis of definitions of direction reveals four important factors namely, communication,leadership, supervision and motivation.

Direction helps management to initiate actions in the organisation. At all levels of management the function of direction is performed. It is a continuous process. It is the responsibility of manager to motivate his subordinates and lead them giving proper direction. Direction plays a dual role by getting things performed by subordinates as well as providing opportunities to superiors to engage themselves in more important tasks. Almost all the actions of organisation are initiated through direction. The integration of individuals effort in an organisation is a highly complex problem. Direction initiates action and integrates employees efforts. Direction helps in getting maximum out of individuals potentialities through leadership, communication and motivation. In a dynamic society, the organisation has to face changes in environment and direction through motivation helps the individual to face this change. Direction is the heart of administration and thus provides stability and balance in the organisation.

B. Principles of Direction

As management has to directly deal with people, direction is the most complex function since the nature of people's is complex and most unpredictable. The managers however have to follow some principles while directing their sub ordinates. These principles are related either to the purpose of direction or to the process of direction.

The principles of purpose of direction and process of direction

Direction is the most complex function of management. The basic purpose of direction is to get the objectives fulfilled by the sub ordinates. While getting this achieved, the following should be borne in mind;

a) Principle of maximum individual contribution

b) Principle of harmony of objective. This aims at esta blishing the harmony between sub ordinates objective and that of the firm.

c) Principle of unity of command. This reflects the desirability of sub ordinates to be responsible to one superior.

d) Principle of efficiency of direction. The direction should always aim at cost reduction, while at the same time it should provide adequate satisfaction to sub ordinates.

e) Principle of appropriateness of direction technique. The techniques adopted could be of three types, namely authoritarian, consultative and free rein. Each technique has its own relative strength and its application depends upon the environment.

f) Principle of managerial communication. An effective communication both ways makes direction effective.

g) Principle of comprehension: correct understanding between sub ordinates and superiors avoids unnecessary queries from superiors.

h) Principle of leadership. Effective leadership is necessary for direction. The managers need to become leaders so that they can influence the activities of sub ordinates by maintaining high morale.

The technique of directing may be done either by giving effective order or through delegation of authority. In a formal organisation set up, the superior is vested legally to issue orders to sub ordinates to execute the work as desired. The orders given must be right type of order depending upon the psychological behaviour of subordinates. Adequate leadership alone can ensure maximum motivation in the sub ordinates.

The order should be in accordance with the demands of this situation. Where ever possible the reason for the order should be indicated. The order should be brief and clear. At times suggestion is likely to stimulate better acceptance than command.

Delegation of authority could be a more general form performing the same function as order, provided delegation is within limits.

Directing is a powerful step in the management process. It creates an appropriate work environment. It pre- supposes an understanding of human behaviour. Individuals are much more than a productive factor. They are not only producers in the organisation, but they are consumers in the market. Direction is the heart of management in action.

C. LEADERSHIP

Prof. Peter Drucker observe that "Leadership as a human characteristic which lifts a man's vision to higher sights, raises a man's performance to higher standards and builds a man's personality behind its normal limitation". In the organisation, effective utilisation of the capacity of human resources depends upon management. A leader has the function of guiding sub ordinates towards reliable objectives of the organisation. Prof.Bernards points out that"leadership is the quality of the behaviour of individuals whereby they guide people or their activities in organised effort". An organisation can get its objectives achieved either through the exercise of authority or by winning the support of the people.

The latter is always preferred; and this is possible only when that manager becomes their leader to influence their behaviour in the right direction. Leadership is an essential ingredient of successful organisation. Prof.Keith Davis says that "Leadership is the ability to persuade others to seek defined objectives enthusiastically; it is the human factor which binds a group together and motivates towards goals. "Prof.Robert Tannenbaum observes that "Leadership is inter-personal influence exercised in situation and directed through communication process towards the attainment a of specialised goal or goals".

1. The basic characteristics of Leadership

The following characteristics of leadership hold good in any organisation-political,religious, or business.

a) Leadership is basically a personal quality motivating individuals;

b) A leader through his dynamic leadership should influence the behaviour of individuals;

c) A leader must have followers and there should be a working relationship between him and his followers;

d) A leader by his own personal conduct should set an ideal and there should be community of interests between him and his team workers.

e) Leadership is exercised in a particular situation and the variables also affect the effectiveness of leadership.

The leaders are of various types namely

1) Autocratic leader,

2) Democratic leader,

3) Laissezy Faire leader.

According to Alford and Belty the following are the types of leaders.

a) Intellectual leaders

b) Institutional leaders

c) Persuasive leaders

d) Creative leaders

The main function of leadership is to build confidence, enthusiasm and zeal.

2. Importance of Leadership

In the absence of a good leader, organisation can not function effectively and efficiently. Since the organisation is the creation of human beings to achieve certain definite objective, it is quite necessary to direct or lead its members in the right direction. For work performance motivation is necessary. An efficient leader by himself is a motivating force in the organisation. A good leader should create confidence in the work force and get good results in the organisation. In the absence of confidence, the workers fail to recognise their ability to work. Ethics is the science of morale. Higher the morale, higher will be the production. Ethics in work force improves organisational ability and stability. Good leadership ensures success in the organisation and it is indispensable for managerial functions, may be motivation, communication or direction.

Courage, will power, integrity, intelligence, initiative, creativity, managerial ability, sense of responsibility, zeal and enthusiasm, mental maturity, paternalism, moral qualities, dignity, faith, technical skill of the essential qualities necessary for good leadership. He should encourage team work, inspire sub ordinates, interpret objectives, ensure coordination and strengthening personal qualities. Thus, leadership forms the basic requirement for the success of an organisation.

3. Theories of leadership

There are various approach to leadership.

a) Trait approach

Trait is a quality of an individual. This is more or less inherent quality. Between 1930-1950 this approach was popular. It was thought that "a successful leader was one who had specific leadership traits". Mental qualities, moral capacities and physical features constitutes major requirements for a leader. Out of this approach came the popular belief that "Leaders are born and not made".

But it is rather difficult to find out which are the traits more important. This theory ignores the importance of situational factors in leadership. Trait studies describe only behaviour pattern. This theory is mostly based on assumption.

b) Situational approach

This theory places more emphasis on the situation factor or environment in which the leader is operating. This approach tells us that leadership phenomenon are the product of situation or circumstances. Prof. Stogdill's investigation reveals that "the pattern of leadership traits differs with the situation". Work situation and environment should be considered for successful leadership. This approach has simulated executive training and leadership development programmes. An effective leader is one who understands the forces of the situation and emerge as a leader.

Prof. Gouldner observes that a theory of leadership should involve both traits and situations.

Each approach makes some contribution to the understanding of leadership. Any one approach is not capable of revealing the source of leadership. An integration of these approaches could be the best. Leadership is neither a quality owned by an individual, nor a product of situation, or the group. Leadership is a relationship existing by all the three forces namely the leader, the lead and the situation, which could be the strong pillars on which the leadership could be firmly established. Prof. Urwick observes that every situation in which leadership happens is a combination of - the leader, the lead, the time, the place and the environment.

D. MOTIVATION

Performance in an organisation would be high if the ability and motivation are high. Prof. D.E. Mc Rarland defines motivation as "Motivation refers to the way in which urges, drives, desires, aspirations, strivings, needs, direct control explain the behaviour of human beings. "Mr. William G. Seo says "Motivation means a process of stimulating people action to accomplish desired goals". Human behavicur is caused by motivates or needs and motivation is the process to induce persons so that organisational efficiency is achieved. Motivation cause goal-directed behaviour. Motivation is the product of anticipated values from action, which is called values.

Motivation is one of the most important factors determining organisation efficiency. Every sub ordinate in the organisation is to be motivated by the superior. Since an individual is the basic component of an organisation, he requires motivation. A man's behaviour is motivated by a desire to attain some goal.

The mechanism of motivation begins with needs and ends with need satisfaction. The process of motivation involves the creation and sustenance of the desire to work for certain goals among the people in the organisation. The basic problem of industry is how to motivate people to work. Motivation is the driving power which helps the management to enthuse workers to work efficiently. Prof. Stanley Vace says "motivation implies any emotion or desire which so conditions one's will that the individual is propelled in to action".

Prof. Allen says that "Poorly motivated people can nullify the soundest organisation".

The mechanism of motivation starts with need and ends with need. So need is the basis for motivation. Prof. Maslow's hierarchy of needs is as follows:

1. Psychological needs
2. Safety needs
3. Social needs
4. Ego-gratification needs, and
5. Self-actualisation needs.

An analysis of the above needs show that if management sincerely desires to motivate people, it should create needs. The manager has to use different methods of incentives to motivate his employees by considering their levels of needs. Motivated employees give higher performance compared to others, and this is necessary for the success of the organisation. Motivation reduces absenteeism and thereby increases productivity. Motivated employees welcome changes in technology, value system etc. which are essential for the industry to increase production.

There are several models of motivation and the management is in a dilema as to how to motivate their employees to get best results the motivation system should cover the entire human force in the organisation. The system should be simple and practicable for application. Since employees differ in education, attitude, ambition etc. the motivation levels should be such that they do not create frustration and incentives to motivate his employees.

E. INCENTIVES

The needs are the driving force of individuals behaviour. The objects that are made use of to satisfy the needs are termed as incentives. They may be either positive or negative. "Negative motivation is based on force or fear, which are highly detrimental to the organisation in the long run. But in the short run period, it may given rich dividends. Loyality, co- operation and expirit-de-corps are likely to be affected and might even results in demoralisation of the work force."

Positive motivation is based on reward. According to Prof. Filippo the important positive motivations are:

1. Praise and credit for work done;
2. Information;
3. Sincere interest in sub ordinates

4. Competition
5. Participation
6. Delegation of responsibility
7. Pride
8. Monetary rewards
9. Responsibility, placement
10. Recognition of work done
11. Increase in pay
12. Prospects of promotion etc.

All these could be either under financial incentives or non-financial incentives.

1) Financial incentives

Under the modern economic system money is playing a major role as a means to satisfy the physical needs of an individual and also secures a social position and power. The wage structure in an organisation should motivate the employees both present and prospective. The intrinsic motives are those that are present during the employment period like recognition of work, participation, competition etc. The financial motives are associated with money wages, retirement benefits, vacation pay, health insurance, bonus, profit sharing, free medical service, financial compensation for achieving a minimum standard of living. These financial incentives could be either individual or collective.

The individual financial incentives meant for the individual worker is expected to induce the individual to reach higher output and obtain greater financial rewards. Taylor's differential piece rate system, Haslay's efficiency plan and piece rate wages system could be the best example for this category.

The collective financial incentives are worked out on a group basis to motivate individuals in the group to evince greater interest in the productive process collectively. Pension plan, profit sharing bonus are good examples.

2) Non-financial incentives

The top-level management attaches more importance to socio-psychological needs that cannot be provided by monetary factors. Management besides financial incentives provide non-financial incentives for motivating the work force to sacrifice more in the total interest of the organisation. The stress is on to provide emotional and psychological satisfaction than financial.

Ranking of the workers in the organisation status; promotion to increase prestige of the worker; Responsibility transfer to satisfy the workers natural and inherent characteristics; pleasant environment for discharging the work; recognition of work performed; job security to increase the zeal of worker; Team spirit to work in co-operation and co-ordination; competition between different individuals and groups; promotion of human relations in the industry to develop a sense of belongingness in the employee; participation of workers in decision-making process; free flow of communication among the employees; building up the morale in the work force; enforcing the discipline on employees to improve organisational standard and objectives that they can play a positive role etc. are the best examples of non-financial incentives. Prof. Hertzberg's model suggests that management should seek to enrich the job to make it more interesting and important which implies delegation of authority, upgrading of responsibility and challenge in work.

3. Theories of Motivation

As a result on human motivation, several theories of motivation have been evolved. These theories could be analysed under two major heads, namely

1) Traditional theories and
2) Modern theories.

The fear and punishment theory, reward theory, and the stick approach come under the traditional theories. The punishment theory has an authoritarian and military approach and as such to-day this theory is discarded on the ground that its application leads to frustration and tension among the workers. Prof. Taylor's view point theory saya "give a man more money and he will produce more" comes under reward theory. Prof. Drucker says that "satisfaction with monetary rewards is not a sufficient motivation". Even the stick approach which says that rewards are made contingent upon effective performance does not hold good when the worker has reached s subsistence level.

Prof. Drucker refers to "Management by objective" in contrast to "Management by control". An effective organisation is one which favours integration and operation in place of direction and control. Thus, the traditional theories have lost their importance in the modern times.

The modern theory recognises "man as the centre of all economic activities". The motivation concept should emphasise more on personal development, both emotional and intellectual, of participation and belongingness. Prof. Mc Gregor says that "the manager is a teacher, consultant, a colleague, but very rarely a boss". The worker will work hard when he finds that the path he has chosen leads to higher productivity and attainment of the predetermined goal. Thus, the modern theory dwells more upon the personality improvement rather than on compulsion, control and authoritarianism.

CHAPTER - 15

MORALE-COMMUNICATION

A. MORALE

Every employee has attitudes that range over the entire spectrum of human behaviour."Without high morale work is drugery and supervision near slave driving".The spirit and willingness with which work is is done constitute job morale. The concepts of job satisfaction and motivation pertain to the individual and morale to the group. Prof.Mc.Firland says that "morale is basically a group of phenomenon". Satisfaction,dissatisfaction and morale are inter- related. Among the factors which yield dissatisfaction to the workforce, the following are important namely salary, good supervision,benefits, job security, inter- person relation, physical working conditions,fair company policies and administrative policies. Employees with high morale live to work and work to live.

Morale and productivity go together. There cannot be a proportionate increase in productivity when morale is increased. Morale building in the organisation is a continuous process and it is the responsibility of the manager. There is saying that "when morale is lost ,the nation is lost".this is applicable to organisation also. A sound manpower management improves employee morale. The management should make its policies clear relating to rules,procedures welfare activities etc. to the employees. The human relations approach motivates the workers to render their best in the productive process. Every individual should be treated as a human being in the organisation. Good human relations techniques motivates people to work better. Prof.Mayo observes the following key elements of human relations;

1) Treat people as human rather than a bundle of skills;
2) Understand people better and communicate effectively;
3) Make them feel useful and important in the organisation;
4) Create sense of satisfaction among people.

Every worker in an organisation feels that he should be treated with dignity and respect and he should not feel that he is an orphan in the industry. He wants recognition, desires security and aspires for trust and confidence. The greatest assets to a business are its human assets and it is obiligatory on the part of the management to protect this. The management should realise that the producers are the ultimate consumers. A worker or an individual should not be treated as "a cog in the profit-making mechanism". The human factor is the most important factor in the productive process. Every problem and every decision in the organisation involves the human element. The human potential is always high and it should be utilised to the maximum extent. Morale is contagious, because people learn through communication and connection. The first -line supervisor is a key-factor in morale building because his morale has multiplier effects on sub-ordinates. The management can use persuasion, effective communication,leadership and sincere interest in the employees to boost morale in the organisation. Even the organisational structure has an impact on morale building. Flat structure increases morale by shortening the length of vertical communication. The sub-ordinates should be associated with decision making process. Participation, job enlargement and job enrichment remove monotony and fatigue and thus increases morale. The management should eliminate conflicts and misunderstanding through negotiation, concilation and mediation rather than resorting to other methods.

Collective bargaining and joint consulation are the best methods to resolve conflicts. Thus, morale is a major factor in modern business organisation to achieve the cherished objectives. Diplomatic and tactful handling of workers' problem and affording all social security measures to workers will go a long way in maintaining morale in the organisation. Morale could be ensured through 'Industrial Democracy' and assurance of protection to workers from 'cradle to the grave-yard'.or as Lord Beveridge says "From the womb to the tomb".

B. COMMUNICATION

The most vital management tool is communication."The number one management problem to-day is communication" says prof.Alvin Dodd the president of American Management Association. The failure of communication facilities would result and largely responsible for distruption, frustration and bankruptcy for management. Communication is the force that binds the people of an organisation and it is the heart of the process of organisation. It is vital in the relationships between the executive and their sub- ordinates. Every executives should know how to communicate. It involves imparting a common idea or understanding.

a. Definition:

The word communication originates from the latin word "Communis" meaning there by common. When we communicate, we try to share our thoughts and ideas with others.

Prof.Keith Davis says " communication is the process of passing information and understanding from one person to another".Communication includes transporting and receiving information. From the point of view of organisational efficiency, the correct interpretation and understanding of the message is very important.

Mr.Dale Beach defines communication as "communication is the transfer of information and understanding from person to person".

Mr.Louis Allen says "communication is the sum of all the things one person does when he wants to create understanding in the mind of another".

It involves a systematic and continuous process of telling, listening and understanding.

Prof.M.W.Cumming observes "the word communication describe the process of conveying messages, facts, ideas,options and attitudes) from one person to another so that they are understood".

Mr.Mac Farland says "communication may be broadly defined as the process of meaningful interaction among human beings. More specially it is the process by which meanings are received and understandings are reached among humanbeings".

Mr.Meyer F.G says "the act of making one's ideas and opinions known to others."

Prof.H.Simon explains "communication may be formally defined as any process whereby decisional premises are transmitted from one member of an organisation to another".

b. Communication process and types

It is a process of changing concept. Since events, relationships are dynamic, flexible and continuous, they are affected by various events. It involves various elements from sender to receiver as follows; sender - ideas - encoding - channel - receiver - decoding and feed back.

A sender passes on information and ideas to others; and these ideas become the subject matter for communication. If the above communication is abstract and intangible, encoding through symbols, pictures etc. become necessary. These symbols are transmitted through channels like radio, telephone etc. The receiver receives the ideas or information and the symbols are converted or decoded. Finally the process of feedback takes place to ensure that the original message is correctly received.

The communication structure is of different types;

1. **Upward communication** where the participative management encourages this process as it helps the management to find out whether its orders are being carried out as desired.

2. **Downward communication** where the required information is passed on from the top to the bottom and this communication downwards is more or less directive and the sub ordinates have to initiate the action as directed.

3. **Diagonal communication** emphasises more on vertical communication rather that horizontal communication, which can create line-staff conflicts.

4. **The grapevine or informal communication** exist in most organisation. Through this channel a person can get information quicker which would take otherwise a longer time through official channels.

5. **Formal and informal communications** The formal communication channel is officially enforced to regulate the flow of organisational communication to make it more orderly, accurate and timely. The formal communication can be either through a single channel or multiple channels. When it is through single channel, the path is only" through proper channel "and through the line of superior sub-ordinate authority relationship only and on essential information. This method helps the management to exercise control over sub ordinates and fix the responsibility. Formal communications are established, officially recognised organisational channels. They include

department meetings; conferences; telephone calls; company new bulletins; and special interviews etc.

The informal communications refer to"grapevine "because of the existence of group interest in the individual in the organisation. This type of grapevine communication is very popular due to its credibility, spontaneity and quickness. The main danger being its successptibility to distortion. The management at times supplement formal information with the grapevine method.

C. Oral and Written communication.

The communication could be either oral or written. The manager invariably restores to oral communication through personal contacts, telephone, public speech, intercom system and other artificial media. This is a more effective communication method since the superior can convey his view point clearly to the sub ordinates, who invariably appreciate this system. The human voice has a greater and soothing influence and effect than written communication. It can change the sub ordinates attitudes, feelings and beliefs.

Oral communication enjoys the following advantages. It saves time; it provides opportunity to ask questions; it can be easily understood; it can foster a friendly and co-operative spirit; it can improve the understanding and trust of the receiver; it provides all opportunity for response and fed back; it develops a sense of belongingness and it provides the communication for his personality development.

But oral communication gives scope for being misunderstood and often distorted and demands on the part of communicator to be more effective in his approach and if the executive is in experienced, he may be at a great disadvantage and may lead to legal difficulties. Since the communication is informal, it may have less weight and the decisions may not be binding and the spirit of authority cannot be easily transmitted.

Written communication is more appropriate and binding. It is a extensively used in respect of reports, research information, policy statements and it is a well thought out communication.

Rules, agreements, memorandum, instructions have to be in writing. It is permanent record for future reference. To be effective, the written communication should be clear, concise and accurate. In the case of complicated and vital issues, written communication is absolutely necessary. As it is formal, it carries more weight and less likely to be mis-understood. For lengthy message containing financial, production and other statistical data, this type is more suitable.

But this written communication suffers from certain limitations. The main defect being that it encourages excessive formality and results in rigid personal relationships. There is scope of red tape and inordinate delay. It may be tedious and difficult to keep written communication up-to-date and does not foster co-operative spirit as it fails to convey the feelings of the communicator. Written communication should be supple mentary and can not be a substitute to oral communication.

D. Communication Barriers

The main problem of communication is one of transmitting meaning from one individual to another. It is the sole responsibility of the communicator to use such a language that is easily understood by the receiver. The language should be simple,understandable and intelligible and also free from ambiguity. The number of barriers impending the flow of communication in the organisation could be classified under three heads, namely;

1. External barriers,
2. Organisational barriers and
3. Personal factors

all these problems are inter-related and mutually influential.

1) External barriers

These problems could be external to the parties involved or might be internal to them. The external barriers may be in the form of "Semantic barriers". Language consists of semantic bodies of signs, signals, or symbols used in conveying meaning from one person to another. These barriers arise form the linguistic capacity of the parties involved. Words, in view of their several meanings fail to convey the real meaning. If the message is badly expressed, lack of clarity, precision; lack of coherence; inadequate vocabulary and implications;faulty translations; unclarified assumptions; wrong perceptions creating distortions in reality etc., the result would be utter confusion and chaos.

Emotional or psychological factors are the main barriers in inter-personal communication. Pre-mature evaluation of the message ;the pre-occupied mind of the receiver; decreasing accuracy during the transmission of the message from person to person; dis-trust of communicator are the source of the psychological factors- creating problems in communication. Written communication should be considered as supplementary to productive personal face to face relationship. Prof.Chesser Barnard says that a communication must appeal to the receiver that it is important to him and as well as for the organisation,.

2) Organisational Barriers

The organisational hierarchy affects communication channels. This crates rigidity and hardship to members. The day to day operations of an organisation are regulated by management for the attainment of pre- determined objectives. Certain official measures like prescribing of various policies,rules, regulations, norms, institution of rewards for good work, punishment for inefficiency and bad work etc. are undertaken by the organisation. These prescriptions affect communication in different direction. Orgaisational policies relating to communication serves as guide lines for every individual to behave and act. The rules and regulations prescribe the channels to be adopted in communication for free flow of information. Status provided is reflected by special privileges provided to the individual, like telephone facilities, cabins between hierarchical positions, greater the possibility of the breakdown of the communication line. It gets delayed if there are large number of managerial levels in the organisation; and under such circumstances the communication also gets disturbed. The existence of communication gap should be bridged immediately to avoid distrust.

3) Personal Factors

Effective communication could take place smooth provided the media adopted like meetings, conference, complaint box, suggestion box, open door system, social and cultural gatherings etc. are efficiently organised. Communication is an inter personal process. Attitude of superiors towards sub ordinates, fear of challenge to authority, lack of confidence in sub-ordinates, by passing the channel of communication, lack of time to talk to sub ordinates and lack of awareness etc. are other factors affecting communication. these are all personal barriers which should be eliminated in the best interest of the organisation.

E PRINCIPLES OF EFFECTIVE COMMUNICATION

The organisation has to follow the guidelines listed below to make the communication efficient and result oriented.

1. There should be adequate communication planning to achieve the best results. One should find out exactly what one wishes to communicate and the objective of that communication. Sufficient information should be collected well in advance so that question from the other side could be answered properly and to the point. Once the objective is clear, the communication has a chance to succeed. The language used should be well understood by the receiver.

2. All levels of people in the organisation need to be familiar with the communication. The quantum of communicator should be such that it is neither more nor less and just sufficient to convey the required information.

3. The medium used, the subject matter, the situation and the person involved are to be carefully balanced. The medium of communication, oral, written or visual must be judiciously selected. At times charts and illustrations and diagram help towards better perception of communication. The tone, expressions and emotions have an impact on positive communication.

4. In a climate of trust and confidence, the communication is always received. One of the rules of human relation is "to praise in public and to scold in private", prof.Rogers observes,"each person can speak for himself only after he has related the ideas and feelings of previous speaker accurately and to that speaker's satisfaction".

5. It should be remembered that communication is a two way process. A follow up of communication helps for the feedback to ensure full understanding of message. If actions contradict words,then words are likely to be discounted. "What is preached should be practiced".

6. It is also necessary to provide adequate training facilities for improving skills in oral and written communication to the communicator and this will enable him to acquire the leadership qualities.

7. Communication helps the manager to develop authority and structure. "Communication may cement an organisation or disrupt it". It is the basis of decentralisation and delegation. A good communication can democratize the management or organisation.

   For good external communication, the basis is the internal communication. It should be remembered that employee productivity and communication are inter- related and inter-dependent. It can promote good union relations and thus boost morale in the work force.

8. An effective communication is a cementing force in the organisation and contributes for a well balanced development of productive process.

   Summarisation(points at a glance)

DIRECTION - LEADERSHIP -MOTIVATION - MORALE- COMMUNICATION

1. To lead means to create confidence in the subordinates so that they could contribute the best in them to the progress of the organisation. Leading promotes personality development. Management is a dual-model theory, that is to say, that they are to be a model to the subordinates and model to themselves. In order to harmonise objectives of a enterpreneurship, it is necessary for managers to analyse and digest the behavioral patterns of subordinates and of themselves.

2. "Man is the product of environment"; so also the manager, "the product of situations", like the power of the leader,the task ahead and the relationship existing between the group and the manager. Since situations are subject to change depending on national and inter- national forces,

the leadership style of the manager, which depends on situation, cannot be streamlined in a particular fashion.

3. Several principles hide leadership qualities of managers. The effectiveness and efficiency of enterprise depend on the capacity of management leadership in bringing about harmonisation between the personal goals of individuals and the goals of the enterprise.

4. The managers should try to integrate the system of managing the organisation so as to make the motivation programme effective and result oriented. The incentives,the reward structure, the principle of allignment between the superiors and subordinates should be inter-woven with the entire system of management. Here lies the leadership qualities.

5. The managers could be efficient and effective leaders in an organisation, when they understand the technique of motivation that can bring subordinates together, closure and enthuse in them the spirit of work consciousness. Then only, the managers could be good leaders.

6. "Language is a vehicle of thought". The communication with clarity and bravity could bring good understanding in the organisation. The informal communication is more effective than formal communication, which is like a command. The informal communication is faster and more effective, which could be later supported by formal communication.

7. Communication could flow not only upward and downward but also horizontally and vertically and could be in any form. Group communication are more productive and result-oriented than in writing and committee meetings.

8. Motivation could in the form of offering money; encouraging participation; improvement of the quality the work; job enrichment; improvement of organizational

environment and better working conditions; better placement, democratic leadership; relaxing rigidity; introduction to flextime and greater security through pension, insurance and fringe benefits, etc.

9. The leadership quality of the manager could be judged through his capacity to boost morale in the working force. Morale is basically a group phenomenon. The manager should treat the workforce (personnel) with a milk of human kindness and as the centre of business activity.

10. A sound man power planning improves employee morale. Diplomatic and tractful handling of personnel problems will boost the leadership qualities. The manager should infuse courage and confidence in the workforce. Democracy in industry is the modern slogan and this is the responsibility of management as the leader and guiding spirit of the industry.

CHAPTER - 16

CONTROL

1. Introducton

Prof. George R.Terry defines control as " controlling is determining what is being accomplished, that is evaluating the performance and , if necessary, applying correct measures so that the performance takes place according to plans".

Mr.Robert Anthony says "Management control is the process by which managers assure that resources are obtained and used efficiently and effectively in the accomplishment of an organisations objectives".

According to Hayens and Massic " control is any process that guides activity towards some predetermined goal. The essence of concepts is in determining whether the activity is achieving the desired results".

"Controlling implies measurement of accomplishment of events against the standard of plans and the correction of deviations to assure attainment of objectives according to plans".

"Adequate control may result in setting new goals, formulating new plans, changing the organisation structure, improving staffing, and making major changes in techniques of directing".

"Control measures deviation from plans and then suggests corrective action. It is the function that closes the loop in the system of managing".

"Control compares the actual performance with the planned performance with the objective to discover whether all is going well according to plans and if not why".

All organisations face this problem of control. With the resources being very scarce, control is necessary to see that these scarce resources are subject to maximum capacity utilisation and thus achieve the targeted objectives. The manager at the planning stage decide how the resources would be utilised and at the controlling stage they try to find out whether the resources utilised are according to pre-determined plan. Control thus completes the entire sequence of management process.

The control process finds out deviation from the planned performance and suggests corrective measures. "Where as planning sets the course, control observes deviation from the course or to an appropriately changed one".control is a continuous process. The control system is a co-ordinated and integrated system. The nature, scope and limit of control various from and different to managers at different levels. Control is of various types like quality control, inventory control, production control, budgetary control and administrative control etc.

2. Process of control

Controls involves three steps viz..

1) Establishing standards,

2) Measuring performance against these standards and

3) Correcting deviation from standards and plans.

1) Standards are established to be the basis for judging and measuring the result. For evaluating the departments performance as also the total performance of the organisation standards are necessary. These standards may be in physical terms,that is on man hour basis or they may be in monetary terms such as the cost of production per unit. These standards are set at strategic points. They

may also be expressed in measurable terms. If the employees are aware of the prescribed standards they themselves can evaluate their performance. Prof. Newman has pointed out three guidelines for selecting strategic points ; and they are

a) The control points should be subject to economical observation ;

b) The control points should provide comprehensive scene to executives and

c) The control points should promote balanced performance.

There are many types of standards available for measuring performance, and among them the following are important;

1. Physical standards;
2. Cost standards;
3. Revenue standards;
4. Capital standards;
5. Intangible standards.

The physical standards arc non-monetory measurements and generally used at the penetrating level where materials are utilised, labour employed and goods manufactured. They may be quantitative or qualitative. The quantitative standards refer to number of units produced per hour etc., where as the qualitative standards refer to the durability of the product etc.

Prof.Goetz analyses these standards as "the building blocks of managerial planning".They also constitute the physical standards for control of the productive process.

The cost standards are monetory measurements and they assign monetory value to the cost of operations. Direct cost or indirect cost per unit produced, materials cost and selling cost are good examples. They are very good controlling devices used by management in the process of production.

The revenue standards have a monetory value to the sale affected for a specified period. The capital standards are reckoned in terms of capital invested, the ratio of current assets to current liabilities are some of the examples of capital standards. In an organisation intangible standards do exist and they are neither monetory or nor physical. They refer to the competancy of the managers and employees, who contribute their share for the success of the organisation and they are more relative in character.

3) Measurement of Performance

It is necessary to make proper arrangements for measurement of performance to compare standards. To detect deviation from the expected levels and to institute remedial measures, this is the best system thought of. This is the second major step in the control process. This is more necessary to prevent occurrence of future deviation by appropriate actions. The methods of performing measurements should be precise and expressed in monetory and physical terms, like sales volume, production units, profits etc.

The qualitative and intangible performance, like human relations, morale of the employees are not measurable. Psychological tests and opinion surveys are good measuring rods for intagible performance. According to Prof.Drucker, it is very much desirable to have clear and common measurements in all key areas of business. The measurement must be clear simple rational, relevant, direct attention and efforts; reliable and understandable and these methods would be necessary for both tangible and intagible performance.

4) Correcting deviations from plans and standards

The next step in control is to find out the extent of deviations and identify the causes for such deviations. Variation in performance are revealed when adequate standards are developed and actual performance is measured accurately. The control process is complete when the standards are achieved and the management will have no further action. The extent of variation differs from case to case and such standards are not obtained in all cases. Managements can take proper control actions, if causes of variations are completely ascertained. Measurement of performance and analysis of deviations and their cause cannot be identified, unless the person responsible is able to take corrective action.

Correction of deviation is the last step in the control process. An organisation is not a self-regulating system and any type of automatic control cannot be established since many factors influence the system. therefore, some additional control actions, like

1) review of plans,
2) review of goals,
3) change in the assignment of tasks,
4) change in the system of techniques adopted
5) Change in the organisational structure etc. would be necessary. Koontz and O' Donnell emphasise that the overlap of control function with the other demonstrates the unity of the manager's job as an integrated system.

5. Basic Requirements of Adequate Control

The principles of control are universal but in their application there could be differences. The chief manager should keep in mind the essential requirements of control in the process of tailoring and designing. Prof. Kootz and O' Donnell have stressed upon the following requirements.

a) Control should be suitable and reflect the nature and need of the activity. Besides the control system being different in different business, they vary from department to department and from one level of the organisation to the other. There are several techniques of control like budgetary control, break-even points, financial ratios etc.

   The manager should use the right technique appropriate to the situation and the size of the departments. Budgeting is the formulation of plans for a given period. "Budgets are statements of anticipated results, in financial terms or in non-financial terms". Budgetory control is a powerful instrument. " If budgeting sets up a target, control measure the accuracy of the shot". Control helps in comparing actual results with the budgets or planned targets and if deviations are found from the planned budgets the manager has to take suitable actions to rectify the same. Budget not only requires planning but it is an instrument of planning. "Only when plans are completely co-ordinated and developed to fit into departmental operations, then only departmental budgets are prepared as an instrument of control".

b) The control system must be understandable. The information and the details of the control system supplied should be very simple and clear so that it is easily understood by the individuals to whom it is meant for. It is quite possible that top managers may understand complicated statistical charts and mathematical formula, while it may not be possible for the low level managers to digest them and under such circumstances the control systems becomes ineffective.

c) The cost of control system should be economical leading to possible savings. Undue complexity of the control system should be avoided in order to economise the expenditure.

d) The system must be highly flexible and adjustable even if the plans undergo change. Unforseen circumstances can force an alteration even on the highly approved plans and the control system should be capable of accommodating such changes. Prof.Goetz points out "that the control system should report such failures and should contain sufficient elements of flexibility to maintain managerial control of operations inspite of such failures."

e) It is difficult to correct deviations which have already taken place. The system should identify such deviations immediately and expeditiously to minimise such happenings in future.

f) The control system should be forward looking and the managers with their vast experience and knowledge forecast and anticipate deviations so that corrections could be incorporated. The financial manager should be in a position to foresee the cash requirements and provide necessary funds well in advance.

g) The control data and system should confirm to organiastional structure, since the activities of the organisation are carried on by people. The control data should be prepared in such a way that it should be possible to fix the responsibility for the deviations. For effective management, organisation and control cannot be separated. Thus organisational conformity is an essential requirement.

h) The control system should be indicative of exceptions at critical points and it is necessary that the critical areas should also be fixed for the most effective control. This will help the management to be vigilant and cautions in its approach to problems.

i) The measurements used in the control system should have objectivity. Mere subjective approach will not solve the problem and it can only cause displeasure to sub-ordinates. The use of indefinite terms to the sub-ordinates can only create frustration to them. The observations made against the employees should be specific and objective and not subjective in its approach.

j) An adequate control system should be suggestive of corrective action. The system should not only detect errors, failures but it should be in a position to identify the actual causes for the decline in profits such as increase in costs or fall in the volume of sales. The control system will be effective only , if it can pin down the particular factor responsible for increasing the cost or in which market area the sales have shown a declining tendency.

6. The control devices could be of two types namely

a) Traditional control devices and

b) Special control devices.

a. Traditional control devices

1. Budgetary control

For a managerial control budget is an important tool and very widely used. "A budget is a financial or quantitative interpretation, prior to a defined period of time, of a policy to be pursued for that period to attain a given objective". Budget not only requires planning but by itself it is an instrument of planning. The success of a budget depends upon the person who prepares it. The budgetary control will be successful only when sufficient authority is delegated to personnel incharge of preparing the budget.

Generally the functional heads prepare budgets for their departments. The budget officer co-ordinates the budgets of different departments and prepares a master budget for the whole organisation to be approved by the competent authority. The competent authority, the budget committee, gives assent to the budget after making necessary modifications if necessary.

The budget period depends upon several factors like the nature of business, the type of customers, the stability of the business conditions etc.,Shorter the period, better will be its accuracy.

The budgets prepared are of various types like sales budget; advertising budget; production budget; materials budget; administrative budget; etc., The preparation of budgets of various departments require a careful study and analysis of costs for previous years together with the plans and responsibilities of each department for the specific period required.

If the budgetary control is to be successful, it is necessary that the top management should support the programme; employees participation in matters of operation is important; fixation of responsibility and proper delegation of authority are essential; a system of incentives for good and creditable work and penalties for intentional wrong doings are to be stipulated and adopted; correct accounting, reliable accurate statistics are to be insisted upon.

2. Traditional non-budgetary control

Proper statistical analysis of various aspects of operations and presentation of comprehensive, accurate and reliable statistical data are very important elements for control system.

Preparation of special reports for problem area help the control system to detect the lapses and to plug the loop holes.

Determination of break even point is an eye-opener to the control system as it indicates at what volume revenues cover expenses.

Internal audit and personal observations are also very important tools of control, as they help the management to identify the deviations and seek out remedial measures.

b) Special Control Devices

Among the several special control devices, PERT(programme Evaluation and Review Technique) and CPM(Critical Path Method) are important. PERT is concerned with shortening of the project execution time rather than cost. On the other hand CPM is concerned with optimising resource allocation and minimising over all cost. PERT can be used for projects like the establishment of a new department, introduction of a new product, for R & D etc., PERT helps the management to plan carefully and to concentrate attention on key projects and identify areas which could increase efficiency, reduce cost and accelerate profits.

"One of the interesting special areas is measuring critical human variables on the valid fact that the human organisation of any enterprise makes the most difference in end results".

Prof. Thomas Wilson observes that "planning and physical controls have become so closely associated as to be regarded as almost inseparable. Planning has, therefore, been said to imply a command economy.

There are two ways in which the management may exercise control over the organisation. Direct controls through orders and instructions, which could be positive or negative. Indirect controls attempt to influence through the adoption of indirect measures.

CHAPTER - 17

CO-ORDINATION

1. Meaning and Definitions:

Co-ordination is considered as a vital phase of control. Prof.Allens observes that "Co-ordination as one of the managerial functions along side planning, organisation, motivating and controlling. It is the orderly arrangement of group effort to provide unity of action in the pursuit of a common purpose". It is further pointed out that " co-ordination, in short, is administration, at its most creative".

Prof.Henry Fayol points out that "co-ordination as an important function of management. Because, it is the orderly synchronisation of efforts of the sub-ordinates to provide the proper amount, timing and quality of execution. So that their unified efforts lead to the objective, namely, the common purpose of the enterprise".

"Co-ordination is less a by-product of the routine functions of management and more a process which must be purposed as a conscious policy if management is to be successful in the modern world".

Co-ordination is superior to co-operation and co- operation is not a substitute to co-ordination. "Each for all, and all for each" is the basic idea of co- operation and it aims at working together to reach a common destination. Where as in co-ordination, different activities of each individual are directed by the manager till the pre-determined objective, as specified by the plan is achieved.

Co-ordination means harmonious combination or interaction of various factors responsible for production. The various infrastructure (men, material, money, marketing, machinery and management) have to be co-ordinated in the productive process. At each managerial level integrating and balancing the various factors is necessary. It is rather difficult to achieve co-ordination without effective leadership. "Co-ordination is an ongoing process whereby a manager develops an integrated, orderly and synchronised pattern of group of effort among his subordinates to achieve a common purpose".

The various definitions of co-ordination reveal the following essential points :

1. Co-ordination is an important function of a managerial leader;
2. It is a never ending process in the field of organisation;
3. It is applicable to group effort only;
4. It emphasises on collective effort;
5. The ultimate goal of co-ordination is common purpose.

2. Need for co-ordination

A large scale organisation requires number of persons engaged in different functions. Managers have to reconcile differences in approach and effort to achieve the goal. The existence of complexities of activities in a modern organisation emphasises for the need of specialisation and division of labour. An organisation has both individual goals and group goals and the management has to integrate both through co-ordination.

Co-ordination is either in the form of co-ordination of various activities or of individuals. Since the individual nature is highly complex, co-ordination of individuals is a greater problem. The management should have the capacity to appreciate the value of co- ordinating its activities; secondly it should have the will to co-ordinate and thirdly the management should encourage in co-ordinating activities. The object of co-ordination is to bring all the parts to the highest perfection possible and to weld them in to a smooth working, efficient organisation of the enterprise as a whole. To achieve internal co-ordination, every tool of management should reach every phase of industrial operation.

External co-operation deals with the problems that are created outside the factory having an affect on the organisation. Labour, demand and supply, science and technology, international economy etc. are external factors having a tremendous affect on the enterprise and it becomes the responsibility of management to promote co-ordination in these factors also.

3. Principles of Co-ordination

Mary Parker Fellett discusses the following basic principles of co-ordination as;

"Co-ordination can be achieved by direct contact among the responsible people concerned". She stressed on the point that co-ordination can be obtained more easily by direct international horizontal relationships and personal communication which could bring about accord on methods, actions and achievements." It is easy to achieve co-ordination in the early stages of planning and achievements in policy making. It should be a continuous process and a voluntary process. All factors are reciprocally related and influence on another. "Good co-ordination will attack the problems as they arise. Excellent co-ordination will anticipate them and prevent their occurence". Co-ordination is the very cream of managership and it can integrate individual efforts for achieving the group objectives. Knowledge and understanding of enterprise by every one can contribute for the overall growth of industry.

4. Techniques of effective co-ordination

The fundamental objective of any managerial activity is to achieve the ultimate objective through a co- ordinated effort of all individuals involved in the productive process.

Supervision in its real sense happens to be the best and the oldest technique to achieve co-ordination. "Because the span of a management limits the member of sub-ordinates that a supervisor can properly direct and because enterprises may be of a size which requires the services of many supervisors, organisation is a very important device for achieving co-ordination". A supervisior's study and careful application of co- ordination can bring about interaction in the activities of the organisation. The following could be the techniques for achieving co-ordination.

a) Co-ordination by chain of command. Prof.Weber has indicated" that in a controlled administration, co-ordination is achieved automatically through chain of command since all the sub ordinates working under one superior are co-ordinated by him". Only under bureauratic organisations this technique is successful.

b) Co-ordination by leadership can bring together individual motivation and can persuade the group efforts. Prof. Ordway says "that top management should practice leadership because without it, no co-ordination is possible".

c) Co-ordination by effective communication helps in improving understanding between individuals or groups. This helps every individual to know his scope, limits and responsibilities and relationships. Effective communication is capable of providing both vertical and horizontal co-ordination provided there are no restraints on the flow of communication.

d) Co-ordination by committees, which enjoy the authority to take decisions and make recommendations provide co- ordination among various functions of the organisation. Committees are useful for co-ordinating, planning and the execution of programmes. "A committee permits the individual concerned not only to obtain a first hand picture of overall plans and of their place in them but to contribute suggestion on the spot for improvement of plans. The committee also furnishes a place where agreement may be reached on the steps in the co-ordination". The modern enterprises are under the pressure of dynamic environment and as such there is a great burden on managers to integrate, plan and co-ordinate their activities.

e) Co-ordination by general staff is specially created for the purpose of co-ordination. This STAFF enjoys a special position and privilege in the field of communication work. The staff centre consists of individuals rich with knowledge, experience and expertise and as such it can distribute the information to various departments and that information is pooled from the departmental heads. It is a reservoir of communication and the co-ordination is achieved by channelising inter-departmental information.

In some organisation, special co-ordinators are employed, whose responsibility is to co-ordinate certain specified activities of the enterprise.

For instance a project co-ordinator is desired to co- ordinate the various activities of the project, which is executed on a contract basis within a specified time bound programme.

In conclusion, it may be observed that "with complications, change and numerous specialised departments, it is difficult to co-ordinate every activity, every sub-routine plan and every expenditure with others".

A balanced co-ordination of various infrastructure in the productive process can assure the management with maximum profits through minimisation of cost. Reduction of cost of production is the best and the most acclaimed method for profit maximisation. And this is possible through the best efforts of co- ordination. Thus, co-ordination plays a major role in the modern industrial organisation, which is beset with very many dynamic problems.

CONTROL & CO-ORDINATION

Summarisation (points at a glance)

1. To determine the extent upto which the plans are being executed, control is necessary. Planning has four phases, namely,-formulation, adoption, execution and supervision and this is through control.
2. Among the various types of control measures, financial controls through budgets, breakeven analysis, ratio analysis, quality control, time-period control, technical control, production control, cost control are very important.
3. The control measures have to be applied right from the chairman to supervisors at different levels and at different time periods. All control measures aim at three objectives, namely- **(a) Establishment of standards; (b) asuring performance and (c)correcting variations with reference to plans and standards predetermined.**
4. Controls should be tailored made to work effectively and efficiently and to be flexible with reference to objectives, climate and corrective action. The managers make use of different tools and techniques to control the process.

5. The latest methods of control pertain to variable budgeting, zero-base budgeting, the PERT (Programme Evaluation and Review System) and (MIS).

6. Management of productivity is an important step in the control process. The achievement of skilled workers could be measured easily as compared to the turnover of managers. In a dynamic society, where there is competitive environment, managerial productivity measurement is very essential.

7. Management of production embraces all the activities that contributes to total production like, purchases, sales, ware-housing, transportation, inventory, inputs, outputs and the feed back, etc.

8. An efficient controlling today demands an efficient information system supported by research and development and a scientific method to study and analyse the various problems confronting the productive process and to find out remedial measures to obviate any eventuality.

9. Most of the controls are financial in nature. The budgetory control, which aims at controlling revenues and expenditure, is the most important. The cost control, control through P and L account (profit and loss), Investment-output-ratio methods are some other important measures.

10. "Prevention is better than cure". Thus, preventive controls are resorted to at every stage in the productive process to prevent, as far as possible, the occurence of deviations from standards already pre- determined and pre-planned. The usual direct control methods are applied by evaluating the achievements with reference to standards fixed earlier. This is more a corrective measure.

11. Social control and this is the result of the society's reactions, responsiveness and sensitivity. Just like social audit, social controls are there. "Production is a means to consumption and consumption is the end of production". Thus, the object of production is 'consumers' satisfaction". Hence, consumers, who determine the density of the producers, control the production process.

12. To understand the actual principles of control, it is necessary to analyse the purpose of control, the structure and process of control. They together determine the scope of control.

    a) The purpose of control is to watch whether production has taken place in accordance with pre-determined plans, and correct them in time so that they do not recur.

    b) Forward control is more beneficial than relying more upon historical data and facts. Since the management today produces goods on a large-scale production, through specialisation and in anticipation of demand, to an international competitive market, and where gestation period is involved, a forward control method is more important and advantages, than relying on feed backs.

13. Responsibility and authority are vested in the managers, who delegate them to sub-ordinate supervisors, who are in independent charge of the departments. Thus, control would become more necessary at several stages.

14. If controls are inefficient, cost would rise due to inordinate delays at various process of production, like purchase, sales, deliveries, etc., If managers are well experienced and knowledgeable, the deviations and delays could be avoided and quality would increase.

15. If the planning process is clear, unambiguous and well integrated, and if the plan forecasting is well designed, the controls would be productive and result- oriented.

16. Besides planing, the organisational structure should be well defined, complete and integrated to make the control techniques work effectively and efficiently. The techniques of control should be simple, understandable and easily applicable, so as to achieve the targets. They should simplify and not complicate the productive process.

17. The standards that are fixed should be accurate, objective, reliable, and within the reach of the management, otherwise they become beyond measurement. If they are abstract, inaccurate and subjective, they remain as standard only beyond measurement. Since the individuals or personnel implement the plans, the controls are to be achieved by them.

18. The most important point to consider in using controls is the extent to which the information that is provided timely. Because controls are useful only to the extent that they provide data to the managers, so that immediate corrective actions could be taken before deviations become insurmountable. The data should be simple enough so that the people responsible to implement them should know why discripancies have taken place and investigate them, and avoid their recurrence.

CHAPTER - 18

SOCIAL RESPONSIBILITIES OF MANAGEMENT

A. OBJECTIVES AND GOALS

The Gettys Burgh speech of Abraham Lincoln "Liberty, Equality and Fraternity", the clarion call of "The French Revolution" and the "Russian Revolution of 1917" under Karl Marx emphasised on one major issue namely that "Man is the centre of all economic activities. He is a producer in the industry and a consumer in the market. Among the five 'M's, Man is supreme and an animate factor. He pocesses dignity, respect and honour in society. His contribution in the productive process in an organisation depends upon how best the management assures and safeguards his role, as a human factor. The subject of "Industrial relations", harmonious human relationship in the industry between labour and management, has developed so much both in content and popularity with the organisation of trade union movement and development of management thought.

The contributions of Dr.Mc.Gragor, Fayol and Peter Drucker to the concept of management thought and the role of man in the productive process have revolutionalised the organisational processes. The individual has come to play a vital role contributing his physical and mental power, to augment the managements resources. The management on its part has started recognising its obligations to society. Personnel management is more complex and industrial psychology become more effective in its application. The managements, which were autocratic and despotic in their approach have now become more paternalistic and their attitude towards employees is more congenial and affectionate and helpful. This has resulted in providing employees more fringe benefits, reasonable salaries and wages and a conducive, atmosphere to work. The morale of the workers being gradually increased and the approach of employers towards employees undergone a morbid change. Better working conditions, scope for collective bargaining and joint negotiations and the innovations of industrial democracy have all resulted in bringing about a revolution in the attitude of management. To-day the worker no longer feels that he is an 'orphan' in the industry. He is proud under present management because he feels he is recognised and his work is appreciated. The managements social obligation to the worker and towards the society have improved to a very great extent. The advent of professional managers and the efforts of government have contributed towards the growing awareness of social responsibilities. The social security measures; the health insurance schemes; provisions of subsidised meals and transport facilities; old age pension scheme; the un-employment benefits; workmen's compensation for accidents during and after the job; free medical facilities; protection to labour from the "Womb to the tomb"; several types of bonus to employees as incentive etc. have all brought a sense of belongingness and motivation to workers in the modern industry.

The social obligation is by individuals and not by institution, because individuals create institutions. Just like the management has certain social obligation to the workers, in return the workers in an organisation have a social responsibility to discharge towards the managements. "Rights and privileges should go along with duties and responsibilities". The social responsibility could be positive, natural and negative, but all the three are equally important.

B. To-day management has a multiplicity of social responsibilities. Maximisation of profit is one of the objectives of management and to-day the more important than that is economic obligation and social obligations of management to varied groups, who are the architects of the institution.

The varied groups that might affect the functioning of the business organisation are share holders, workers, consumers and customers, creditors, suppliers, society and government. Thus, it is the responsibility of management to discharge its obligations to these varied groups, so that the organisation could have a well balanced development.

1. The real owners of the organisation are the share holders, who have contributed the initial capital expecting a fair return on their investment. It is management's responsibility to project the interests of share holders, who have taken risks and responsibility in promoting the industry. The management has to effectively and efficiently function and at the same time provide sufficient profits to the share holders, who have a direct participation in the management.

2. Workers have genuine interest in the organisation and they are the real back bone of the industry. They can make or mar the institution. The organisation's growth and future are in their hands. The management should satisfy them and protect their interests.

   By developing administrative process, the management should promote co-operative endeavour between employers and employees. They should adopt progressive labour policies, recognize trade union rights, provide opportunity for labour participation in management, co-partnership scheme and, if possible, profit sharing facilities, improve their living and working conditions, provide all possible financial reliefs and assistance etc.

3. The primary activity of any business unit is consumers and customers satisfaction and on whom the future of the organisation depends. "Once a customer is always a customer". The management should bear this in mind while producing commodities and fixing their price. To build up a customers and consumers clientale, the company should charge a fair and reasonable price; the supply of goods and services should be of uniform standard; the management should not indulge in unfair practices like hoarding, creating artificial scarcity, black marketing etc.; the advertisement should conform to public morals and culture etc. Thus, customer's and consumer's satisfaction happens to be the rock-bed of management objective. "Production is a means to consumption and consumption is the end of production". The management should bear this in mind in all its business activities.

4. The management should protect the interests of suppliers, who determine the functioning of the organisation. The suppliers provide materials, raw materials, machinery, science and technology, semi- finished products etc. to the management as required and it is management's responsibility to make prompt payments for such supplies.

5. The creditors supply funds for the purchase of science, technology, capital assets and even provide funds for revenue expenditure, if necessary, in times of need. "Finance is the back-bone of commerce". It is management's responsibility to honour such credits with prompt payment of interest on credits and make sufficient arrangements for repayment of funds (capital) borrowed.

6. Business management cannot think of its independent existence, without the government patronage, help and continued support. After all, the government is the parent business organisation managing the whole country. It is government that provides environment and infrastructure to the organisational work. The management has to reciprocate this patronage of government by law-abiding measures. It should pay all the legimate dues and taxes to the government honestly. It should not corrupt public servants and sabotage the democratic process. It should aid the government in times of need and provide correct statistical information and establish a parental relationship with the government.

7. Managers have a social obligation to the society as a whole. "Social equity and social justice" are the watch-words in a developing democratic set up. Organisations exist for the society and the social system creates an environment for organisational functioning. The management should adopt socially desirable standards of living and avoid wasteful expenditure. The gains from increased productivity should be equitably shared by workers, management, share holders and the society. The management can even adopt "one village" or 'one locality" and develop it in all directions. It can build schools, hospitals, townships, parks in its locality and thus provide amenities to the needy public. They should keep pollution at minimum level and contribute their share in the nation building activities.

Maintenance of integrity of business conduct, morale and character and the discharge of obligations to the society are the primary responsibilities of modern managements. Under no circumstances, the management should shrink from this responsibility and avoid performance.

CHAPTER - 19

MANAGEMENT BY OBJECTIVES

The subject of management by objectives (MBO) has gathered more momentum since one decade in view of speedy development and expansion in the field of management education. The MBO in view of its operational thrust and its vast application to reality and concrete practice has gained more appreciation and implications, while other contributions remained only on conceptual and theoretical aspects.

A. Though it is difficult to identify a particular person responsible for the innovation of this concept (this concept being evolutionary) the credit should go to Prof. Peter Drucker, who presented this concept in modern style. He observed that "objectives needed in every area where performance and results directly and vitally affect the survival and prosperity of business; and the performance that is expected of the manager must be derived from the performance goals of the business". If this goal is to be achieved the management by objectives is required. The G.E.C. of U.S.A. applied MBO in its re-organisation programme. Even Prof. Mc Gregor supported MBO in place of traits. Prof. Odiorne published a book on MBO which emphasised on management philosophy. To day MBO is a way of life to managements. MBO is also necessary for performance appraisal for integrating the individuals with the organisation (i.e. belongingness) and for long range planning objectives of the whole business. The manager's performance results are the ends, goals, targets or mission. Business performance requires that each job be directed towards the objectives, results have to be measured by the contribution he makes to the enterprise. The size of potential market, legal restrictions, competition etc. provide limitations in determining objectives.

The following areas require determination of objectives of performance namely ; innovation; market standing; physical and financial resources; profitability; manager performance and development; worker performance and attitude and public responsibility.

The main purpose of business is production and marketing of economic goods and services. The management should define the key areas in the enterprise, decide what needs to be measured and determine tools of measurement. The main objective of any management is to earn profits. In an enterprise where there are number of managers incharge of various departments, no one manager could be singled out as responsible for this profit. It is the collective responsibility of all the departmental heads involved right from the marketing manager to machine shop foreman. Thus, in the process of attaining the main objective, the different sub-goals are correlated and all these require clarity to avoid confusion and side tracking. If the objectives are not well defined and ambiguous, they may lead to confusion among the various departments leading to infrastructural wastages and inefficiency having an impact on profits.

B. The process of management by objectives

MBO is both a philosophy and technique of management and it is a process where supervisors and sub-ordinates jointly identify the common objevtives, determine the results to be achieved, evaluate the contribution of each individuals and integrate individual effort with the organisation efforts making the best use of all the potentialities available. MBO requires the key administrative personnel to contribute their maximum to achieve the objectives. It attempts to integrate and balance the goals of key personnel. It establishes a self-evaluating mechanism to measure the contribution of each individual. A participative management is a pre-requisite for MBO. The following steps are to be followed in the process of management by objectives;

The first step is the classification of objectives aimed at by the organisation. The top management has the responsibility to point out the objectives bearing in mind the dynamic nature of the environment. There could be any type of time stipulation and the objectives are preliminary in character subject to modification. While operational objectives are measurable, the strategic goals are not so.

The individuals are contributory factors in achieving the organisational objectives, and every individual should know in advance what is expected of him. The superior can set his sub-ordinates' objectives with their consultation and agreement in the light of preliminary objectives and resource availability. Such a step would create confidence in the sub ordinates. Any manager at any level requires capital, material, human resources to accomplish goals.

By relating these to the goals themselves, the superiors are better able to see the need and economies of allocating them. The allocation of resources and their direction should be done with the knowledge of subordinates. The goals and the resources availability should have a relationship. There is no meaning in fixing objectives without reference to potentialities available.

Goal setting is not only a job process but also one of interaction which requires recycling since sub ordinates are involved in determining the goals. In recycling, sub ordinates at every level are involved and influence the recycling process. Since self commitment of individuals / sub ordinates is there, the completion of target is always possible. Prof.Ordiore states that " the power of commitment is what makes MBO work and the absence of such commitment can cause it to fail". Thus, it can be said that setting of objectives is joint venture-superiors and sub-ordinates, the result of interaction and recycling of ideas. People involved have a better understanding of their target and their role in the performance of the organisation.

Appraisal is the last step in MBO. The objectives should clearly define the vital signs of an organisation, which should help in measuring the achievements. In an MBO management system, performance review must be directly related to goals and result statements. MBO has enkindled the interest of managers through out the world in the field of business organisation.

It has many benefits. It helps in the better management of organisation. Each organisation stands for certain specific objectives and management has to direct its efforts in attaining those objectives. A result- oriented planning is absolutely necessary. Objectives have the capacity of inquiry and introspection. They provide standard of control and an yard-stick for measurement. MBO helps in identifying the key result areas in the organisation, which help both the employers and the employees. It helps in clarifying the roles and structure of organisation and removes deficiencies. MBO emphasises on "Commitment performance" and thereby provides psychological satisfaction to the sub ordinates. Of late, more organisations are moving towards appraising by objectives and results rather than traits.

C. Limitations of MBO

Like any other system, the MBO also suffers from certain limitations and weakness, which are found in the system itself, others are due to defective application. Thougly the system is simple and easy to practice, the managers, who have to implement, are found wanting in the entire understanding of the system. They feel that MBO is merely another management exercise for controlling the behaviour of sub ordinates. The managers should have a sound knowledge of planning and control. Due to communication gap and understanding, and want of corporate knowledge, the system has not deeply penetrated in to the organisational structure.

Most of the objectives are set for short time periods and more emphasis is laid on current objectives, where as the managers are expected to have a long period expectations and trends. Quantitative goals may be given priority over qualitative aspects. In the absence of support by planning, organising, directing and control, MBO may not achieve its goals. Some times MBO presents the danger of inflexibility in the organisation. In a dynamic society, a particular goal may not hold good.

D. Conclusion:

In spite of these weaknesses, the MBO has grown in-popularity recently due to its remarkable potentialities in managing an enterprise effectively. U.S.A is a pioneering country in the application of this concepts. The industrially developed countries like Britain, France, U.S.A, japan and Germany have given impetus to the development of this concept as a system. Prof.Drucker says that "objectives are needed in every area where performance and results directly and vitally affect the survival and prosperity of the business". Prof.Mc.Gregor made a strong plea for appraising on the basis of objectives. Mr Edward Schleh emphasised that objectives should be set for all personnel including foreman, salesman, accountants, industrial engineers and chemists. With the development of professional managers, the business community and organisation are feeling the need for "Scientific management", for the success and prosperity of the business. For developing nations managements by objectives is a boon and seems to have no alternative.

CHAPTER - 20

MANAGEMENT THEORY JUNGLE

In recent years, management developed a number of approach to its study. Their variety and the large number of persons, particularly from universities, who espouse them have resulted in much confusion to what management is, what management theories are, and how management should be studied. "Virtually, in management theory, a jungle is created".

1. DIFFERENT APPROACHES TO MANAGEMENT

The various approaches to management may be grouped as here under :-

i) The operational approach (management process)

ii) The human behaviour approach

iii) The empirical or case approach

iv) The social system approach

v) The decision system approach

vi) The communications centre approach

vii) The mathematical approach

i) Operational Approach:

It attempts to relate the management knowledge to the managerial task. Management as a universally applicable body of knowledge with principles and theory applicable to all types and levels of enterprise. This approach is propounded by Henry Fayol.

The following are the fundamental beliefs of the approach:

1. Managing is an operational process.
2. Long experience can be the ground for basic truths or principles.
3. These principles could become focal points for useful research,
4. Can furnish elements of useful theory of management.
5. Managing is an art.
6. Management principles are none the less true.

ii) The Empirical Approach :-

"The empirical approach analyses management by a study of experience to draw generalisations, but usually as a means of transferring knowledge to the student".

iii) The Human Behaviour Approach :-

Emphasises study of human beings in the concern but centred on interpersonal relations. This school brings to bear "existing and newly developed theories, methods, and techniques of the relevent social services upon the study of inter and interpersonal phenomena". This approach focuses on the individual and his motivations as a socio-psychological being.

iv) The social system approach :-

It is closely related to human behaviour approach. It recognizes enterprise as a social organisation. It describes the cultural relationship of various social groups and attempts to integrate them in to a system".

v) The Decision Theory Approach :-

It concentrates on rational decision - the selection, from among possible alternatives of a course of action". It is apparently an outgrowth of the theory of consumer's choice. It has arisen out of such economic cosiderations as utility maximisation, indifference curves, marginal utility and economic behaviours under risks and undertainties.

vi) The Communication Centre Approach :

It considers manager as a communications centre and building knowledge of managing around this concept. In this, manager's role is seen as that of receiving information, storing and processing it, and determining it. It emphasises the role of communication in managing as well as the central importance of decision making.

Since the time of Fayol and Taylor, a universally applicable theory of management has been developing at an increasing rate. the following are the main contributions :-

1. Public Administrators
2. Business Mangers
3. Behaviouralists
4. Social Scientists.

2. Result-Oriented Concepts :

The well known American management consultant, Mr. Raymond C. Lexon, in his popular book captioned 'More by doing less', has outlined seven concepts for getting results through people; and they are

i. Management by communication.

ii. Management by system ;

iii. Management by results ;

iv. Management by exception ;

v. Management by motivation ;

vi. Management by objective and

vii. Management by participation.

i) Management by communication :

It has been estimated roughly that a manager spends 90% of his official time in communicating, either receiving or sending information. The importance of communication lies in the fact that it is a continuous process and is not a one-way traffic. "Only with good communication can misunderstandings be ironed out, long-term plans achieved and the various activities co- ordinated and controlled". The success of a manager depends largely on the success and the effectiveness of his communication with the sub-ordinates and superiors.

ii. Management by system :

It is a philosophy of management or an approach to management problems whereby experimentation and analysis displace the blind acceptance of things, traditional and conventional.

iii. Management by Results :

"The thesis of this concept is that management in industry deals broadly with control, that is with getting the work done through co-ordinating the co- operative efforts of people who have been properly organised into working groups for the accomplishment of specified purposes". The improvement can be evaluated by only comparison. This comparison is made by putting side by side, earlier and later records expressed in the same terms and identical units.

iv & v. Management by Exception and Motivation :

It relates to the creation of will or linking to work. The experts like Urwick and Breach emphasised the importance of motivation.

Man is a complex factor of production which can be best utilised only when he is motivated. Hence, this thesis centres around motivational factors.

vi. Management by objectives (MBO)

This new approach is based on quantitative, measurable goals that are often set jointly by superiors and subordinates. It is also based on the principle of management that gives full scope to individual strength and responsibility. And at the same it also provides common direction of vision and effort, establish team work and harmonise the goals of individual with the common weal. "It makes the common weal the aim of every manager". It motivates the manager to go for timely action because the goals and objectives of his task demand it.

One of the major functions of MBO is to review and rewrite the company's job descriptions for managers as they must show precisely that objectives can be allocated to each executive.

MBO is also considered as one of the very successful rating methods of performance appraisal. Instead of requiring the superior to rate his subordinates, under this approach each time subordinate is requested to establish for himself, short-term performance goals or targets, ways in which he can improve his own efficiency against standards that he has set for himself.

It is a result-oriented performance appraisal technique.

vii. Participative management

One of the pioneers in developing means of measuring human variables is Ranis Lakert. His research as a Director at the institute for social research at the university of Michigan indicated that the best managerial producers :-

1) are supportive in that they lend support to those reporting to them ;

2) facilitate people's work with the necessary tools, training, inside or outside help, and other things necessary to assure that assigned task will be accomplished;

3) encourage interaction, talk, and mutual help among all members of the work group;

4) expect high performance standards.

The above type of Likert designed management is called as "system 4" or participative management.

Prof. Likert stresses the importance of improvement in goal performance and also in satisfaction of subordinates.

Participative management indirectly touches the human psychology. The priorities of the worker is studied as that of a human being but applied to the human being working as a main factor of production.

On the whole, under this approach, employees are treated not as a hostile group or exploiters but as indispensable part of themselves (employers). Under participative management, the board of decision-makers includes the representatives of :

1) Investors
2) Workers
3) Consumers
4) Government and
5) Management.

CHAPTER - 21

MAIN CONTRIBUTORS TO MODERN MANAGEMENT THOUGHT & TRENDS IN MANAGEMENT PRACTICES.

1. Introduction

Skill seperate from technical knowledge and experience is remarkably close to current understanding of the function of management.

In the early times some of the principles of management were effectively used by the Roman Churches. The military organisations have also contributed immensely towards the development of management thought. A number of principles of management have been adopted from the working of military organisations. It is recorded of Napolean, that he never gave an order without explaining its purpose, and making sure that this purpose was understood. He knew that blind obedience could never ensure the intelligent execution of any order.

A large number of scholars in recent years have contributed to the development of modern management thought.

2. Charles Babbage (1792-1871)

He was born in 1792 and graduated from Cambridge in 1814. Babbage was a profilic writer. His most important contributions are :-

1) Benefits of division of labour :-

Babbage explained the benefits that can be obtained from division of labour and intelligent organisation of workers.

2) Use of science and mathematics :-

He was perhaps the first to perceive that the methods of science and mathematics could be applied to the operation of factories.

3) Emphasis on cost of production :-

He advocated that each employer should make determined effort to reduce costs by :-

i) the discovery of improved methods ;

ii) the knowledge of the precise expense of every process ;

iii) the knowledge of which process offer the greatest possibility of cost reduction through study.

4) Babbage is credited with anticipating the mechanism of time and motion study for scientific management practices.

5) His most significant contribution was the building up of "Difference Machine" which he hoped would make it possible to extend tables of interest or insurance premiums or tables of tidal ebb and floods indefinitely and automatically.

Babbage worked for an automatic recording device.

Babbage is regarded as one of the foremost early british thinkers on management. It has been mentioned that Babbage was a pioneer in operations research. It is surprising to note that most of the American writers have not even mentioned his name, even casually in their standard works.

3. F.W.TAYLOR(1856-1915)

Taylor was born in 1856 in a middle class family in Philadelphia. He joined Midvale Steel Works in 1878 and became ultimately its chief engineer.

The basic philosophy of Taylor's " Scientific Management" was that there was a need for a fundamental change of attitude on the part of both managers and men. Taylor wanted that management should take the responsibility of planning, directing and organising work. Taylor stated that the best management rests on the foundation of high wages and low costs. Taylor introduced the concept of functional foremanship. The importance of Taylor's work can be assessed from the fact that even Lenin of Russia considered it of immence benefit. Lenin wrote in PRAVDA-"We should try out every scientific and progressive suggestion of Taylor system. There is need for introduction in Russia the teaching of the Taylor system".

4. HENRY FAYOL

If Taylor is to be regarded a the "Father of Scientific Management", it would be fair and just to call Henry Fayol the "Father of Principles of Management".

Fayol was born in 1841 in a french bourgeois. At 19 he graduated as a Mining Engineer. From 1888 to 1918 he worked as a Chief Executive of a coal and steel combine. When he took charge of this combine, it was on the verge of bankruptcy.

At the time of his retirement the concern was financially most sound. This tremendous success is regarded as " one of the romances of "French industrial history".

Fayol concentrated on the " Top Management " and worked downwards. He was more concerned with overall control than with mere supervision.

Fayol divided all activities of industrial undertakings into six groups-

i) Production ii) commercial
iii) financial iv) Security
v) Accounting vi) Managerial.

Fayol summarised the qualities required by persons of various undertakings as under-

i) Physical ii) Mental
iii) Moral iv) general Education
v) Special Knowledge vi) Experience

Fayol pointed out certain basic principles of management. The most well known principles are- Division of labour; Authority and responsibility; discipline, unity of command; unity of direction; subordination of individual interest to general interest; centralisation; scalar chain; order; equality; initiative; stability of tenure of personnel, and esprit-de-corps.

Fayol divided Management functions into-

1) Planning, 2) Organisation;
3) Command; 4) Co- ordination; and
5) Control.

He considered planning as the most important and difficult Managerial function.

Thus, Henry Fayol made a pioneering contribution to management thought.

5. HENRY.L.GANTT

Considerable tributes have been paid by Management writers to GANTT, for his contribution to management thought. His "wage incentive plan" has been regarded as an improvement on Taylor's "piece-rate system." His Task and bonus system of wage payment has been considered as most satisfactory among differential wage systems of reducing labour costs. Gantt also made a substantial contribution to management planning and control. Gantt has a much clearer understanding of the place of trade unions in an industrial society and tried to co-operate with them rather than oppose them.

6. FRANK BUNKER GILBERTH

Gilberth's most significant contribution in the field of management was to "develop management as a social science with the human being the centre of interest". He was the first to apply the motion picture camera to the recording and analysing of operations, the first to classify the elements of human motions. He devised methods to show up wasteful and unproductive movements. He used flow-process charts which break up work done into five basic elements : operations, Transportation, Inspection, Storage and Delivery.

Gilberth's work and achievements were outstanding. The main theme of his work was that there is a best way to do a job and this should be searched for, and discovered and implemented. This philosophy is sound and widely accepted by management.

7. MARY PARKET FOLLET(1868-1933)

Mary Parket follet was born in Boston in 1868. She was educated at Radcliffcollege, Massachusetts U.S.A. By about 1920 she gained wide recognition as a political philosopher.

Mary Parket Follet has been praised for her practical observations about the value of human relations for the basic principles of organisation. She contended that the final authority vested in the chief Executive should be replaced by an authority of function in which each individual has final authority for his own allotted task. She felt that service should become the dominant motive in management. To Follet, the secret of leadership was the art of thinking ahead. Follet felt that leadership is not a matter of dominating personality and therefore, leaders should not be autocratic.

To Mary Follet the whole concept of final authority at the apex of the hierarchy appeared to be an illusion. She showed that authority in terms of subordination of one man to another offered human emotions and can not be the foundation of good industrial organisation. She wrote-"Authority belongs to the job and stays with the job".

Metcalf and Urwick have paid tributes to her work by pointing out that she was a political and business philosopher of the first rank.

8. GEORGE ELTON MAYO

Mayo was born in Australia in 1880, and was educated at St.Peter's college, Adelaide. In 1926 he became professor of Industrial Research at Harvard Business school.

The main contribution of Elton Mayo can be stated as under:-

1. Human Relations Approach:-

His studies at the Western Electric company at Hawthorne plant has revealed the importance of human and social factors in industrial relationship.

2. Non-Economic Awards:-

His experiments at Hawthorne showed that non-economic incentives are sometimes more important in determining the attitude of workers towards their work and management. To workers, the sense of participation, belongingness, morale, security and recognition are sometimes more important than pure economic incentives or better environment.

3. Personal Counseling:-

Studies conducted at Hawthorne stressed the value in the talking out process in alleviating personal stress and preoccupation, and in bringing about co operative relation with in work groups.

4. Informal Group:-

A major contribution was to show that the factory was a social system and that informal groupings in the work situation vitally affected human behaviour and provided an effective channel of communication and a means of direction.

5. Teaching and practice of Management:-

These experiment provided course material and a focus for research to many Industrial Relations Departments in major colleges and universities during the past quarter of a century.

To conclude-Hawthorne experiments made by Elton Mayo indicated that major productivity gains might be achieved through and improved understanding of the human factor in organisation.

9. L.R.URWICK

As English consultant and educator, Urwick is recognised as an outstanding authority in the field of management. Urwick has been a prolific writer on organisation and on management subjects. Urwick is regarded as a leading exponent of the traditional classical approach. He formulated a set of rules known as principles of administration. Urwick made it clear that in an organisation rationality should take precedence over personality.

To solve the problem of relationship between line and staff, Urwick made a distinction between staff specialist and the general staff. The main function of the staff specialists consists of planning, thinking and advising, while the general staff are expected to lighten the burden of the Chief Executive by assisting in the details of command, control and co ordination,

Most of the principles formulated by Urwick deal with the formal structure of organisation. He gave much attention to the "Delegation Principles", and states that the "lack of the courages to delegate properly and of knowledge of how to do it is one of the most general causes of failure in an organisation". He maintains that at all levels authority and responsibility must be coterminus, co-equal and defined. He also warns against the use of committees for purposes of administration.

Though Urwick relied heavily on earlier writers, it would be uncharitable to say that his contribution in the field of management was not significant.

10. H.A.SIMON

Simon is an American political and social scientist. Simon criticised the principles of management formulated by writer such as Urwick and others. He rediculed their principles as "homely proverbs", "myths", "slogans".

Simon is the principal exponent of the "decision making approach". To him, management means decision making. He envisages three stages in decision-making activity-

1) The intelligence activity,
2) Design Activity
3) Choice Activity

Simon criticises those whose theories are based on the assumption that man is completely rational. He maintains that man has only"bounded rationality". In view of this relation, managers do not insist upon "optional solutions" but are satisfied with good enough solution. Simon also makes a clear distinction between programmed and unprogrammed decisions. Simon pays considerable attention to the problem of communication in an organisation system.

The essence of simon's concept is that Managers should efficiently utilise all forms of external influence for manipulating the personality of an employee, for changing him in such a way that he will act as desired "by his own motivation rather than by the stimulus of moment-by-moment instructions".

11 RENIS LIKERT

Likert is a leadingsocial psychologist. Likert has developed a number of group-related theories. After extensive research he concluded that "employee-centred" rather than "Job centered" superivision is necessary for higher productivity. He discovered that general, rather than close supervision tended to be associated with high productivity.

His research findings show that firms which adopted "truly participative form of Management having complete confidence and trust in sub-ordinates"-showed high productivity, lowscrap loss, low costs, and excellent labour relations.

12. PETER F. DRUCKER

Drucker was born in Vienna in 1909. He was educated in Austria and England. he was, for sometime, an economist for the International Bank. He become professor of Management in the New York University in 1950. He is widely known for his writings on Management.

Drucker introduced the concept of "Management by objectives" (M.B.O.) and viewed performance as the ultimate test of management. He maintains that management can never be an exact science or a profession. The concept of scientific management of human relations approach has been sharply criticised by Drucker. According to Drucker, the basic purpose of a business is to create a customer.

13. CHARIS ARGYRIS

C.Agryris is a social scientist and prof. of Industrial administration at Yale University.

The basic contention of Argyris is that formal organisation requires " behaviour that ends to frustrate, place in conflict and create failure for psychologically healthy individuals. A large majority of the people in modern organisations are created as immature human beings in their working environment, and are encouraged to be passive, dependent and sub ordinate. In such organisations creativity, innovation, involvement and human dignity is sacrificed.

Argyris finds three main mechanisms through which organisations frustrate mature employees and encourage immature ones to stay that way. They are ; formal organisation structure, directive leadership and managerial controls such as budgets, incentives systems and time and motion studies. Argyris suggests that the employee must be provided with more " power' over his own work environment and therefore must be given responsibility, authority, and increased control over the decision making that affects his immediate work environment. He must become self-responsible.

Argyris feels that what is needed is a philosophy of management that views the individual and organisation not only as inter related but actually inter penetrating one another.

MODERN TRENDS IN MANAGEMENT PRACTICES

Summarisation- (Points at a glance)

1. Today business and industry are more concerned with innovation than they were in the early part of the fifties of the twentieth century. With the advent and impact of the forces of economic dynamism, change in every field of economic activity has become evident and essential. Today growth depends on change and adoption of new techniques and methodology. Products trends and developments have necessiated the companies to employ creative scientist and engineers. Today managers have to spend more of their time representing their companies to out-side agencies and individuals like government officials, labour unions, financial interest, customers, suppliers and group

organisations etc., to impress upon them their products and prices. They should possess public relations techniques. In recent years, companies have evinced more interest in the whole process of decision making among their executives.

2. Large-scale industrial development and high standard of living have brought benefits of industrialisation to many parts of the world.

3. The concepts of operation research and scientific management techniques enable management to optimize by allocating scarce resources in the most profitable way. Forecasting techniques and quicker information through computerisation have contributed for substantial development in the work-process. Automation has made possible greater output with lesser man-hours of labour, of course not creating any unemployment.

4. Tomorrows manager will have to be more knowledgeable in many areas. He should have enough knowledge of technology and social sciences to evaluate the advice of his experts. He must have knowledge of social trends of his own country and the outside world.

5. Managerial practices differ from country to country depending upon the socio-economic environment and which vary from country to country. Multinational corporations have sprung up with different orientations. Though managements perform same functions in all the countries -planning, organisation, staffing, co-ordination, leadership-motivation, direction, co-ordination, control, innovation and representation- the practices adopted are different.

6. Business is a privilege, not a right, granted by society and this privilege could continue only till it serves social needs

and society. Besides economic performance (profitability) the modern business must demonstrate social awareness, sensitivity and responsiveness as well as social performance. A socially responsible management should respond to the needs and desires of customers, employees, suppliers, shareholders, bankers, government and the general public, Excess profittering, un-fair trade practices, environmental pollution etc., are destructive activities not palatable to the society and also to the firm in the long run.

7. The pressure of organised labour; recognition of human dignity and element; growing public opinion; increasing participation of labour in decision making process; the threat of natioalisation; the development of consumerism; the managerial revolution; democratic management etc., are some of the salient factors to be recognised by modern management; and toning down the pure economic objective of profit maximisation.

8. Management in a social system has to discharge certain obligations to the society. It has to canalise the infrastructure namely- men, material, money, machinery and marketing and utilise them to their optimum point through an optimum combination; achieve the pre-determined objectives by motivating the personnel through incentives and inducements; satisfy the consumers needs by producing quality-goods at reasonable cost; maintain a balance between the flow of income in order to achieve economic stability and integrity and to prevent the recurrence of business recession, inflationary or deflationery trends harmful to the society etc.

9. Work is a way of life, it gives him dignity, status and recognition in society besides providing mental happiness and physical development. Thus, the need for opportunity to develop his personality, skill and knowledge and satisfaction in his work.

Management should try to achieve the goals set for its own development and success, namely,- to produce goods to the satisfaction of consumer needs; provide ample opportunities for employment and income generation; earning reasonable profits for its own survival and to the satisfaction of share holders and make provisions for employees satisfaction by boosting morale.

10. Modern managements have to face certain serious challenges in the productive process. They are -

    a) Authorative and dominant labour organisations affiliated to different political parties and ideologies;

    b) Ever challenging competitions waiting opportunity to weed out the weak and the meak organisations through fair or foul means;

    c) Pre-dominant, disgruntled and critical public always aiming at better standards and quality;

    d) the forces of challenging consumerism (consumer assistance and resistance) demanding the best quality goods at the lowest price; and

    e) The continued governmental constraints and restraints working as bottlenecks to industrial organisation, expansion and developments. Thus, the modern managements have to promote and safeguard the interests of share holders, the employees, the customers, the society and the government.

11. The national and inter national economic environments are changing so fast today, that managements have to adjust and accommodate to the changing economic scenario, otherwise they are " a fish out of water".

A BIRDS VIEW OF MANAGEMENT FUNCTIONS

A) Planning to deal with:

a) Forecasting

b) Determination of objectives

c) Application of strategies

d) Defining policies, procedures and programmes.

e) Fixing schedules.

f) framing of rules and regulations.

g) Accurate and reliable budgets with reference to total firm and each department.

h) Methodology for implementation.

B) Organisation:

a) Determining job requirements.

b) Grouping of jobs to suit

1) Individuals
2) Sections
3) Departments
4) Divisions

c) Delegation of authority to different levels of managers.

d) Defining and fixing powers and responsibility.

e) Providing communication system to help decision making, co-ordination and effective control.

	f) To prepare the organisation to meet the challenges of changing environment.
C) Directing, Staffing, Motivating & Communication Leadership:	a) recruitment, coaching and training, counseling, promotion, evaluation of performance of employees (personnel).
	b) Direction and supervision.
	c) Fixation of renumeration perks, fringes benefits compensation etc.
	d) Participation, motivation incentives, protection, safeguards, employee morale etc.
	e) communication-both formal and informal communication.
	f) Co-ordination and leadership.
	g) Management Development.
D) Controlling:	a) Fixing performance standards.
	b) Appraisal against standards fixed.
	c) Control through return on investments-capital-output ratio.

e) Measuring deviations from pre-determined standards and goals.

f) Corrective measures against feed back.

E) innovation and representation:

a) Introduction of modern techniques into the productive process.

b) Automation and computeris-ation for quick communication and results.

c) Benefits to personnel (work force) through representation-democratic management and participative investment-profit-sharing-co-partnership (Industrial Democracy).

CHAPTER - 22

MISCELLANEOUS CONCEPTS RELEVANT TO THE SUBJECT.

A. INDIFFERENCE CURVE ANALYSIS:

1. Meaning

Prof. Edgeworth, Pareto and Slutsky originally developed this theory, but subsequently refined and popularised by Profs.J.R. Hicks and Allen. The marginal utility analysis is defective in respect of-

a) It tries to measure utility in quantitative terms;
b) It makes utility additive and;
c) It assumes that the marginal utility of money to be constant.

In this approach, the cardinal measurement of utility has been discarded on the basis of scale of preference and the ordinal method of preference has been accepted.

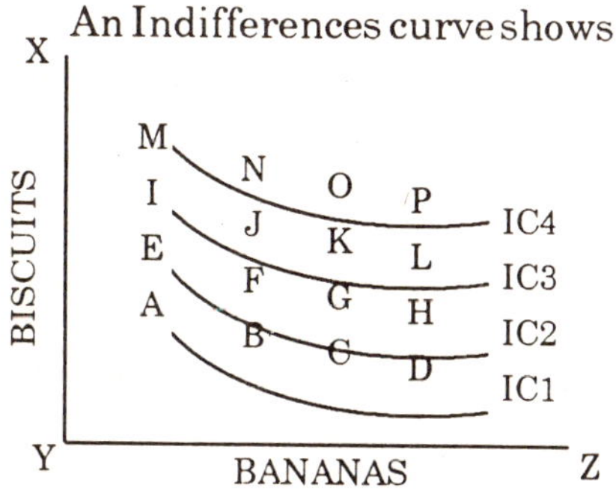

An Indifferences curve shows different combinations of two commodities, which give the consumers an equal satisfaction. This curve is drawn on the basis of the "indifference schedule" which is a statement of various combinations of two goods that will be equally acceptable to the consumers. That is to say the consumers is indifferent to various combinations as they give him same and equal satisfaction.

An indifference map represents a collection of many indifference curves where each curve represents a certain level of satisfaction. The higher indifference curve shows a higher level of satisfaction and the lower indifference curve shows a lower level of satisfaction. The different indifference curves in the indifference map will be named 1,2,3,4 etc., in an ascending order. Prof. Stonier and Prof. Hague observe that "an indifference curve is a contour line on map which shows all places of the same height above sea level. Instead of representing height, each indifference curve represents a level of satisfaction. The total satisfaction of utility derived from any of these combinations on an indifference curve remains constant".

2. ASSUMPTIONS

a) Assumes that the consumer has complete information about the economic environment (ie., about prices and markets).

b) The consumer behaves rationally to maximise his satisfaction with the given income.

c) That the consumers are capable of ranking all combinations of goods according to the satisfaction they yield.

d) That the consumer is interested in a combination of goods and capable of comparing satisfaction of different combinations.

e) That his scale of preferences will remain constant.

f) That the consumer has a fixed amount of money to spend on two goods completely; and

g) That the prices of these goods are given in the market and are assumed to be constant.

3. MARGINAL RATE OF SUBSTITUTION

Every indifference curve represents one satisfaction. All points in the same indifference curve represent equal satisfaction, because one commodity is substituted for another commodity, while the consumer moves down on an indifference curve. The loss in 'Y' commodity is counter balanced by gain in 'X' commodity. This is called marginal rate of substitution. This concept is an important tool of indifference curve analysis. The Marginal Rate Of substitution may be defined as the rate at which an individual will exchange successive units of one commodity for another, so that his level of satisfaction remains the same. As the consumer travels down on the indifference curve, he reduces the rate of substitution, and this is called Diminishing Marginal Rate of Substitution.

Indifference Schedule With Rate of Substitution

Combination	Bananas	Biscuits	Rate of Substitution
1	1	20	—
2	2	15	1.5
3	3	12	1.3
4	4	10	1.2
5	5	9	1.1

In the figure given below, the rate of substitution is shown between points ABCDE by means of vertical lines denoting Y commodity (Biscuits) and the horizontal line indicating X commodity (Bananas). The length of Vertical line is decreasing showing thereby that the Marginal Rate Of Substitution is diminishing. The principle of diminishing Marginal Rate Of Substitution can be explained as follows:

a) One commodity will have to be decreased while the other is increased, if the consumer has to have the same satisfaction.

b) The commodity which is increased has lower marginal significance and therefore, cannot substitute for the same amount of the other commodity, but only for less and less of the other; the rate of substitution will have to decline.

c) The commodity which is decreased has higher marginal significance and, therefore, cannot be substituted in the same ratio by the other commodity, the rate of substitution will have to decline again.

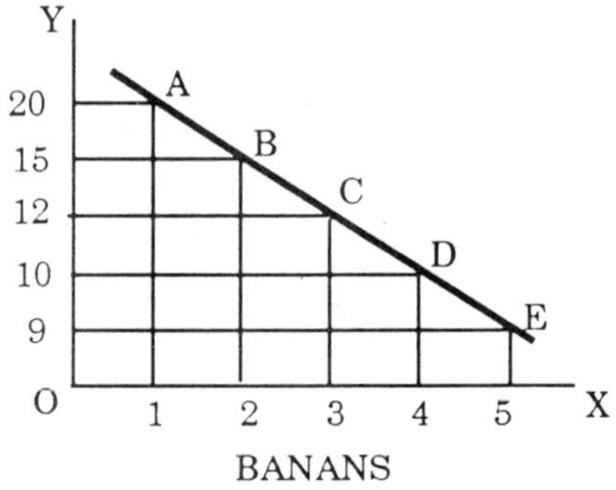

It is because of this principle of diminishing marginal rate of substitution that the indifference curve slopes downwards from left to right, rather steeply in the beginning, but later at a lower rate and finally it will tend to be almost horizontal that is the indifference curve will be convex.

4. PROPERTIES OF INDIFFERENCE CURVES

There are three important properties of indifference curve analysis.

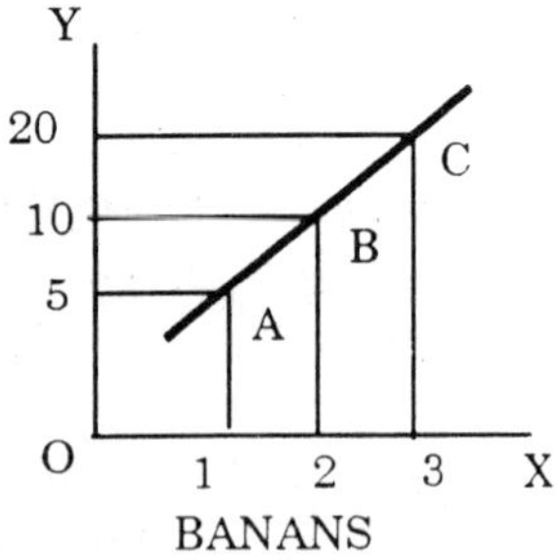

a) The indifference Curve always slope downwards from left to right. This is based on the assumption that different combinations of two goods will give the consumer the same amount of satisfaction. If one commodity is added, the other commodity will have to be decreased. An upward sloping difference curve is impossible and absurd.

A. 1 Banana + 5 biscuits
B. 2 bananas + 10 biscuits
C. 3 Bananas + 20 Biscuits

It is clear from this diagram that all these combinations of bananas and biscuits cannot give the same satisfaction, because the 2nd combination gives the consumer greater satisfaction than the first as it has more of both goods and so on. Since we assume that indifference curves represent only one satisfaction, it cannot slope upwards, nor it can be horizontal.

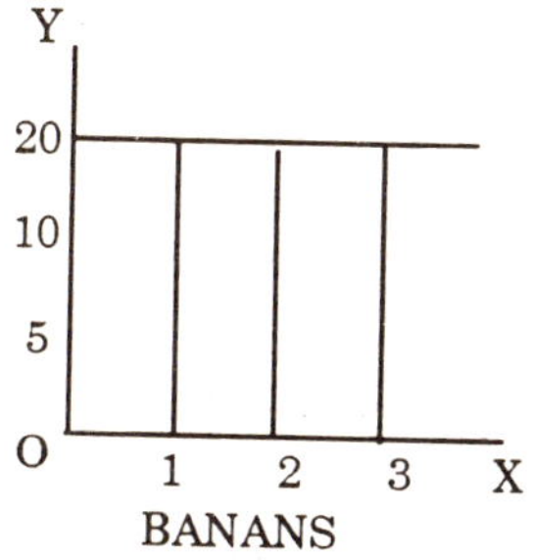

All these combinations of bananas and biscuits are said to represent the same satisfaction. This is also absurd. If indifference curves cannot slope upwards or horizontal, the only possibility is, it can slope downwards from left to right.

b) Indifference curves are convex to the point of origin to the two axis. The left hand portion is normally relatively horizontal. This concept is based on the assumption of diminishing marginal rate of substitution.

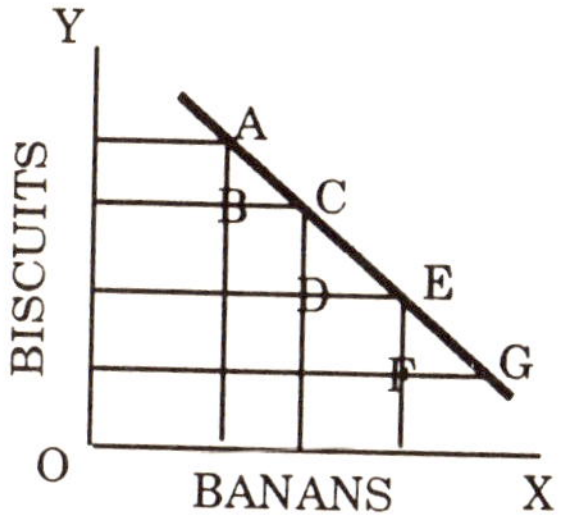

Here the indifference curve is convex to the point of origin to the two axes OY and OX.

BC Bananas substitutes AB Biscuits

DE Bananas substitutes CD Biscuits

FG Bananas substitutes EF Biscuits.

It may be noted here that BC=DE=FG. But AB>CD and CD>EF. This shows that the rate of substitution of bananas for biscuits is diminished and this is responsible for the convexity of indifference curves.

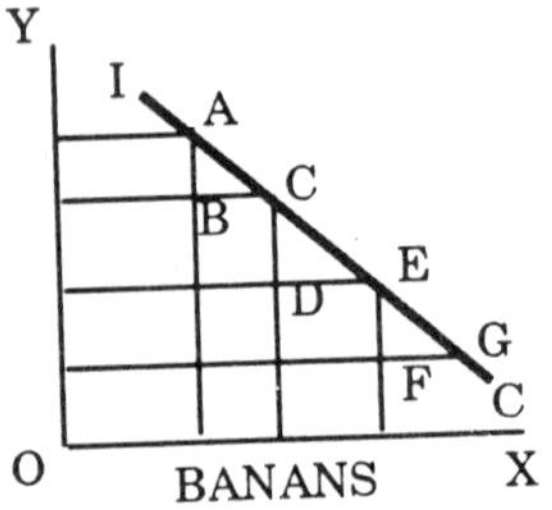

It is easy to prove that an indifference curve cannot be concave.

Here, where the IC is concave,

BC Bananas substitutes AB biscuits

DE Bananas substitutes CD biscuits

FG Bananas substitutes OAF buiscuits

The only possibility is, it can slope downwards from left to right.

While BC=DE=FG; AB <and CD<EF. The concave indifference curve is based on the assumptions that the same amount of X commodity will substitute for an increasing amount of Y commodity, and this concave indifference curves possible only under the assumption of, -

1) That marginal utility of a commodity will increase, when the consumer has more units of it, and secondly,

2) That marginal utility will decrease when a consumer has less unit of it. These two assumptions are totally wrong and against facts of human behaviour. Thus concave indifference curve is impossible.

In the absence of a curve, it could be a straight line curve or a right angle curve, as below;

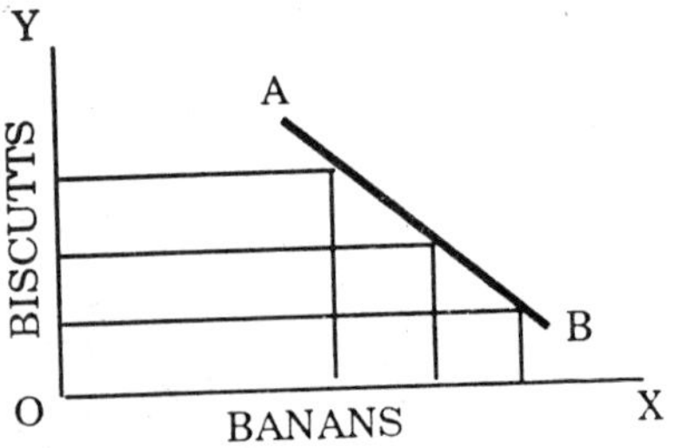

STRAIGHT LINE CURVE

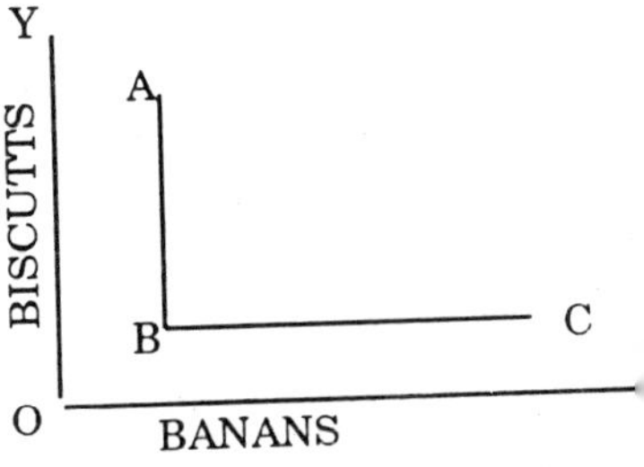

RIGHT ANGLE CURVE

If it is a straight line, it implies that both the commodities are perfect substitutes, and if they are perfect substitutes, they could be considered as one commodity. If it is a right angle, they are perfectly complementary goods, and it is difficult to come across complementary goods. So, it could be only convex to the origin.

c) Two indifference curves never intersect each other.

This property is based on the assumption that each indifference curve represents one utility and that different indifference curves represent different utilities. One satisfaction may be higher or lower than the other, but cannot be higher and lower, as well as equal to the other, at the same time.

Suppose two indifference curves cut each other at K. This means points K and T, which are on the same IC2 show equal satisfaction. Similarly points K and S, which are on the same curve,

IC1 shows equal satisfaction.

Thus, K=T

K=S

∴ S=T.

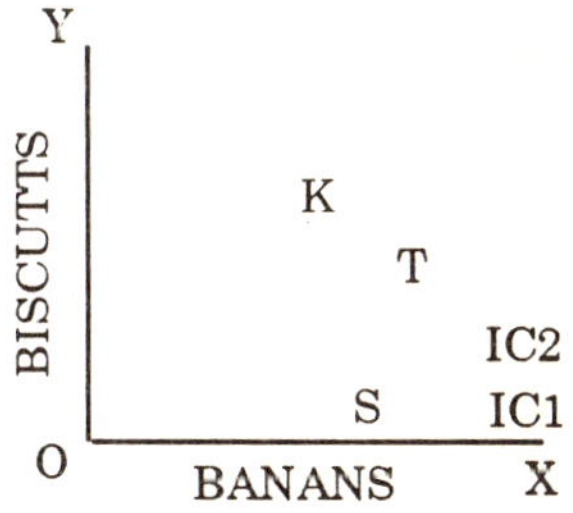

Since K is common to both the curves, points S and T show equal satisfaction. But this is contrary to our assumption, that points on a higher indifference curve shows greater satisfaction than points on a lower indifference curve. Therefore, two indifference curves cannot intersect each other. Thus, all the three properties of indifference curves are proved to be valid.

5. Consumer's Equilibrium

This represents the point on the indifference curve, which the consumer considers most advantageous to him and there will be no tendency on his part to move either way. The different points on the indifference curve show different combinations of two goods, which are equally welcome to the consumer. But which combination he choses depends on the prices of two commodities and resources at his disposal. This has given rise to the concept of Price Line or Budget Line in indifference analysis. This line indicates all possible combinations for the consumer to buy with given income and the prices of two commodities. The combination beyond this line cannot be reached by the consumer. Whenever there is change in price or income, this budget or price line will change. The consumer will come to equilibrium when the price line is tangential to a particular indifference curve. Only at the point of tangency, the consumer will be at the highest indifference curve. If he moves on either way, he has to come down to a lower indifference curve and thereby losses his higher satisfaction derived by being in a indifference curve.

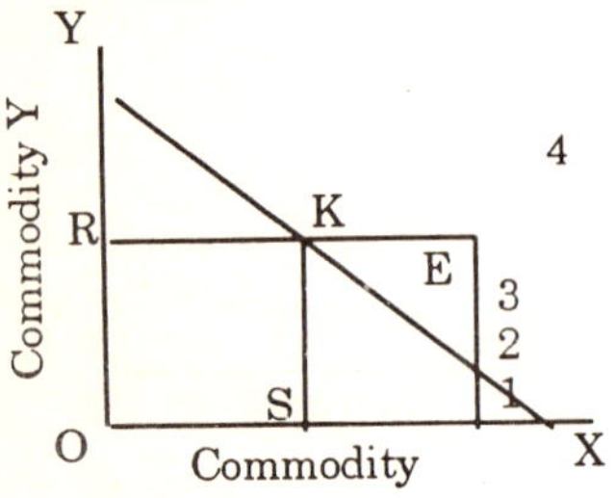

With given prices and income, the consumer can move up and down on the price line. He cannot go behind the price line. The position K is the most advantageous one, because only at that point the consumer can be in curve number 3 and attain maximum satisfaction. If he moves on either side, he has to come to a lower indifference curve number 2 or 1. He cannot reach curve number 4. So point K is equilibrium point. At this point, the consumer will have OR units of 'y' commodity and OS units of 'X' commodity.

For a consumer to be in equilibrium, the two conditions detailed below are to be fulfilled. The budget line should be tangent to the indifference curve and secondly the indifference curve should be convex to the OX axis or to the origin point O to imply that the marginal rate of substitution is diminishing.

THE INCOME EFFECT

This may be defined as the effect on the purchases of the consumer caused by changes in income with prices of goods remaining constant. An increase in income shifts the equilibrium position of the consumer to a higher indifference curve and vice versa. By joining the various equilibrium points, we get income consumption curve, which indicates that the larger the income the larger will be the purchases of X and Y commodities.

THE SUBSTITUTION EFFECT

This means the change in the purchases of a commodity as a result of a change in relative prices above, while the income of the consumer remains constant. Substitution leads to extension in demand when the price falls and to a contraction in demand when the price rises.

THE PRICE EFFECT

This means the change in the quantity due to a change in the price of a commodity. The price is the combination of income effect and substitution effect.

The price effect=income effect+substitution effect

The several effects could be classified as follows :

Types of effect	Money income	Price	Real income	Level of satisfaction
1. Income effect	changes	constant	changes	changes
2. Substitution effect	changes	changes	constant	constant
3. Price effect	constant	changes	changes	changes

6. Criticism of indifference curve analysis

1. The analysis makes an impractical assumption that the consumer is capable of possessing complete knowledge of his scale of preference. This is wrong.

2. The analysis is imaginary and not amenable to empirical research. It is not easy to collect data regarding the preferences of individual consumers. The consumer may not be a free agent when subjected to experimentation.

3. Prof. Samuelson points out that the concept is defective and imaginary. He developed the "Revealed preference theory" observing the market behaviour of the consumer.

4. The consumer can express his preference in simple cases of combinations between two commodities. If it is a question of 3 or more commodities, the illustration becomes difficult and leads to complicated mathematics.

5. This concept is micro-economic in character. It deals with one consumer and two commodities only. In case of studying group behaviour, this concept is not of much utility.

6. Prof. Armstrong observes that the consumer is indifferent between the combinations of two goods because of his in ability to perceive the difference between alternative combinations.

7. Prof. Armstrong, Neumann and Morgenstan observe that the indifference curve analysis cannot explain the behaviour of the consumer satisfactorily. If "uncertainty" of expectation with regard to the consequences of choice get in, the whole analysis will break down."

7. Practical Utility

1. In the production theory, this concept is used to arrive at equal product curve. To find out the producer's equilibrium, this concept is made use of. In the case of production, the equal product curve shows different combinations of two factors of production between which the producer is indifferent, because any of these combination is capable of producing the same output. The

basic aim of a producer is to attain a low cost combination so that he could make the highest profit by keeping down cost of production. Indifference curves are used in the theory of production, they are called Iso-product curves. Producers equilibrium is obtained at the point where producer's budget line becomes tangent to one of the Iso-product curves on the map.

2. In the field of exchange, the indifference curves can be used to determine the position of equilibrium, when two persons are entering into a market and dealing with each other. Prof. Edgeworth used the technique of indifference curves to indicate the mutual gains from the exchange of two commodities between two consumer's. In the field of inter national trade in which two countries produce goods and exchange between them, this concept is useful.

3. In taxation, this concept is used to judge the welfare effects of direct tax and indirect tax on the individual. With the help of indifference curves, it could be determined that a direct tax is preferable to an indirect tax with regard to its effects on the consumption and satisfaction of tax payer. It is assumed that indirect taxation reduces individual welfare more than direct taxes.

4. In price control and rationing, this concept can be used to know the different preferences of the consumers for the rationed commodities and the fixed supply for them could be arranged in the order of preferences.

5. In the field of savings, this concept shows the preferences of an individual between present and future goods and his intensity of desire for present goods over future goods.

6. Consumer's surplus can be measured with the help of this technique without any need for making unrealistic assumption in arriving at the Demand theorem without ambiguity. This concept forms an integral part of the modern welfare economics.

SUMMARISATION

Indifference curve analysis:

a) *To overcome the innate defects of the marginal utility analysis, the indifference curve analysis was propounded. It shows different combinations of two commodities of two commodities which give equal satisfaction to the consumer. The indifference curves always slope downward's to the right, do not cut one another and are always convex curve and to the origin. The indifference curve analysis is also based on certain assumptions like that consumer is rational; there is original utility; the marginal rate of substitution is applicable ; there is consistency and transitivity of choice; and that total utility depends on the commodities consumed.*

b) *The indifference curve analysis is useful in determining the quantity of each commodity that the individual will buy and helps in the knowing the quantity purchased of a commodity when its price changes; it helps in arriving at the position of equilibrium , where the price line touches an indifference curve giving maximum satisfaction. The technique of indifference curve is useful to the theory of production; the theory of exchange; in the field of rationing; in the measurement of consumer's surplus and in the field of taxation.*

B. ELASTICITY OF SUPPLY

Supply refers to total supply offered for sale at a price by retailers and whole salers. Suppply factor will be just the opposite of demand factor. The price factor is the resultant of both supply and demand factors. "Supply depends on scarcity, just as demand depends on usefulness". Scarcity in the economic sense means only in relation to its demand. Supply is also related to time, place and price like demand.

1. Law of supply

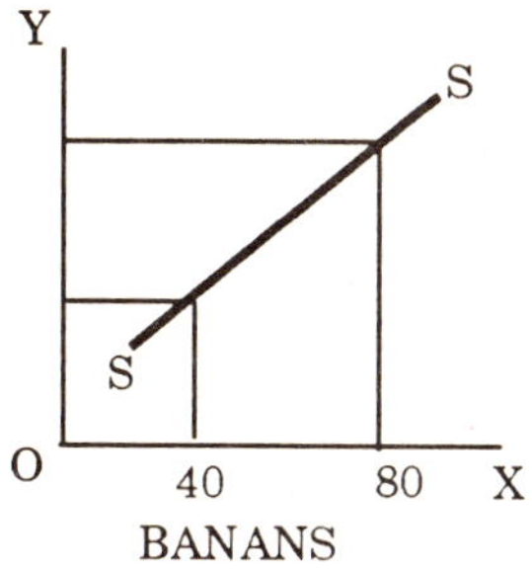

There is functional relationship between the price and quantity supplied and this relationship is stated in the form of a law called the law of supply. The law states "that other things being constant, the price of a commodity has a direct influence on the quantity supplied. As the price of a commodity increases, its supply extends and vice versa".

The supply curve SS slopes upwards from left to right - larger supplier at higher prices.

2. Assumption of supply schedule

a) Number of firms or sellers, Larger the sellers, higher the supply. Tthe quantum of supply depends upon the number of outlets (firms) available.

b) **Cost of production.** This is an important item affecting the supply position. The basic non-price determinants of supply are given and do not change. The technique of production, resource prices, prices of other goods, price expectations, and the number of sellers in the market should not change. A change in any one or more of these determinants will cause the supply curve for a product to shift to either the right or the left. A shift to the right indicates an increase in supply and a shift to the left indicates a decrease in supply.

c) **Prices of related goods:** It is assumed that supply of a commodity depends purely on its price and not on the prices of other commodities related to it. If prices of related goods fall, the firm producing goods may increase the supply of a particular product even though its price has not gone up.

d) **Price expectation:** It is assumed that the seller supplies the commodity on the basis of the prevailing prices. If he anticipates a higher price in future, he will reduce the present supply; if he anticipates a fall in price in future, he will be tempted to sell more at the current prices.

e) Natural factors, labour problems, change in government policy are all factors determining the supply position.

C. INPUT AND OUTPUT ANALYSIS & RELATIONSHIPS:

1. This concept was first developed in the 18th century by Prof. Quesney in the name of Tablen Economique. It was Prof. Leontief who developed input-output analysis in a refined fashion to give a shape to Prof. Walrs equilibrium analysis. This analysis may be described as a mathematical study of the production structure of the economy considering the various production sectors constituting the economy. This analysis is a very useful instrument for economic forecasting in the developed economies and for economic planning in the developing economies. This concept tries to predict the total production per sector, given the amount of consumers spending on each sector. Various industries are mutually interdependent; the output of one industry becomes an input for another industry. Even the by product of one industry, could be the raw-material for another industry. This concept explains this inter-relationship and inter-dependence among the various industries. This concept is also called "Inter-industry Analysis".

2. **Main Features:**

There are three main features of this analysis.

a) This analysis is concerned only with production and does not take into account the demand for goods. It explains only the technological problem. Given the amount of available resources and technological knowledge, this analysis describes the use of inputs to obtain the possible output.

b) This analysis is based on empirical facts only, that is to say, the estimates of input and output quantities are made on the basis of empirical data, therefore, this input-output analysis differs from general equilibrium theory as propounded by Prof. Walras.

c) This analysis takes into account the mutual dependence of planned production of various industries in the economy. For example, manufacturing industries depend on agriculture for raw-materials and agriculture depends on industries producing fertilizers, cement, pesticides, tractors, etc.

3. Assumptions

a) It is assumed that the available resources, the demand for finished goods, and the prices of all inputs and outputs are given and constant and their variations are not considered.

b) It is assumed that the technical co-efficients of production, that is the input proportions or ratios to produce a given output, are fixed. Technical substitution and techniques of production are not taken into account in this analysis.

c) It is assumed that there exist constant return to scale in the economy. One percent change in input would bring about one percent change (Equal change) in output is presumed in this analysis.

d) It is also assumed that demand for the finished product is large enough to keep production going in its full capacity. No input is either unutilised or under utilised.

4. Working operation of the analysis:

To work the system, the economy is divided into several manageable sectors. Each sector is assumed to produce only one product. Since each sector has number of industries producing closely related products, the products of these several industries are grouped together. The similarity of factor inputs is an indication that these products are similar.

After dividing the system into sectors, number of equations are framed to establish relationships between various inputs of each sector to the output of its product. Subsequent to this, further equations are framed to relate the output of a sector to the outputs of other sectors, which are treated as inputs. Thus, the final output available for consumption demand is determined. The framing of equations and the technical co-efficients of production take place on the basis of empirically obtained data. The help of computer is availed of to frame input-output models, otherwise it would be a voluminous process.

Since constant returns to scale assumed in input - output analysis, as mentioned earlier, there will be a linear relationship between inputs and the resulting output of any product. Inspite of number of outputs, there will be only one combination, which will be consistent with the available resources and with the final demand for consumption and capital accumulation.

5. METHODOLOGY

(A Model of Input-Output Analysis-Matrix)

Hypothetically an input-output matrix is being prepared taking into consideration only three sectors from among the available innumerable sectors, as an example.

TABLE-1 INPUT-OUTPUT MATRIX

To Sector

From sector	Agric-ulture	Indu-stry	Serv-ices	Consu-mers	Total
Agriculture	2	4.50	0.40	3.10	10
Industry	4	12	2	32	50
Services	0.4	6	3.60	30	40
TOTAL VALUE OF INPUT	6.40	22.50	6	65.10	100

The services sectors includes services like banking, insurance, transport, etc. Each firm should be placed only in one sector. A large part of production goes to the consumer, who buys from all these sectors . The above matrix indicates about how much each of the sectors bought from and delivered to each of the others. A horizontal review indicates the following; The annual value of agricultural output went from agriculture to agriculture itself by Rs.2 crores; output worth Rs.4.5 crores to industry; to services Rs.0.4 crores and Rs 3.10 crores to consumers. If vertically analysed, agriculture receives Rs.2 crores worth of output from itself, industry receives Rs.4 crores and Rs.0.4 crores went to services. The total value of output for the agricultural sector is Rs.10 crores and the total value of output is Rs.6.40 crores. The balance of Rs. 3.6 crores may be refereed to as sector income, which includes the incomes of those, who provide labour and capital for this sector. The sector income is technically called "Primary Input".

If the primary input is added, the Matrix appears as follows:

TABLE-2: INPUT-OUTPUT MATRIX WITH PRIMARY INPUT

(In crores of Rupees)

From sector   To sector

	Agric-ulture	Indu-stry	serv-ices	Cons-umers	Total
Agriculture	2	4.50	0.40	3.10	10
Industry	4	12.00	2	32	50
Services	0.40	6	3.60	30	40
Primary Input	3.60	27.50	34	-	65.10
TOTAL	10	50	40	65.10	165.10

After the preparation of input-output matrix (Revised), the next step is the job of computing technical co- efficients, which play an important role in the input- output analysis. Inspite of the technical co- efficients changing, due to economies and dis economics of scale and technological changes, the input output analysis remains considerably constant.

TABLE 3 : TECHNICAL CO-EFFICIENTS

From Sector   To Sector

	Agriculture	Industry	Services
Agriculture	0.4	0.18	0.02
Industry	0.8	0.48	0.96
Services	0.08	0.24	0.18

As per Table-2, the total production in the agriculture sector is Rs. 10 crores. To produce Rs.10 crores it is necessary to purchase agricultural goods worth Rs. 2 crores, industrial goods worth Rs.4 crores and services of Rs .0.4 crores. If these three amounts are divided by the total production of Rs.10 crores , we get 0.4 0.8 and 0.08 respectively. Similarly, co-efficient can be determined for other sectors also. These nine ratios are the technical co-efficients, that is to say, that a unit of output of a sector technically requires a certain fixed and given percentage of inputs from each of the sectors.

6. Utility of this analysis

This analysis is no longer a research and academic project. It is a very useful tool of economic analysis. In the determination of economic policy; for the preparation of development plan; for economic forecasting in developed countries, for comparative analysis of growth; for the increase in defence expenditure and its impact; and for the readjustment of the target of production, this concept is of great use. From the business point of view also this concept is useful as it provides detailed projections and reduce the degree of the uncertainly.

D. COST BENEFIT ANALYSIS

1. Meaning and Importance:

The cost-benefit analysis is the most appropriate method in appraising the achievements of the projects. This analysis is the most scientific and useful basis for evaluation of projects. This analysis helps the planning authority to make correct investment decisions and to achieve optimum resource allocation to bring about a wide difference between the cost of projects and the present value of benefits. This analysis requires the process of enumeration, comparison and evaluation of benefits and costs. The higher the cost- benefit ratio, the higher will be the priority attached to a project. Since capital and other investible resources are scarce in under-developed countries, it can maximise output by using them on a project, so that its benefit-cost ratio is higher than that of the alternative project.

Prof. Anthony, while commenting on U.S. Government experience, observes that cost-benefit analysis had its impact in all governments since 1960's. He says "cost- benefit analysis focused on those consequences of a proposal which can be estimated in quantitative terms. Since there is no important problem in which all the relevant factors can be reduced to numbers, cost- benefit analysis will never provide a complete answer to any important problem. The resulting analysis narrows the area within which managingjudgment is required even though it does not eliminate the need for Judgment".

In the past much attention was not given to this concept and much attention was not bestowed on government spending. Of late, to improve efficiency in government expenditure to achieve the objectives of public policy, and to fix the responsibility on the officials to whom the task is delegated; to measure performance standards; to introduce competitions among the units in governments; to reduce public expenditure, this concept is widely used.

It should be remembered that market mechanism beside on marginal utility and marginal cost cannot be applied to public utility undertakings like public transport, electricity, education and health etc.

2. Classification of the Analysis:

The cost-benefit analysis could be classified into:

a) Objectives and goals:

b) Exploring and determining alternative methods to attain the pre-determined goals:

c) Identifying the goals and measuring the achievements and taking steps to correct deviations;

d) Fixation of responsibility on each government officials to discharge the obligation entrusted to him and with results; and

e) Providing incentives for good work and results and offering dis-incentives for non-completion of tasks assigned within a time bound programme.

In the process of introducing the cost-benefit analysis, the authorities have to follow a methodology and they are faced with planning, programming and budgeting factors, which they have to widely analyse and execute. Budgeting is more important in cost- benefit analysis in the government than in private organisations. Since that happens to be a very important tool to control the operations of government expenditure effectively and to guarantee the proper and optimum utilisation of resources. Dr. Novic observes that" Performance Budget "is an innovation and should be strictly adhered to, as it would help in identifying, judging and implementing the alternative methods to achieve the goals. Performance budgeting is synonymous with "Strategic Planning" in the sense it helps cost-benefits analysis to be analysed carefully and delegently. In cost-benefit analysis judgment is always very important, since it should supplement cost accounting and statistical analysis.

3. Evaluation

A project is evaluated relying upon the benefits obtained from it. Benefits refers to the addition to the flow of national output. A project, which is executed, is said to be beneficial, when it is in a position to contribute an increase in production and consumption. These benefits may be real or nominal, direct or indirect and tangible and intangible. In cost-benefit analysis one is concerned only with the real benefit from a project, direct benefits and tangial benefits that are computed and measured in monetary terms.

In similarity with benefits, there are various types of cost like the project costs, Associated cost, Real cost, nominal cost,

Primary or direct cost, secondary or indirect costs etc. The primary or indirect costs are very important for the cost benefit analysis.

In project evaluation, comprehensive data extended for a long period is required, since gestation period is involved. It is also necessary to make comparisons with similar projects executed elsewhere. This data will also be helpful to assess the contribution made by the project to national output and to national employment scheme etc.

4. Conclusion

Direct benefits and total direct costs of a project are to be computed in the process of evaluation of a project to find out whether it is beneficial to execute that project or not. To arrive at the aggregate direct costs and benefits, the following steps are to be followed; Data are to be collected and calculated on the basis of physical quantities of goods and services produced and consumed; the money value of these goods and services is to be computed on the basis of price indices in different markets through weighted average method giving weight to inflationary and deflationary situations and finally, while calculating annual costs, due regard is to be given to the durability of capital assets and their depreciation. The annual costs are calculated by dividing the totals costs by the expected life of the capital assets. Likewise, annual benefits are calculated by computing the money value of direct benefits flowing from the projects after deducting from it the associated costs of the project.

Inspite of certain limitations like difficulties in cost assessment and difficulties in benefit assessment and the problem of measuring the present and future benefits from a project and costs incurred in obtaining these benefits; this cost-benefit analysis is of immense use to undertake projects, programmes and to determine the budgeting system.

E. MULTIPLE PRODUCTS-NEW PRODUCTS

Today there are no firms, perhaps which would produce a single product. Almost all firms produce atleast multiple models and sizes of their output. In the modern economy, every firm has to determine these important policies namely-products policy, promotional policy and pricing policy. It is a social and financial obligation of a firm to determine, first its product line policy. With reference to product opportunities, the management has to deal with two important factors, namely,-

1) Whether the firm has adequate economic promise that is, its technical feasibility; and

2) Can the company appropriately exploit this economic opportunity and this factor relates to " multiple products" advantage.

The most important cause for adding a new product to the product line is to reinforce the strength of the company to meet any type of challenge in the process of competitive strength and to accelerate profits. A firm may have more resources but under exploited. By adding a new product to the product line, the excess capacity of the plant, which has remained under exploited, could be availed of to produce maximum output. That is to say, idleness of the plant could be profitably made use of by adding new products. This excess capacity becomes the source of the competitive advantage cost-wise of the multiple product firm.

Unexpected secular shifts bringing about demand fluctuations and technological advancement are the main determinants of excess capacity and they demand for a new produce line at every level of production. This excess capacity may be seasonal, cyclical or may run for a long period resulting in the shut down of the firm creating unemployment or profit acceleration due to the utilisation of the by-product neglected so far. Changes in the technology of production; Variations in selling techniques; Shifts in raw-material supply due to transport development; research and competition in the field of using raw-materials; changes in the location of markets and new devices in the productive process etc., can bring about secular shifts resulting in excess capacity. Vertical integration is the source of excess capacity that promotes multiple product lines, where the company has made investments in several levels of production and distribution. Research creates excess capacity by making current products absolute and research also helps in developing new products to absorb excess capacity.

2. POLICY ON ADDING NEW PRODUCTS

Companies which use product development as a major competitive weapon, have to face three problems, while adding a new product, namely-

1. Maintaining a list of potential product additions;
2. Appraising these proposals and make a selection of the product; and
3. Launching new products to get maximum profit.

The top management has to prepare a long list of proposed new products, Which may be supplied by inventors, corporate research departments, professional product founders, customers, from marketing staff etc. Prospective profitability is to be the basis for selecting a new product. Items to the addition of the product line should be ranked in a priority ladder according to profitability- yield from the top to down, of course with an exception under strategic consideration. As regards profit calculation, incremental profits have to be considered rather than net profits. Incremental profits refer to the difference in the firms profits with and without the addition of the new product, and the cost burden of existing products are waived. If the new product fails to yield "Minimum Profitability", it should be rejected. Thus, capital budgeting should be rigorous and strict. While determining the profit standard, the total rupee income over the whole life of the product minus the total outlay (including investment) to produce is to be considered. In measuring profit prospects, the problem that is posed is in estimating profitability through projections of revenues and costs; and while doing so, it is necessary to cover the expected life span of the product ranging from three to five years. As regards profit determination, some consider historical returns on investments, some require minimum return equal to the company's ten-year average and some others are interested in an arbitrary standard of adequate profits.

Prof. Joel Dean suggests the criteria for new products, - namely the new products should bring benefits to the existing products; they should have common product facilities; common raw-materials, common distribution channels and common technical and production know-how. They should also have substitute and complementary relationship with the existing products and should match the existing product line. Thus, a right combination of products, new as well as the existing products, in the product line has a powerful promotional value.

3. Policy on dropping of old products:

This problem is as important as the problems of selecting new products. Deletion of old products is partly due to past mistakes in over-product lines additions and partly from inadvertent additions and acquisitions. Deletion is also due to absolescence caused by rapid changes in consumer taste or improvement in rival's products. The decision of management to drop or delete a product should be based on net profit analysis.

To improve financial competition and to organise properly the market segment, it is necessary to improve the existing product line. Products which have to face competitive comparisons and which bring higher profits, should receive very special care and attention. In every firm, there should be a screening committee to identify sick products before eliminating them. It is also necessary to find out whether the product is giving only net profits instead of incremental profits. The firm has only one choice among different alternatives, namely, - improve the product, buy or drop the product. There are certain indicators that can help the management to determine whether or not to eliminate a particular product and they are-

a) Reduction in product effectiveness;

b) Innovation of a superior substitute products;

c) Consumption disproportionately of the executive time;

d) Sharp decline in trade trends;

e) Sudden fall in the price-line; and

f) A downward trend in profits.

These indicators are sufficient enough to take a decision. Thus, it could be concluded that an addition of a new product to the product line or a deletion of a new product from the product line should be done after careful analysis, screening and judgment and decisions, since this action had a lasting effect on the firm and management.

F. MULTIPLIER AND ACCELERATOR MECHANISM

1. The multiplier concept was first introduced to economic theory by R.F. Khan, a renowned economist of the cambridge school. It was later expounded by Dr. J.M. Keynes. Dr. Keynes' investment multiplier is one of the key concept in Keynesian models of income determination. Prof. R.F. Khan developed employment multiplier on the

other hand. The employment multiplier measures the ratio of the change in total employment to a given change in investment; while the Keynesian investment multiplier measures the ratio of the change in total income to a given change in investment. Multiplier is a very important element of the theory of employment. The multiplier is a concept which expresses the relationship between an initial increment in investment and the ultimate increment in national income. It refers to the fact that an autonomous increase or decrease of expenditure for output can increase or decrease total expenditure for output by some multiple by inducing a change of consumption expenditure in the same direction. The Keynes investment multiplier has been propounded by economist to explain the cumulative effects of changes in investments on income via, their effects on consumption expenditure. According to this theory, changes in investment will lead to changes in consumption through income, which in turn leads to changes in income. Thus, the principle of multiplier attempts to measure the final change in income as a certain multiple of the initial cause, namely change in investment. To find out the size of multiplier, it is necessary to clear the two important concepts, - the marginal propensity to consume (MPC) and the marginal propensity to save (MPS). Every person gets an income which he can either consume or save, or partly consume or partly save (Y=C+S).

Whatever one consumes through spending will become others income and the others will also do the same. The multiplier effect of an initial increase in investment depends upon, MPC, when income increases, the consumption is bound to increase, but need not be in the same proportion or ratio. In other words, an individuals propensity to consume decreases with an increase in income.

Since what is not consumed is saved, the marginal propensity to save is the reverse of marginal propensity to consume. The investment multiplier is connected with the change in investment on consumption expenditure and related to the MPC or inversely to MPS. The value of multiplier lies in the fact that it is determined by the MPC. Equilibrium income is found on the assumption that a part of total income goes to consumption expenditure and the rest is kept in saving, which is invested. The simple model is,

Y = C-S	I	= investment
Y = C-I	Y	= stands for national income
S = I	C	= consumption
	S	= savings

An initial rise in investment creates employment for workers engaged directly in capital projects and their spending then gives rise to secondary employment in industries producing consumer goods. The ratio between overall rise in employment and the primary employment is called the employment multiplier. This employment multiplier also depends upon the value of MPC, because larger the part of additional income used for consumption expenditure, the higher will be the level of demand for goods and the rise in the level of employment.

2. The accelerator is another important tool of economic analysis. This concept is generally associated with the name of Prof. J.N. Clark (An American Economist), though

it was Prof. Albert Aflation (French Economist), who first propounded this concept in a crude way. In recent years Profs. Harrod, Hansen and Samuelson have further developed this concept. They have tried to integrate the principle of 'Accelerator' with Dr. Keynes 'Multiplier' analysis. Prof. Kenneth Kurihara has evolved the new concept of 'Super-multiplier'.

3. Accelerator and multiplier are parallel concepts. While the multiplier shows the effect of investment on consumption via. income and employment; the accelerator shows the effect of a change in consumption on investment. Multiplier shows the dependence of consumption on investment, while the accelerator shows the dependence of investment on consumption. The accelerator measures the effect of an increment (or decrement) in the rate of consumption on the volume of investment. It expresses the ratio of the net change in consumption to the net change in investment. In other words, the consumption goods industries constitute the basis of investment goods industries. Dr. J.R. Hicks observes that "the theory of multiplier and accelerator are two sides of the theory of fluctuation, just as the theory of demand and the theory of supply are the two sides of the theory of value".

These two concepts are very important for managerial economics. The managerial economists have to take resource to consumption, expenditure, savings and investment in the determination of the scope of his business. Income determines consumption; consumption determines savings; savings determine investments; investments determine production, the volume of production determines employment and finally employment level determines wages and income. All these concepts are vital to the science of managerial economics.

G. CAPITAL BUDGETING - AN ANALYSIS

1. "Finance is the back-bone of commerce", Business Finance is different from agricultural finance. Whatever may be the size of the business enterprises, a modern business unit, may be a firm or an industry, demands a huge capital expenditure right from the starting of the project till the goods (manufactured commodities) reach the market for sale. The capital expenditure required by a business enterprise is for various items. The initial capital, the fixed capital, maintenance capital, the operational capital, the developmental capital, etc., are the types of capital that a modern firm requires. The capital expenditure has to be incurred before the commercial production begins and after also. The quantum of capital required vary from company to company depending upon the nature of production and the purpose of production, whether the goods are required only for the domestic market or for exports to international markets. Modern industries are giant industries and they require huge capital expenditure.

2. The managerial economist has to take very important decisions regarding investments in fixed assets and these decisions are to be taken judiciously in order to get maximum returns at the minimum cost. He has to canalise the resources for the project with minimum liability to the enterprise and utilise the financial resources effectively and efficiently. Unused financial resources would mean capital blockade and it is a stain on the profit resources of the company. The enterprise requires balanced flow of capital. Capital planning should be a long term planning and demands designing a systematic investment programme. The management should select a capital proposal, which allocates the resource in the most efficient

manner. "Minimum liability with maximum effective utilisation" should be the guiding principle in capital budgeting. The capital budget is an estimate of cost each project approved by a competent authority and arrived at after consideration of several alternative factors before finalisation. Thus, capital budgeting is a major factor for the managerial economist, since all the operational activities of the enterprise hinge around this factor.

3. Prof. Milton Spencer says "capital budgeting involves the planning of expenditure for asset, the returns from which will be realised in future time periods". According to Prof. C.T. Harengren "capital budgeting is long-term planning for making and financing capital analysis". Prof. R.N. Authony says "Capital budgeting is essentially a list of what management believes to be worth while projects for the acquisition of new capital assets together with the estimated cost of each project". The main problem of capital budgeting is to decide; how much money will be required for the capital expenditure to execute the projects, how much money will be available and how should financial resources be spent and allocated to various competing projects. Capital budgeting can help:

   1. In the replacement of current obsolete equipments with upto-date efficient equipment;
   2. Can help to estimate the capital requirements of the firm for selecting the best proposal for investment;
   3. Can help in taking long term investment decisions;
   4. can help in evaluating the various proposals of capital investment to avoid loss on the basis of their profitability, and;

5. it can help to ascertain the effect of depreciation, insurance, etc., on the profits of concern and to avoid and reduce unnecessary expenditure.

6. Prof.R.M. Laymor says "capital budgeting consists in planning the development with available capital for the purpose of maximising long-term profitability of the firm". Capital budgeting (CB) involves three major problems, namely,-

   a) The demand for capital,-It is necessary to survey the need for capital and analyse with precision the good investment proposals for development. The quantum of capital required and the channels for its distribution by visualising their earnings, since the gestation period involved and the unknown technical advances, market development and irrational changes in relative price have an impact on the entire enterprise.

   b) Supply of capital,- This is a major problem for the enterprise. Where to get funds and how to get it? The managerial economist while harnessing financial resources, he should strictly observes "the least- liability cause" that is, the funds should be mobilised by creating least liability to the enterprise. The financial resources may be internal or external. The chief internal resources are depreciation charge and retained earnings (ploughing back the profits). The external earnings comprise of shares and debentures from the public, besides borrowing in the form of loans, advances, deposits, etc., As far as possible equity shares are to be resorted to, as they create minimum liability. The external resources largely depend upon the state of capital market and the sound financial position and good-will of the company.

c) Capital Rationing - Capital has a scarcity value and has a cost. The return on investment should be more than the cost of capital and it determines the cut-off point in capital budgeting. The aim of capital should be to maximise the profit potential and it has, thus to choose a project, which is the most profitable one. Thus to conclude, capital budgeting consists of determining the cost of capital, the rate of return on investment and ranking the various proposals on the basis of their profitability-yielding position.

Thus, capital budgeting is a major issue for the company. A proper and sound budgeting can help the management to keep down the cost of capital, which is an element of cost of production, and maximise returns in the form of profits to be distributed to the management, worker and investors.

H. PROJECT ORGANISATION OR MATRIX ORGANISATION

A special "Task Force" is appointed to complete a project work by a firm or industry with a project manager as the leader and with a team of experts from several experts from several functional departments. A project organisation is also called as a grid or matrix organisation. Authority flows vertically and horizontally and this two way flow of authority is with a project manager and his staff, who are responsible for the success of a given project, within a given time schedule and cost. Item which require designing, building a huge plant, involving product innovation, highly complicated and tight timing schedule are referred to matrix, which lacks unity of command.

Advantages and disadvantages of matrix:

a) Matrix achieves a co-ordination in the execution of a project. It combines the functional and product patterns of departmentation in the same organisation structure. It consolidates the diverse interests in the organisation to obtain the objective. Creativity through interaction of specialists and functional department. Development of strong team work to achieve the project. To make matrix effective functioning, it is necessary to clearly define the objective of the task; to clarify the roles of authority and responsibility of manager and his team; to select an experienced manager with knowledge and information; to apply controls on time, quality and cost and to reward project managers and the team appropriately.

b) the disadvantages in the system could be absence of unity of command; insecurity and fear of unemployment after the project is completed; danger of over- specialisation; transfers from project to project reduces loyalty to the functional department from where specialists are absorbed; absence of economies of scale resulting in under utilisation of resources; a state of conflict between functional and project managers; an imbalance of authority and power and involving number of frequent meetings to arrive at decisions and thus loss of time.

I. AN ANALYSIS OF SELLING COSTS

Selling costs distinguishes monopolistic competition from pure competition. The firm has to take a decision about selling cost which is a very important variable in determining the equilibrium firm. The selling cost may be defined as that cost which persuade buyers to purchase its product in preference to others. According to Prof. Chamberlin "selling costs are costs incurred in order to alter the position or shape of the demand curve for a product". Advertising, salesmen's salaries, expenses of sale department, margins granted to retailers and wholesalres, expenses incurred, window- dressing, samples, demonstration expenses etc., constitute selling costs.

Equilibrium of the firm with selling costs

It should be remembered that while selling costs add to the demand for the product of the firm, they add to the increase in total costs also. The concepts of managerial analysis also applies to the selling cost. The addition to the revenue made by an increase in selling expenditure should be balanced against the increase in total costs. When once the product and price given is assumed, then it is very easy to indicate the optimum volume of selling costs for the firm.

XT	=	Assumed price level of the product
COC	=	Combined cost curve
APC	=	Average production cost
ACC	=	Average selling cost curve.

The above figure indicates the equilibrium of the firm with selling cost and out-put. Both price and product are given. XT is the given level of price and the U shaped APC is the average production cost curve of the product. the average selling cost curve (ASEC) is also U shaped. The COC is the combined cost curve. It is obvious that the selling cost and the corresponding output is optimum, when the total profit is the maximum at Y. The line ET shows the assumed price level of the product at which it is sold. When selling costs are increased, total costs go on increasing. That level of selling costs gives the maximum profit where the last unit sold in the market adds to the total cost must equal assumed price. COC intersects ET at Y, BN is the equilibrium output and the area EYZO is the maximum profit. If the firm produces and sells beyond BN, the excess of marginal cost (MC) over price will reduce its total profit; nor beyond the point and advertise at the given price.

J. RECENT TRENDS IN MANAGEMENT EDUCATION & TRAINING IN INDIA

1. Professionalisation of Management

India's greatest asset is manpower. This must be channelled into increasing productivity. What is required is a pooling of managerial and engineering resources on co-operative basis so as to tackel on a large scale the problems of technology for development. The institutes of research and engineering must work in collaboration with industrial organisations both in public and private sectors and develop a technology suited to the needs of the country.

Mary Parker Follet once concluded a paper entitled management as profession - as follows:-

"What does all this imply in regard to the profession of business management?' It means that men must prepare themselves as seriously for this profession as for any other. They must realise that they, as professional men, are assuming great responsibilities, that they are to take a creative part, a part which I believe, only trained and disciplined men can in the future hope to take with success".

Now management can justifiably lay claim to be a profession.

A professional is a person who has undergone a certain rigorous training to acquire a body of knowledge and develop certain skills with the objective of rendering service to society - the financial objective being a subsidary one.

Professionalism involves two basic elements namely :-

1) the acquisition of certain knowledge and skill;
2) the right mental attitudes.

In management, the nucleus of a body of knowledge has now been formed. Techniques useful to managers exist and newer one are being developed in our country. Educational institutions have emerged for providing this knowledge and skill to young students and executives.

Regarding the right mental attitude, there is a growing awareness in India of an organisations social responsibilities-to the share holders, employees, the customers and society and community.

The owner managers are attending courses abroad and in India to acquire management education and sophistication. They are also encouraging their children to obtain similar knowledge and skills. Computer points and complete education and training are developing very fast especially in the field of "Soft- Ware".

2. Management Education and Development

The claim to professionalisation is further supported by the growing management consciousness in India. A committee was set up as early as in 1949 by the All India Council of Technical education to examine the possibility of including industrial and business management as a subject for various educational institutions. This resulted in the formation of a board of management studies in 1953 with the objective of formulating courses of study in business management. Particularly after the first five year plan, the managerial gap became obvious and the mid-fifties saw a movement towards improving managerial skills through proper educational facilities. Apart from the administrative staff college at Hyderbad, formed on the lines of Henley, which trains nearly a thousand managers a year, three national institutes of management were formed at Ahmedabad, Calcutta and Banagalore with the help of Harvard business school and M.I.T. in the case of Ahmedabad and Calcutta respectively.

Management courses and subjects have now been introduced in various universities at undergraduate and post graduate levels, as well as in other educational institutions. Some universities in india offer business administration courses of 2 to 3 years duration full-time or part-time. The institutes of management, the universities and other institutes offering training courses in management generally have their sights on the pre-recruitment type of training. Post-Graduate diploma courses in business management, personnel management and marketing management are being started in universities.

As regards training facilities for working managers in india, such facilities are provided not only by a few educational institution such as Bombay Management Associations, which have been formed in different parts of India and are tied together in to a loose form of Federation by the All India Management Associations with its head office in Delhi. All these Management Association hold various management seminars aimed at different management levels to provide them with orientation as well as in depth courses and help strengthen the management movement in India.

In addition, there are other agencies like the National Productivity Council (NPC) and the Local Productivity Council (LPCs) like the Bombay Productivity Council (BPC) providing educational facilities aimed at increasing productivity through the use of scientific methods of management as well as modern concepts and techniques of productivity.

There are about 47 local productivity councils in India. Besides, some companies like Tatas and Hindusthan Lever, have started their own management development facilities which are either used exclusively or in combination with external agencies for the development of their own managers.

Most experts agree that there is undoubtedly a perceptible trend towards professional management, though it has a long way to go before it can be said to stay. In the case of Tata Iron and Steel company, the tradition of professional type of organisation was achieved long ago. The creation of Tata Management service and the establishment of the Maftlal Service private limited, have among others, accelerated the trend towards professionalisation of management.

In spite of these happy trends, it has to be admitted that even now management in India is mostly controlled by families. While the need for rapid professionalisation have been sufficiently recognised, the progress towards it has been rather slow and halting. However the hopeful sign is that the second generation of industrialists who are today in charge of running many large plants trend to be more realistic in their approach to managerial problems and are becoming increasingly aware of their limitations. They are thus much more receptive to professional advice.

3. Need for greater role by Professional Managers

The managerial community in India is expected to play a more important role during the last decade of the century. This class will not merely have to be leaders in production and marketing but also in society as a whole. The manager of tomorrow will have to be more concerned about social justice and equitable distribution.

Mr. P.T. Kuriakose, Director, International Youth Centre, New Delhi, speaking at a recent seminar on the subject of 'Managerial Role in the Future', stated - "First of all, India is likely to be more technology oriented than it has been so far. Industrialisation is bound to be on a larger scale than it is today. Therefore, there will be a consequent increase in the rate of urbanisation. Class consciousness amongest India's people is bound to grow. As industrialisation progresses and as poverty continues, the working class is bound to grow and become more conscious of its nature...."

Another participant in the seminar A.D. Moddie also outlined the role of a manager in the context of the leadership requirements of India. The job of the leaders will be intricate, challenging and complex.

The future managers will be effective if they contribute not merely to their organization but also to society. One of the major lacuna in the management education in our institutes is the lack of adequate importance to the area of social perspective and the need of business. The emphasis quite frequently in business schools is on management techniques and skills rather than on the problems of a manager operating in Indian society. Perhaps this is partly due to the fact that with the exception of one or two management institutes most of them are modeled on and operate on the lines of their foreign collaborations.

With the recent changes in the government policy towards gradual privatisation of productive sector and change in the Industrial Policy, the responsibility of professional managers has increased rapidly. They have to face great challenges with the advent of twenty first century, when Science and Technology are expected to make a quantum jump.

4. Future of Management Education

It should provide opportunities for comprehensive discussion of the imperative because the manager has to work within the overall frame work of the society he lives in the manager cannot insulate himself from the socio-political processes that are shaping the attitudes and values of the citizens. Persons who are well-versed in the political and social science can make significant contribution to the development of greater sensitivity and awareness among management students.

The studies which are used in business schools should be based on Indian problems and issues so that the students have some familiarisation with the problems they are going to encounter later in their careers in industry. The management students should also be encouraged to involve themselves actively with social and community work. Such involvement should be compulsory part of the curriculum and adequate weightage should be given to it. For example, a business school may adopt a village and make it a model in terms of education and literacy, housing, health, recreation, political awareness etc. This will make the students more aware of the problems of the rural areas and will also help them to be more in tune with social needs.

The large scale and medium scale industries should involve themselves in furthering the cause of management education. Mere theoretical knowledge is not sufficient. The students of management studies should be forced to undergo training in industries and other areas, in which they have specialised. This will help them to understand the practical problems. Even practical training should be made as pre-requisite for awarding degree, and diplomas. Case studies should be a part of curriculum. Mere class lectures may not improve the quality and standard of management education. Students should be exposed to the complexities and challenges of the 21st century.

K. SELECTED READINGS

1. K. Boulding : Economic Analysis
2. Stigler : Theory of Prices
3. J.R. Hicks : Value and Capital
4. P. Samuelson : Economics
5. J.M. Keynes : General Theory
6. S.E. Harris : New Economics
7. Joel Dean : Managerial Economics.
8. Varsheney Marheswary : Managerial Economics.
9. Spencer M.H. : Managerial Economics.
10. Writhr and Wilson : Forecasting Profit.
11. Mrs. Joan Robinson : Imperfect competition
12. J.R. Hicks : Trade cycle
13. C.L. Sehultze : National Income Analysis
14. M.L. Seth : Micro Economics
15. M.L. Seth Macro - Economics
16. Principles of Management : Peter F. Drucker
17. Essentials of Management : Koontz and O'Donnel
18. Essentials of Management : Josaeph. L. Massie
19. The Mnagement Process : Davas
20. Management Theory and Practice : E. Dale
21. A System and Contingency.

    Analysis of Managerial Functions. : Koontz and O'Donnel

22. Professional Management : Haiman.

23. Personnel Management and Industrial Relation : Dale Yoder

24. Business Administration : S.A. Sherlekar

25. Principles and Practice of Management : L.M. Prasad

26. Magazines and Reports on Management Studies

27. Management of tomorrow : Louis Allen

28. Management : Stoner Jame.A.F.

29. Tasks, Responsibilities and Practices : P. Drucker

30. Other Periodicals.